D0094030

# HELPING THE ABUSER

## Intervening Effectively in Family Violence

# HELPING THE ABUSER

## Intervening Effectively in Family Violence

## BARBARA STAR

**Family Service Association of America, New York**

Library of Congress Cataloging in Publication Data
Star, Barbara.
    Helping the abuser ; intervening effectively in family
violence.

    Includes bibliographical references and index.
    1. Family violence—United States. 2. Family social
work—United States. I. Title.
HQ809.3.U5S777 1983      362.8′2      83-48129
ISBN 0-87304-202-6

Book design by Charlotte Staub

Printed in the United States of America

To Edith and William Star
Bless you for all time

# CONTENTS

## ACKNOWLEDGMENTS

The writing of this book would not have been possible without the support of the Levi Strauss Foundation, Haven House, Inc., and the people who participated in the study, especially those whose programs are described in these pages. To them all, my deepest appreciation.

# INTRODUCTION

**M**ost family violence incidents go unreported. Those that do reach public attention are usually so serious they warrant legal action. Typically, the criminal justice system has been assigned the task of dealing with the perpetrators of family violence. Often the only options available to the court have been to incarcerate assaulters, place them on probation, or release them. However, many programs for assaulters *do* exist, although most are not known beyond the communities they serve. A grant from the Levi Strauss Foundation in May 1979 enabled the initiation of research to identify and examine those community-based programs throughout the country that offered alternatives to incarceration. Specifically, it focused on programs that were developed to deal with both males and females who physically or sexually abuse one or more members of their family.

The original goals of the study included both identifying the range of programs that existed and comparing the treatment approaches found in order to determine their effectiveness in eliminating destructive behavior. Unfortunately, the latter goal could not be attained because so few programs attempted formal evaluations of their services. However, it was possible to obtain information about the treatment modalities used, the content of the services offered, a general profile of the people who used the service, and the techniques found by the staff to be most (and least) effective when working with abusive clients. This book, in Part One, presents a synthesis of that information. In addition, in Part Two, it offers several in-depth descriptions of some of the less traditional programming models that were discovered. It is hoped that the book will suggest ideas about programs that agencies, groups, or individuals interested in family violence can implement in their communities.

Unlike many studies, which focus on only one form of violence that can occur in families, such as child abuse or wife battering, this study attempted to include the whole realm of family violence from infant abuse to granny-bashing. However, since the purpose of the study was to identify the types of programming that exist, it was not necessary to locate all programs designed to assist abusers. Instead, efforts were made to find a variety of programs in a variety of settings that dealt with one or more types of family violence. Toward that end, agencies and individuals listed in directories, newsletters, and research bulletins as well as names provided by clearing houses, major organizations, and word of mouth were contacted. The settings included family service, child welfare, community mental health, conciliation court, juvenile and adult corrections, hospitals, shelters for battered women, neighborhood centers, salvation army, YM and YWCA, specialized community organizations, and private practice.

The main criteria for inclusion in the study were (1) an identifiable program or service specifically for family violence abusers, and (2) a program that had been in operation for at least six months. Several hundred telephone calls were made which ultimately resulted in a sample of 116 programs, sponsored by 111 agencies, that met the research criteria. All administrators of programs that met the criteria were willing to participate in the research project so none of the programs that qualified had to be eliminated from the study. To avoid the delays and poor return rates that are typically associated with questionnaires, telephone interviews were held with the head of each program (or with an appropriate program representative) in the sample. Each telephone interview lasted 45 to 60 minutes and gathered information about the format and content of the service offered to the abuser, number of people who use the service, referral sources, client characteristics, techniques used, type of personnel who provide the service, program philosophy, location and funding of the program, administrative structure, program evaluation, methods used to prevent worker burnout, and how the program was received in the community. Appendix A contains a copy of the research instrument.

When all the interviews were completed, the programs were categorized into general programming approaches and forms of service. Site visits were made to those agencies whose formats offered alternatives to the more traditional service delivery approaches.

## RESEARCH SAMPLE CHARACTERISTICS

Of the 116 programs surveyed, 7 dealt with all forms of family violence, 4 dealt with three types of family violence (spouse abuse, physical child abuse, and sexual child abuse), 30 dealt with two forms of family violence (28 with physical and sexual child abuse, 2 with spouse abouse and sexual child abuse), 29 focused specifically on spouse abuse, 24 on physical child abuse, and 22 on sexual child abuse. Appendix B contains a further breakdown of the sample characteristics.

The agencies and individuals offering the services represented fifteen different settings. Family service agencies provided the setting for the largest number of programs (28) while community organizations, hospitals or medical facilities, child welfare agencies, and criminal justice settings, *each* constituted approximately 10 percent of the sample. Together they comprised 70 percent of the sample. The other 30 percent were mental health facilities, community consortiums, protective services, private nonprofit agencies, shelters, community centers, YM and YWCA groups, social and religious ministries, community action programs, and private counseling services.

One-third of the programs were located in large urban centers with populations of more than one million. More than 20 percent were located in areas populated by 500,000 to one million, close to 40 percent were located in communities with populations from 100,000 to 500,000, and less than 10 percent were located in communities containing fewer than 100,000 residents.

None of the assaulter intervention programs had been in existence for more than ten years; the largest percentage (43 percent) had existed for one or two years. Fifteen percent had provided service for more than five years, and 11 percent had operated for less than one year. Generally, programs offering services to physical child abusers had been in existence the longest, and services for spouse abusers were the most recent.

Not all agencies that were discovered to offer services to family violence abusers have been included in this study. During the initial sample selection process we found that many agencies and organizations were concerned about the problems of violence in families and had initiated in-service training devoted to one or more aspects of family violence. They tended to assign victims and abusers randomly to available workers, as they would any newly entering case. Consequently, in those agencies family violence assaulters became integrated into the workers' general caseloads and could not be identified easily (if at all) for research purposes. Even though that type of integration may be the ultimate goal in dealing with violence in families, for the research project it was necessary to focus on separate programs or components of programs that dealt specifically with the assaulters.

One other feature that limits the representativeness of the sample was the tendency to locate more programs in the western states than in the eastern part of the nation. This probably occurred because the researcher was based in Los Angeles.

The people who participated in the study sounded dedicated, involved, and enthused about the work they were doing. They believed that their work was important and that they were making a significant contribution toward the rehabilitation of worthwhile human beings and the reduction of pain in families. They were uniformly cooperative about sharing their time and expertise with the researcher. However, many were unaware of the existence of other family violence programs and felt that they were working in a void. To reduce their sense of isolation, the researcher developed and distributed to the research participants a booklet, *Services for Abusers in Family Violence Situations,* which listed the names of the programs in the study and information about the services they provided to encourage the sharing of ideas among these practitioners.

## THE NEED FOR PROGRAMS THAT FOCUS ON THE ABUSER

Rarely is violence in the family confined to a single incident. Without intervention, violent episodes will be repeated. Even when the family structure changes through divorce, separation, or removal of the identified victim, abusers continue the pattern of abuse when they remarry or take on new family responsibilities. The problem does not go away on its own; it requires active intervention to stop the pattern of abuse. Victim-oriented programs may teach victims how to survive, but they do not teach abusers how to stop. Assaulter-focused programs are more likely to reach the people whose behavior needs to be changed the most.

In addition to reducing the incidence of violence by confronting the perpetrators directly, programs for abusers save money. The victims of abuse usually feel too intimidated, vulnerable, or physically incapable of stopping the abuser themselves. When they do initiate action, it often takes the form of external pressure applied by a third party such as the police or the courts. Because new state laws are calling for more stringent prosecution and sentencing of family violence abusers, the courts will be asked to deal with greater numbers of physical assaulters in the future. According to information provided by the National Criminal Justice Reference Service, the average annual cost of incarceration per inmate is $10,486. Outpatient counseling or educational services cost only a fraction of that. Many administrators who participated in the research estimated that it cost them less than $1,000 to provide complete service for an entire family unit.

Just as we cannot ignore the problem of family violence, neither can we hope to correct the problem by ignoring the abusers. Providing services for abusers may prove to be the most effective and efficient way of dealing with problems caused by violence in the family.

# HELPING THE ABUSER

## Intervening Effectively in Family Violence

# PART ONE

# Understanding and Treating Violence in Families

This section describes the personality and demographic characteristics of the assaulters, program formats that are being used to intervene with the abusers, administrative issues in program development, treatment issues encountered by line staff, and techniques for working with abusers.

# I
# APPROACHES TO FAMILY VIOLENCE

**A**lthough instances of violence in the family date back at least to Cain and Abel, the concept of family violence is relatively new. The earliest identified, and best known, form of family violence is physical abuse against children, but increasingly society has become aware that among family members no one age level or relationship is immune from violence. From infancy through old age, violence is a fact of family life. However, it is a fact of life few people wish to acknowledge because it so blatantly contradicts the sanctity of the family. Traditionally, families have been associated with caring, loving, and protective behaviors. The family mystique leaves little room for understanding the use of physical or sexual abuse to children, spouses, or parents. Consequently, there is a tendency for everyone (victim, assaulter, and general public) to minimize or deny the extent of violence in the home.

However, statistics indicate that the existence of family violence is both real and extensive. Police respond to more family disturbance calls than to all other categories of serious crimes combined.[1] Between 20 and 25 percent of homicides nationwide involve victims and offenders who are related to each other.[2] And where the victim–offender relationship was known, 14 percent of all aggravated assaults, those that involve serious injury or the use of a weapon, were between family members.[3] So prevalent is violence in the family that it prompted members of the National Commission on the Causes and Prevention of Violence to comment that the general public had more to fear from family and friends than from violence in the streets committed by strangers.[4]

## TYPES AND INCIDENCE

Family violence usually refers to the threat or actual use of physical force on one or several members of a person's nuclear or extended family. In practice the term also encompasses adult sexual abuse directed toward children, whether or not force is used. The word *family* is used loosely to include men and women who perform spousal or parental functions regardless of their legal right to do so (e.g., boyfriends, common-law marriage partners). Family violence contains several categories, including child abuse, sibling fights, spousal assaults, sexual abuse, parent battering, and abuse to the elderly.

- Official estimates from the National Center for Child Abuse and Neglect place the number of abused children at 250,000 annually.[5] Even though violence to children tends to diminish with age, approximately 20 percent of reported abuse involves child victims who are in their teens.[6]
- No figures are available for sibling violence because conflicts between siblings are so common that they are treated as a normal and transitory part of family interactions. However, every year brings new reports of serious or fatal attacks between natural or stepsiblings.
- One study estimated that as many as one out of four couples engage in at least one violent episode during the course of their marriage.[7] The same study reported that 3.3 million wives and more than a quarter of a million husbands each year receive severe beatings from their spouses.[8]
- Sexual abuse includes both sexual assaults to children in the family and forced sexual relations with wives. Every year approximately 100,000 children are sexually assaulted by family members.[9] Marital rape is still too newly recognized to be accurately estimated. However, one study of battered women discovered that in addition to physical abuse, 30 percent of the sample had also been sexually abused by their spouses.[10]
- Parent battering involves children, usually adolescents, who intimidate, beat, or kill their parents. Researchers believe that children in one out of ten American families hit, beat, stab, or shoot their parents.[11]

• Granny-bashing is the term used to describe abuse inflicted by middle-aged adults to their elderly relatives. Although no nationwide figures are available, it is thought to be as prevalent as child abuse.[12]

## APPROACHES TO TREATMENT

Programming efforts to reduce family violence seem to parallel public awareness and attitudes. Although it may be possible to cite programs that began several years ago, for the most part attempts to deal with family violence originated within the past decade. Because program development has been so recent, agencies and organizations are still in the process of exploring which components and techniques work best. Many administrators have dealt with the problem pragmatically, embracing the philosophy, "When in doubt, expand." They add new elements as new concerns emerge. For example, several programs that were originally designed to meet the problem of physical child abuse expanded their services to include sexual child abuse when they discovered that some of their clients were also incest victims or that sexual abuse was beginning to constitute a serious problem in their community.

Programs usually have not developed from planned and integrated community efforts but as the outgrowth of small interest groups. Some programs began, and remain in existence, because of the interest taken in that aspect of family violence by a small core of workers. Their individual effort and willingness to invest time in the project made it worthwhile for the agency to provide services to family violence victims and assaulters. If that core group were to leave the agency or turn its attention to another subject, the program would probably cease to exist.

Some programs operate at the whim of public funding sources. As long as state and federal grants underwrite programming costs, agencies provide service. Without Title XX funds, for instance, it is doubtful that many agencies would be able to offer the same range of services to child abusers. Several agencies were able to develop their programs more fully only after they were awarded city or state contracts to become service providers in their areas. If priorities change within the funding agencies, many programs currently aimed toward reducing violence in families might become defunct.

In some cases, programs developed only after the news media

called attention to the lack of integrated services in the community for family violence victims and assaulters. For example, an Indiana-based community organization that coordinates child protective services originated in response to the death of a young boy whose family was known to a number of local agencies and organizations.[13] Many believed the death could have been prevented had better lines of communication been drawn among the various community agencies.

One discovery made during the sample selection phase of the survey was that several factors in programming approaches to family violence treatment and prevention influenced both the type of service delivery provided for assaulters and the amount of service made available to them. These factors included program availability, program content, program focus, program resources, and program orientation.

**Program Availability**   Even though many forms of family violence exist, not all are served equally by community agencies or practitioners. Some are not served at all. The least known forms are the least represented in the community helping network. Despite a concerted effort to locate programs for every type of family violence, the research survey does not contain the names of programs specifically designed to intervene in situations that involve spousal rape, parent battering, or abuse to the elderly. There have been a few attempts by shelters for battered women, self-help groups such as Parents Anonymous, and adult protective services to provide help for the victims of those assaults, but no programs were found that extended help to the assaulter.

Undoubtedly the criteria used to select the research sample hid to some degree the true extent of services available to assaulters. Because the criteria called for a specific program or component of a program that focused exclusively on the abuser, it eliminated some services in agencies, such as family service, that routinely provide counseling for all types of family problems. Nonetheless, the lack of specific programs points to a large gap in efforts to eliminate family violence.

**Program Content**   Program content refers to those services that constitute the program. Ideally, programs should contain a wide range of services for assaulters so that program content can be shaped to meet the needs of each client. In reality, because of constraints imposed by finances, personnel, or interest, most programs limit their services to one or a few types, such as group counseling or parent aides. Even though the services offered are valuable, they may not suit the needs of every client. Consequently, assaulters are forced to conform to the type of service offered or go without service. Many prefer to go without.

**Program Focus** The single-focus programming model dominates the field of family violence. In the survey it was rare to find programs that were designed to deal with all forms of family violence. Those that did were usually geared toward providing short-term assistance. The majority of service providers concentrated their efforts on one type of violence—spouse abuse, physical child abuse, or sexual child abuse.

Maintaining a single focus offers many advantages to agencies and organizations. It gives programs greater administrative manageability, it permits an in-depth understanding of one particular form of family violence, and it conserves rather than scatters resources. However, programs that focus on only one type of assaulter reduce their ability to generalize about assaulter needs and consequently are less able to understand how to treat assaulters who batter more than one member of the family. By looking exclusively at one form they limit their vision about other forms.

**Program Resources** Although many people give lip service to the notion that family violence is a community problem, when it comes time to plan programs, communities often prefer to delegate the responsibility for dealing with family violence to one or a few agencies. Those individuals and administrators who might otherwise welcome the opportunity to assist in reducing family violence decline to participate if they or their program will have to shoulder the problem alone. During times of declining resources, administrators would be reluctant to apply the bulk of their existing resources toward only one type of problem that affects family functioning.

**Program Orientation** By far most programs that deal with family violence have had a victim orientation. With the exception of the physical child abuse category, it was much easier to locate services for victims than for assaulters. Victims generate more sympathy than do assaulters. They are the underdog. They seem more vulnerable and in need of protection. In contrast, assaulters often present themselves defensively, resist change efforts, and drop out of programs early. Many counseling personnel believe that working with assaulters will bring fewer gratifications. As a result, services generally are given to victims and complying family members rather than to disinterested assaulters, especially when the assaulters are male.

In addition to the sympathy they generate, victims are targeted for service because they are more available to participate in the programs offered. Even when service providers are prepared to treat assaulters, assaulters may not be in the position to avail themselves of the services because they have been incarcerated, have separated from the family, or have left the community.

Finally, victims are favored for treatment because they are less threatening to work with than assaulters. Working with abusers can be dangerous to helping personnel. Not all assaulters confine their anger to family members. Some act out their frustrations, fears, and rage through physical abuse directed toward members of the lay and professional community.

Given the service delivery approaches generally applied to the field of family violence, the alternatives open to assaulters are severely limited. The field is characterized by partial service, victim orientation, and limited program availability. Consequently, few options exist for those people who wish to control their violent tendencies or for relatives, friends, and neighbors who would like to intervene on behalf of the victims by encouraging or pressuring assaulters to get the help they need.

## HOW FAMILY VIOLENCE IS PERCEIVED

Problem ownership shapes program content. The approach to working with assaulters is determined, in part, by the way family violence is perceived. For example, if family violence is considered the product of a deranged mind, then program content will focus on the rehabilitation of mental illness. If family violence is a result of external pressures, then program content will focus on removing the sources of external stress. During the past several years, attitudes toward assaulters have changed considerably. The use of social services and community programs has signaled a movement away from the view of the abuser as a criminal to the view of the assaulter as a person who is in need of help.[14] It has prompted a move from punishment to rehabilitation and in its wake programs have sprung up which attempt to rehabilitate by teaching specific skills, by providing emotional insights, by offering support and concern, and by re-socializing.

Programs operate from an explicit or implicit value base concerning people and their problems. In this survey, the general value premise regarding people who sometimes act out violently within their families was that they should be treated as worthwhile human beings, that their behavior can be changed, and that they deserve an opportunity to avail themselves of the treatment resources that will help them change.

Program philosophies often reflect the specific attitudes held about assaulters. For better understanding of how the research participants perceived family violence, they were asked to articulate the philosophy that guided their program for assaulters. Among the research sample four major attitudes emerged:

1. *Societal.* Family violence reflects the general level of acceptance that violence receives in our society. Some helping personnel perceived violence as an American way of life; others saw it as a socially condoned method that allows some people to maintain a privileged position in society. According to this view, abusers are not emotionally ill; they are a product of a society that condones violence. In such a society the abusers as well as the abused are victims of violence. Programs with this philosophy most often dealt with several forms of family violence. They tended to work with the parents or spouses in the family toward learning new behavior and attitudes.

2. *Family Systems.* Violence is symptomatic of a dysfunctional family unit. What affects one or a few family members affects the family as a system. As with the first attitude, family violence victimizes everyone in the family. If some of the emotional needs held by the family members are fulfilled so that they are able to master their environment, they will let go of their pain. Generally this philosophy was expressed most often among agencies that dealt with physical or sexual child abuse. Program personnel were likely to use a group counseling or family therapy approach.

3. *Socialization.* Family violence is the result of inappropriate sex-role socialization. Violent behavior is learned and can be unlearned only through resocialization. According to this view, family violence is the assaulter's problem and is not an outgrowth of family or marital interactions. Programs with this philosophy

most often focused on people who physically abused spouses or children, and the problem was dealt with by means of an educational approach and building social skills.

4. *Early Experiences.* Violence is produced by early life exposure to family environments that are rejecting and violent. These unsatisfactory early experiences lead to impoverished relationships and a generational cycle of violence. The best way to break the cycle of violence is with support and nurturance. Programs that provided services for physical and sexual abusers tended to embrace this philosophy. They used peer groups and reparenting approaches to deal with the problem.

# 2
# PROGRAM OPTIONS FOR ASSAULTERS

The range of program options for assaulters in family violence situations far exceeds what might be anticipated. Rather than one or two standard programming methods, the survey revealed at least four different models and more than a dozen program services. In addition, several programs (some of which are described more fully in Chapters 5 through 10) offered formats that differed substantially from the more traditional individual or group therapy arrangement.

Programs for assaulters were found at both the primary and secondary interventive levels. Primary intervention refers to methods that prevent violence from occurring, and secondary intervention consists of remedial efforts to stop the further spread of violence once it has begun.

Providing general community education fits the primary intervention category. Most programs in the survey provided speakers for community groups. Their job was to sensitize the community to the magnitude of the problem, the signs of its occurrence, and ways to cope with it. Their aim was to raise the level of public awareness about the problem of family violence and suggest the means to prevent or stop it.

Another form of primary prevention program revolved around concepts of marital and family life education. Many of these programs were offered to young adults and to teenagers. The hope was to present a realistic picture of problems that occur in marriage along with ways to deal with those situations nonviolently. Some-times these programs focused on parent education and were hospital based to reach new parents, especially mothers who were considered part of a high-risk population, those people who were likely to resort to violence. They were offered basic information about child development and child-rearing practices to prevent misconceptions which might lead them to believe that their children were being willful or nonloving.

Programs at the secondary intervention level were largely remedial and sought to stop further abuse among identified assaulters. The most commonly found among the research sample were the counseling programs for individuals, couples, and families who were unable to cope with the violence in the family. Some programs took a short-term, crisis intervention approach which focused on the immediate violent incident. They attempted to understand the triggering mechanisms and offered possible alternate ways of reacting or interacting. The majority of programs saw the problem of violence rooted in a long individual or family history which required a more detailed look at the total life history of the abuser and his or her family. Groups for abusers offered both therapy and education to men and women who, either voluntarily or by court order, sought to stop the abuse against spouse or child. The group members usually examined the violence in their own lives and were taught how to identify and control their anger.

Spanning both the primary and secondary levels of intervention were those programs that combined short-term counseling with useful information about child rearing or marital problems. The use of hotlines and telephone counseling, for example, tends to reach both high-risk populations and those who have already begun to abuse. Support groups also link primary and secondary interventive efforts. They tend to break through the isolation that is so often associated with family violence and provide a support network who can be called upon when tensions build.

## PROGRAM FORMATS

Four major categories of programming formats emerged from the survey: counseling, education, support, and mediation.

**Counseling** This may take the form of individual, marital, family, or group therapy. The goals are to develop inner awareness, understand the basis of behavior, learn alternatives to current behavioral patterns, identify and label feelings, clarify role behaviors, and enhance interpersonal communication. For instance, an agency in Illinois connected with a juvenile court offers sexual abusers and their families long-term individual therapy, marital counseling, and family therapy. A multidisciplinary counseling center in Colorado is also a long-term treatment resource. Its program focuses on weekly marital therapy sessions which deal with the issues of husband–wife communication and self-esteem. Another Colorado program uses only a group counseling approach in its work with spouse abusers. Its program requires at least a four-week commitment on the part of the clients. Since it is usually the first counseling experience for the participants, the group time is structured so that there are opening and closing rounds in which everyone participates.

**Education** The emphasis here is on the acquisition of new information and on skill development. Assertiveness training, relaxation techniques, parenting classes, and anger management instruction belong in this model. A family service agency in Rhode Island offers parents an eight-session child management class that follows a prescribed course based on an approach called the Systematic Training for Effective Parenting. A Michigan program for spouse abusers presents a six-session theme-centered educational group that focuses on marital myths, the dynamics of violence, and the way that people communicate. A private practitioner in Minnesota uses a cognitive behavioral approach that includes assertiveness training, body awareness, and anger management in his treatment of abusers.

A counseling center in a community near New York City offers several educational workshops including one for spouse abusers and another for parents of young children. The workshop for spouse abusers is based on the premise that most batterers do not voluntarily seek treatment; they often avoid or prematurely terminate counseling service and so an educational format would be the least threatening to abusers who were remanded for service by the courts. The workshop is designed to confront the illegality, immorality, and damaging consequences of abusive behavior. The format of the three two-hour sessions includes (1) a description of spouse abuse laws and the role of the police and the courts, (2) a discussion of a film that illustrates the causes and damaging consequences of spouse abuse, and (3) a discussion of nonviolent methods of communication. Because of the amount of material to be covered and the complexity of the topic, the organization is planning to expand the number of sessions to six and also to add three follow-up contacts.

Parent education programs are based on the assumption that greater understanding and better coping will alleviate parental helplessness and rage that can result in child abuse and other family dysfunction. The weekly sessions educate parents in the normal development of young children and help parents deal with interactions around such common areas as limit setting, meal times, nutrition, health, bedtime, siblings, sexuality, cleanliness, and independence.

**Support**  The goal of these programs is to reduce or eliminate the sources of stress that increase the likelihood of violent reactions. The more common program components include homemaker services, support and socialization groups, case aides who provide concrete services, and parent aides who serve a reparenting function. For example, a Hawaiian social service agency offers a broad-based outreach program that uses paraprofessionals who function as homemakers and teach parents budgeting, marketing, and child care skills; lay therapists who provide nurturing and parenting to the adults; and logistic aides who give transportation and other concrete services. This is a long-term service for abusive parents, who, on the average, use the service for eleven months. The Parents Anonymous self-help program provides a well-known model of ongoing group support to potential or actual child abusers. According to its co-founder, PA is like an extended family for people who never had one before. For two hours every week parents have the opportunity both to socialize and talk over life stresses or parent–child problems with their peers who have experienced similar problems.

**Mediation**  The focus of mediation programs is on the immediate cessation of violence by means of defusing the explosive situation and referring the participants to local resources where they can receive help to prevent future violent occurrences. Crisis intervention, assessment, short-term counseling, and resource location are the most common components in this approach. This type of service is usually affiliated with the criminal justice system to assist law enforcement officials when they are called out to intervene in a domestic disturbance complaint. A program in Arizona is housed in the county attorney's office and personnel can be summoned in crisis situations such as suicides, sexual assaults, death notifications, and family disputes. Its workers may be paged 24 hours a day. Two evenings a week, those nights when the largest number of family fights occur, program personnel drive unmarked cars equipped with police radio so that they are available for immediate response to calls for assistance. In family violence situations the main goal is to keep the peace. They offer crisis intervention and seek to determine what happened and what the respondents want. They explain the options available to the victims and the assaulters and try to elicit a commitment to change. Workers usually see the respondents only once, at the time of the disturbance. However, they may spend from one to three hours with the family members until the situation has cooled down. They provide the family with information about community services such as counseling programs or alcohol and drug rehabilitation programs, where they can obtain long-term assistance. Not only does this program help to reduce family violence, it also saves the police department money by reducing the amount of time officers have to remain on the scene.

Few programs use one approach exclusively; most combine elements of two or more models. The most common combination is counseling and support. An incest treatment program in California that operates under the auspices of a juvenile probations department proceeds through several counseling phases, including individual therapy for the child, mother, and father; mother–child counseling; father–child counseling; and total family counseling. In addition, personnel assist clients in locating needed community resources, such as housing or legal aid. An outgrowth of that program, which has subsequently become an integral component, is a support group that offers the abusers and their spouses an opportunity to meet between therapy sessions. The group experience serves as a socialization vehicle as well as a self-help medium.

Another favored combination is the counseling–education approach. A Michigan-based organization offers a counseling–education program for couples who are involved in domestic violence. They hold six weekly theme-centered sessions which last for an hour and a half each. The program developed in response to a state law that requires mandatory counseling programs as a provision of probation for individuals convicted of assault and battery in a domestic situation. The focus of the program is to provide individuals and couples with information, understanding, and skills which enable them to change the assaultive behavior and enhance the quality of interaction among family members. The couples meet as part of a larger group and during the six weeks discuss their conception of marriage, the meaning of domestic violence, how people communicate, how to cope with life, the dynamics of domestic violence, and how to change their behavior. They learn about such things as sex-role stereotypes, the history of domestic violence, meeting communication needs, assessing their coping skills, channeling their anger productively, conflict resolution, and assertiveness training. After the initial meeting, each session begins with feedback from group members about what has been happening during the week and a discussion of any delayed reactions from the previous session. All group members are expected to participate during the meetings and relate their particular situation and behaviors in regard to the topic under discussion.

A third combination is education and support. For example, among its services, a hospital-based community mental health center offers a seven- to eight-week Parent Effectiveness Training course to its clients and also provides supportive services in the form of transportation, day care, recreation, and socialization luncheons. A North Carolina agency developed an early intervention parent education program for parents of newborns. Based in a hospital, the program seeks to foster parent–child bonding. In addition, the agency supplies parent aides who go into the clients' homes two or three hours a week to spend time with the parents. The agency also sponsors a parent support group in conjunction with its day care program. The service is run on a drop-in basis. Each session is self-contained but concentrates on building self-esteem and supplying parents with child development information.

# NEWER FORMATS

Some agencies have been experimenting with alternatives to the more traditional service delivery models. Their programs provide a combination of services within unique formats. Some of the more unusual formats that were discovered during the survey included the following.

**Coalitions** Some communities formed coalitions or consortiums that were established by community agencies to provide a broad-based and integrated network of services to clients. For instance, a group in Indiana concerned with child abuse is composed of a collaboration of 31 community agencies that offer a wide range of services from diagnostic assessment, to sponsoring PA groups, to providing parent surrogates. Another group, in New York State, serves as a coordinating body that prevents service fragmentation caused by inadequate communication between agencies. Every month they hold team meetings comprised of all people who provide service to a particular family, e.g., protective services worker, therapist, teacher, public health nurse. What makes this group truly unique is that the parents are also required to be present at those meetings so that they too can participate. An example of a consortium is described in Chapter 5.

**Residential Centers**   Most residential centers are shelters for the victims of violence, but some agencies have established residences for the total family. In California there is a 72-hour residential facility that offers a warm, supportive setting in which the family can cool off. Tennessee has a two-week residential program that allows time to observe the family's interactional patterns and to initiate treatment. (This program is more fully described in Chapter 6.) A program no longer in existence, but successful as a pilot project, was a four-week program for spouse abusers. They were housed on an inpatient unit in a medical center. During their stay the men engaged in a group that focused on sex-role stereotypes, a coping skills group, physical activities, assertiveness training, and relaxation training.

**In-Home Services**   In this case the service goes to the client's home. An agency in Iowa spends at least four hours a week for eight months providing family therapy and parenting meetings. A midwestern agency offers an intensive in-home service that teaches child management skill training. During the first week personnel make three to five home visits, then three visits the second week, followed by one visit a week for the next two and a half to three months. Another program that works with parents in their own homes is described in Chapter 7.

**Hotlines Plus**   The concept of hotlines is certainly not new, but many organizations are doing a good deal of follow-up with their clients and some are combining crisis counseling with short-term respite care. For instance, a southern California organization offers both a 24-hour hotline and family aides who are trained to serve as caring friends to stressed families. In northern California a community organization helps parents deal with stressful situations by providing hotline service plus emergency baby-sitting, emergency foster care (overnight or weekend), and parent helpers to assist with shopping or apartment hunting.

**Family Camp**  A California family service agency sponsors a family camp accommodating twelve families, who meet for four weekends during a three-month period. The weekends are highly structured and include a therapy group that focuses on the parents' early childhood experiences, self-esteem, and self-fulfillment; an information workshop on topics such as nutrition or budgeting; a parent education class that is aimed at the modification of specific behaviors the parents want their children to change; dance and psychodrama for adults; and recreational activities. This program is described more fully in Chapter 10.

# PROGRAM COMPONENTS

The program components are the services that form the core of the program. Several services were identified in the survey, although not every program uses every type of service.

**Individual Counseling**  In this approach the counselor or therapist sees the abuser alone. The one-to-one interaction facilitates the development of trust and dependence and may be perceived by the client as less threatening than group or family counseling. The individual approach relies on guidance, support, and/or insight techniques to change client behavior. The counselor may guide the client by pointing to the legal options or likely course of events the client can anticipate encountering, or may provide support by building self-esteem, or may develop insight by exploring the client's early life experiences. Because so many perpetrators of family violence have themselves been abused, many counselors encourage their clients to work through their own feelings about the prior abuse which placed them in the victim's role. The counseling sessions identify other problems in daily life that may contribute to the violence and suggest ways to eliminate pressures. One program insists on providing individual counseling for all members of the family so that each person may have the opportunity to understand the impact of the violent behavior on his or her life. Most individual counseling sessions are scheduled on a once a week basis. An exception to that practice is a program for abusive spouses in Connecticut wherein the counselor meets with each client twice a week for three months, then once a week for three months, then does a one-year follow-up. The more intense contact allows the therapist to take a detailed life history in blocks of three or four years and discuss the effects that each phase has had on the client's perception of himself and his attitudes toward others.

**Group Counseling** Group therapy is a popular and less expensive alternative to individual counseling. The group format provides many sources of feedback for the abuser from people who share similar feelings and problems and also exerts peer pressure on the participants to change their behavior. Most group leaders expect the group members to take responsibility for introducing the issues they wish to discuss. However, many are beginning to use a theme-centered approach for each session to channel the groups' thoughts and energies. One major focus in many groups is the way anger is identified and expressed. Another is on the sex-role conditioning related to violence. Groups offer abusers a new perspective about the ways that they communicate, the psychological games they play, and how they present themselves. It also provides them an arena in which they may improve their social skills.

Some agencies bring five or six husband-wife dyads together to form couples groups. The discussion usually centers on marital issues and the effects of abuse on the children. Other programs conduct multiple family therapy in which four to six family units meet as a large group.

**Marital Counseling** Violence in the family often has a detrimental effect on the marital relationship even when the spouse is not the target of the abuse. Many counselors believe that each member of the marital union is equally responsible for the quality of the relationship. Conjoint counseling of the husband—wife unit is offered to improve communication between the couple, to point out areas of collusion, to identify marital problems, and to determine what is left to salvage in the relationship. Conjoint treatment is not always the primary goal; it may be an intermediary step. For example, sometimes the marriage is so shattered that the couple needs marital counseling for a few months before it is possible to work with the entire family unit. Marital counseling offers an arena in which to air pent-up grievances, correct misperceptions about the meaning attributed to the spouse's behavior, and learn new ways of relating to each other. A New Jersey program asks the couple to examine the role that each parent plays with the children and also the way they displace problems on to the spouse or child.

**Family Counseling**   Meeting with all members of the family together is one way to make certain that each person's feelings and point of view are heard and respected by the other family members. It also makes it easier to analyze the dynamics of family interactions and to understand the alliances and coalitions that make up family patterns. For example, a program for sexual abusers meets with the total family for at least six months to discuss reversed roles, power distribution, communication patterns, and the distribution of responsibility. Usually family counseling takes place once a week, but some programs are structured so that workers may meet with the whole family twice a week; in an Iowa agency, program personnel may see the entire family as often as three times a week until the situation is under control. Family counseling may take place with part of the family rather than with every member. Workers in a Texas agency routinely interview the total family for the first few sessions, then work with subgroups in the family for several sessions before returning to work with the whole family again.

**Respite Care**   When there isn't enough money to make ends meet, when the baby cries incessantly, when the world seems overwhelming, people need help, but not necessarily counseling. One administrator believes that more child abusers can benefit from respite care services than can benefit from psychotherapy. Respite care services are designed to give people a chance to take a temporary breather from the conditions that produce extreme stress. The most common form of respite service is day care for children. Clients who are affiliated with a child abuse program in New York, for instance, have one day a week all to themselves without worrying about the children, who are being cared for in a center operated by the agency. Concrete services, especially those that provide homemaker service or transportation, also relieve the feeling of being overwhelmed and make life more manageable for clients. Decreased pressure on the parents often reduces the amount of frustration abusive parents displace on their children and increases the level of tolerance for their children's behavior.

**Parent Aide** Isolation is a common feature among abusers. Parent aides provide companionship and give abusers someone who listens and cares about them. One New York agency supplies each family that it serves with a parent aide whose function is to provide the abuser with support, with budgeting and homemaking assistance, and with social experiences. Because so few of its abusive parents have experienced success in their lives, one family service agency provides parent aides who teach, encourage, and model productive and satisfying behavior for their clients. Parent aides attempt to build the abuser's level of self-esteem and develop a broader support system. They also help abusers obtain more enjoyment from life by going on picnics or outings into the larger community.

**Support Groups** Sometimes no one can understand the needs of abusers better than people who have experienced the problem themselves. Whether as an adjunct to therapy or an entity in itself, the support group serves as both a socialization vehicle and a self-help medium. Sharing is the foundation of support groups. Many times the group meeting begins as a social event around coffee and cake and informal interaction among the participants. Then as a large group they discuss the personal events that caused pain, concern, or joy during the week. To make certain that everyone who wishes to share something with the group has time for discussion, some groups ask their members to contract for a specified amount of time at the beginning of the session to discuss a specific topic or problem. Not all discussions revolve around emotional issues; some include discussion of personal health care and life skills. The groups usually meet once a week and are facilitated by one or two members. Sometimes a member of the professional staff serves as a co-facilitator, but, unlike a group therapy leader, the professionally trained person is there mainly in the capacity of a resource person. Some support groups are created largely for recreational purposes. Their members go on outings or learn art and craft skills. The group gives its members a change from the normal routine and helps them develop better social skills.

**Educational Groups** Many educational groups take the form of classes and most of them focus on interpersonal communication skills and child development information. However, one program for child abusers includes information not only about child development, but also about first aid and toy making. A Delaware agency conducts a nine-week program with each two-hour session focusing on specific content such as how to cope with stress, how to express emotions, family communication, and conflict resolution. A Texas agency conducts a twelve-week parent effectiveness training program that includes the topics of child development, discipline, problem solving, self-esteem, and effective communication.

**Hotlines**   Hotlines have the advantage of instant accessibility so that they can provide immediate assistance for immediate problems. Hotline workers are prepared to offer crisis intervention over the telephone. They help people cope with the flood of fears and emotional feelings that trigger abuse. They point out options that are available in the community for future use. Also, they suggest linkages with family and social support networks. However, not all situations are crises. Hotline workers also provide information about normal human development and local resources. The worker may speak to a person only once, but the outcome can have long-lasting effects.

**Assessment**   An assessment is an evaluation of individual and family functioning in a family violence situation. That evaluation can have far-reaching consequences on every family member. Assessments serve many purposes. They often are made to determine what services are called for in a particular case. They also may be used to determine whether a child should be removed or returned to the home, whether the abuser is too dangerous to remain at large in the community, or whether a specific agency is appropriate for the type of problem discovered. The evaluation is usually based on a psychosocial history of the individual or family as well as involvement with other community agencies. However, many agencies also include medical, neurological, and psychological testing.

**Case Management**   Because many social and health agencies provide service, one family may be connected with half a dozen different community agencies. Case management serves to coordinate services among the various agencies. Case managers act as overseers, making certain that goals and objectives are being met by seeing to it that the family is following through and that the community is following through. In addition, case managers pull together plans and actions which result in meeting case objectives. In some instances they also evaluate service requests or needs in relation to the availability of the needed services.

**Advocacy** Advocate services ensure that client rights and needs are being protected. One program uses former abusers to work as advocates for current abusers. They explain what to expect, go with them to court, tell them what services they are entitled to, and help them negotiate the social service system. Some program advocates talk to community groups to maintain funding for continued service; others talk with judges, lawyers, and police about the enforcement of laws, and some work with legislators in the formulation of needed legislation.

**Community Education** Most programs assign personnel to perform community education functions. The purpose of community education is to raise the level of public awareness. It can be done at all levels of the community from lay public to legislators to professionals. Speakers describe the extent of the problem, how it manifests itself, why it happens, and what can be done about it. Sometimes representatives from several community agencies will form a panel to discuss the problem of family violence from several points of view and suggest ways to tighten the community network.

**Information and Referral** Sometimes a little knowledge can go a long way to help people cope with difficult or frustrating life situations. Information and referral services offer assistance to people who do not know where else to turn for help. This service gives people some idea about the options that are available to them and links them with the appropriate community resource. Many times the personnel who operate the service not only have a good working knowledge of the community resource network, they also are familiar with the laws and procedures that apply to a given situation. Usually information and referral components serve the professional community as well as the lay public, suggesting resources that assist professionals in their work with clients.

**Residential** A residential service enables persons to be removed from the environment that triggers and reinforces violence and be placed in a setting that is safe and protective. Historically, residential services have been used for victims of violence who have needed foster homes, institutions, or shelters. However, for abusers they tend to offer a combination of support and structure that helps to control impulsive acting out. The residence is perceived as a neutral territory in which it is safe to explore feelings and begin to break the pattern of abuse. The length of stay permitted in residence varies with the program and may be as little as 48 hours or as long as two weeks.

**Training** The training component stresses skill development for clients. It teaches clients how to enhance the effectiveness of their interpersonal transactions. Most training programs make wide use of modeling and role-playing activities in which the clients emulate the behaviors demonstrated by the workers. One program conducts its training sessions in rooms furnished to simulate the various living areas in a home. A program in Missouri uses videotape feedback of parent—child interactions as part of its training procedures. Some programs shape specific behaviors with behavioral techniques; the therapists teach their clients how to reinforce desired behaviors from family members and how to extinguish those behaviors that are disruptive.

## SUMMARY

In general, programs for physical child abusers contained the most extensive variety of services. They were also the oldest, many having been in existence since the early 1970's. They offered individual counseling, therapy groups, support groups, parent aides, child development classes, skill training courses, and an array of concrete services. In contrast, most services for battering spouses had begun within the previous two years and leaned toward short-term groups, marital counseling, individual treatment, and crisis intervention. Programs for sexual abusers are relatively new also, most having begun within the previous five years. These programs tended to include family counseling, marital counseling, individual treatment, and support groups.

# ISSUES IN PROGRAM DEVELOPMENT

Program development begins with a good idea, but there can be many pitfalls if some aspects are not well thought through. Some of the issues that might be considered emerged during the interviews with program administrators.

## PARAPROFESSIONALS

Most organizations in the survey hired professionally trained workers, such as social workers, psychologists, or child care specialists, especially when counseling, education, and day care services were part of the program. However, those agencies that provided supportive services often relied on nonprofessional volunteers or paid paraprofessionals for the bulk of their service provision. The most widely used paraprofessionals were those who served as parent aides or parent surrogates. Selection of parent aides is based on certain desirable characteristics among the applicants. Because the parent aide is expected to serve as a role model for the client, the aide is usually a female who has successfully raised children of her own. Because the parent aide is also expected to "parent the parent," applicants should display acceptance, warmth, and maturity. One California agency that considers family aides to be the heart of its efforts to prevent child abuse and neglect looks for people who hold a deep commitment to working with parents in stress, who demonstrate personal maturity, a nonjudgmental attitude, willingness to listen, genuine interest in people, and responsible behavior, and who are agreeable to receiving training and supervision. A Kansas City Parent Aide program looks for people who have had good parenting experiences themselves, both as children and as parents, or who have acknowledged and worked through negative experiences. They need to be well enough "put together" psychologically to give emotionally to others without being drained. Some volunteers do not have children but have had extensive contact with children so that they can understand the pressures attendant in 24-hour-a-day parenting. Motivation for wanting to become a parent aide is also important to consider. Those who lack adequate emotional supports in their personal lives and who see involvement with the parents as a major way to fulfill their own emotional needs or to work through their personal problems are not good candidates.

Most programs require their parent aides to complete a training program that may take from six to eight weeks. Frequently this training includes films and speakers that provide information about the dynamics of the abusing family, the learning of communication and listening skills, and the way to be an advocate for the family; also situations are role-played around the initial interview, a family crisis, or dealing with hostility.

Agencies expect a specific commitment from parent aides. A North Carolina organization, for instance, expects the parent aide to attend an intensive six- to eight-session experiential and didactic training session, spend five hours a week per family, and participate in weekly group meetings, as well as undergo personal supervision, in order to receive the support they need to work with the clientele. An Indiana agency expects its parent surrogates to participate in an eight-week training program (two hours per week), to make a time commitment to the program of three hours a week for a period of a year, and to attend bimonthly supervisory sessions. Another midwestern program expects that its parent aides will complete a 30-hour training course, make a two-year commitment to the program, see the assigned parent at least once a week as well as keep in touch by telephone between visits, regularly attend weekly parent aide group meetings, report any incidents of abuse or neglect, keep logs of time spent related to the program, and fill out periodic data forms for evaluation.

## FUNDING

"Our fund-raising efforts never stop," sighed a program administrator. "We are constantly searching for new ways to keep our programs running. We get a little money from here and a little from there. Our funding patterns look like a patchwork quilt." Although the cost of some family violence programs can be absorbed within the agency's budget, most agencies and organizations must generate funds from outside sources for these programs. In many cases, the program costs cannot even be offset by a fee for service because the majority of family violence programs (at least those in this survey) charge either no fees or very low fees. Financial backing comes mainly through contracts, grants, donations, Title XX, or federal, state, and county matching funds. Some state-mandated programs are guaranteed funds through the state and county legislature. For programs that are not supported by the legislature, contracting is the most favored approach. The organization contracts to provide a certain type of service to clients referred from the funding agency. For example, a county may wish to augment its child protective services but may not want to hire additional county workers or sustain the cost of a particular service as part of its ongoing operating budget. Therefore it contracts for those services from a community agency that already has the needed service. One typical example is a contract with the county child protective services division to provide its clients with parent education, transportation, child care, or counseling services. Another common example is a contract with the state attorney general's office or a city district attorney's office to provide outpatient treatment to spouse abusers as part of a diversion program.

Grants offer another way to underwrite programs. Federal agencies such as the Law Enforcement Administration or the National Center for Child Abuse and Neglect sponsor demonstration projects which enable agencies to develop and test model programs that might otherwise be too expensive for them to attempt. Private foundations seek programs that eradicate social problems or improve the quality of community life and provide the seed money to begin new programs. However, grants tend to be time-limited, usually from two to four years, and grantors expect that continued program operation will come from community support. The competition for grants is stiff and program administrators spend large portions of their time locating appropriate foundations and writing grant proposals.

In contrast to the laments of many administrators came the comment by a few program directors: "We don't need funds. Everything is donated." Many smaller organizations find that they can operate their program successfully from in-kind donations. Furniture, office space, telephone, printing all are donated by local businesses and organizations. Frequently, workers in these programs are unpaid, volunteering a certain number of hours each week to work with the abusers. Because program operation needs are shared, no one group or individual feels overburdened in the provision of goods or services.

## COMMUNITY SUPPORT

Despite the ultimate good that might be derived from the program, not all segments of the community enthusiastically embrace services that intervene in family violence. Some programs for battered women, for example, found that people did not want shelters established in their neighborhoods because they feared destruction of their property and violence from the abuser. In other cases, such as those programs operated by a contract with a specific agency whose referrals come only from the contracting agency, the general public and even the professional community may be unaware that the service exists. However, most program administrators actively seek the good will of the community. They want to operate in an accepting, rather than a hostile, environment. Many program executives believe that a solid base of community support and is needed to sustain a long-lived program. A community committed to the worth of a project can be called upon to provide continued financial support. Also, a professional community that perceives the program as being necessary to an integrated social service base can be counted upon to make continued client referrals. Most administrators strive to maintain community ties through coalitions and meetings which enable them to become viable members of the community power base and have input into the decision-making structure which shapes the policies affecting family violence programming.

## PROGRAM EVALUATION

Mechanisms that evaluate the success with which a program achieves its goals usually receive the least amount of attention during the program development phase. Most agencies and organizations use informal evaluation techniques. The most common criterion used among abuse programs is the recidivism, or reabuse, rate. However, considering the reluctance of people to report abusers, the likelihood of an abusive incident reaching the authorities is low. Another widely used method is based on client feedback. Almost all programs include a follow-up period, usually ranging from three months to one year, during which the workers call or visit the clients to assess the current family situation. Some workers examine changes in the quality of the interactions between the abused and the abuser. Many conduct a case review to see if treatment goals have been met. Others establish a contract with the client when service begins, and they end their service when the contract goals have been accomplished.

Some programs attempt to overcome the distortions found in the use of informal techniques by developing a series of measurable objectives. One child abuse program that uses a group work approach does an ongoing evaluation of client performance. For instance, they assess the client's actions in the group and check to see whether the clients attend at least 50 percent of the group meetings. Many programs have adopted the Goal Attainment Scaling technique suggested in the Rita and Blair Justice book, *The Abusing Family.*[1] Workers and clients first identify main problem areas or areas of concern that require change and then they set goals for the client in each of those areas. Within each problem area goal attainment progresses along a five-point continuum: most unfavorable outcome likely, less than expected success, expected level of success, more than expected success, most favorable outcome likely. The worker and client determine what behaviors belong at each point along the continuum. Some programs use baseline entry tests of knowledge and attitudes. The clients are retested after completion of the program to determine what changes took place as a result of their participation in the program. One program even uses videotape to help their workers evaluate the amount of progress a family has made. They videotape a family session at the beginning of the program and

---

again at the end of the program to determine the extent to which the clients have learned the skills that were taught.

## BURNOUT PREVENTION

"We had a 50 percent turnover in the past year," complained a California administrator. "Two years seems to be the most that our workers can take," commented the head of an Illinois program. Indeed, most of the program personnel surveyed identified burnout prevention as a major issue that was not addressed very well by their programs. However, each had some suggestions for reducing the likelihood of worker burnout.

The first type of suggestion concerned worker support through mutual interaction. "Nothing causes people to burn out faster than working in isolation," said one counselor. Many agencies provide formal activities that enhance mutual support and interaction such as weekly staff meetings, peer supervision, outside consultation, and full staff review of all cases as a team so that one person does not carry the decision-making burden alone. Many agencies also encourage informal supportive activities among their workers such as weekend social recreation, staff retreats, potluck dinners, and picnics. Volunteers require support also, even though most work only part-time. Administrators provide them with easy access to staff and are prepared to be on call themselves. Some programs make it a point to reward their volunteers with dinners and certificates as recognition of their service.

The second way to reduce worker burnout was through training and education which gave information workers need to help them deal effectively with their clients. Many agencies provide ongoing in-service training programs, some hold periodic all-day training sessions, and many encourage their workers to attend conferences that relate specifically to the problems experienced by people on their caseload.

A third suggestion was to reduce the pressure on the line staff. A common way is to use co-therapists, especially in dealing with groups and families. Changing worker functions periodically by rotating job responsibilities also helps to reduce the pressure that builds when one is working with such a crisis-prone client population. Some administrators find that setting concrete goals for each case so that progress is more visible can be rewarding to workers as well as to clients.

A fourth suggestion concerned the line staff's work hours. Many people advocated the need for flexible working hours and compensatory time off. Others believed that the number of work hours spent with abusive families should be limited. Several agencies offer their workers liberal vacation and sick leave policies, such as five-week annual vacations and one-day-a-month cumulative sick leave. Some agency administrators have even instituted the concept of mental health days: free days off that are not charged to the worker's vacation or sick leave. One agency allows its workers to take five mental health days a year.

The final means for reducing burnout was associated with caseloads. Workers suggested limiting or reducing their caseloads, carrying diverse cases rather than only cases that involve abuse, and refraining from scheduling patients back to back. "But," said one counselor, "there always seems to be a 'Catch-22.' There are so few people working with abusers that more of those cases tend to come to us who are willing to work with them."

Some additional words of advice from Oklahoma that were echoed by workers in Washington and Minnesota: Don't exploit yourself or others. Take a break when you feel under stress. Say "no" and stick to it. "There is no sense trying to prevent burnout," contends a program director. "Everybody does eventually. The important thing is knowing when to leave."

# 3
# ASSAULTER CHARACTERISTICS

In the hope that a profile of the assaulters might emerge, part of the research was designed to obtain information about the people who used the services that the agencies provided. Certain characteristics did, indeed, arise from the descriptions workers gave of their clients. Two types of information were generated, one that led to a demographic profile and the other that led to a personality profile. Profiles can aid in identifying general characteristics of a target population which point to high-risk factors. They offer the clues that alert workers to potential abuse and the need for certain types of service. Profiles also have some important limitations. One criticism often leveled at the use of profiles is their tendency to force people into preselected categories. Sometimes the categories are so general and all-encompassing they do not help to point out differences between one group and another. For example, low self-esteem is a characteristic often associated with assaulters, but it has also been associated with victims and even seems to characterize many clinical populations. However, when used as a guide, profiles enhance our ability to differentiate as well as to predict.

A few people in the survey found themselves unable to talk about the "typical" client or "most frequent" clients, saying instead that each one was different or that no pattern was apparent because the program served a small number of abusers. However, the majority were able to formulate, both from the agency's statistical records and from personal experience, those factors that seemed most prevalent among the people who were identified as assaulters of family members.

# DEMOGRAPHIC PROFILE

This sample may not accurately represent the majority of family violence perpetrators in the United States. Nevertheless, the following profile appeared.

**Child Abusers**   Physical child abusers tended to range in age from 17 to the mid-30's, with most in their late teens and early 20's. A high proportion were single parents (female) who received welfare and consequently were in the low to low-middle income groups. College education was rare among this sample. Although many were high school graduates, most had not graduated from high school. The majority of child abusers were Caucasian, with blacks represented to a lesser extent. Where religious affiliation was known, it leaned toward Catholicism and fundamentalist sects.

**Spouse Abusers**   In this sample, spouse abusers tended to range in age from 20 to 40, with most in their mid-20's to early 30's. The vast majority were Caucasian males, although a few females were also included. Most were in the blue-collar to middle income groups. Very few were totally unemployed or on welfare. The majority were high school graduates and some also had college or vocational training. Most agencies did not ask for information about their clients' religious affiliation. Where it was known, Catholic, Protestant, and fundamentalist religions were cited most often.

**Sexual Abusers**   The ages of sexual child abusers ranged from 20 to 50, with the majority in their middle 30's. Caucasions were most represented,· with some blacks and Hispanics. The abusers tended to be males who fell in the lower to middle and middle to upper-middle income groups. Most had graduated from high school and some had graduated from college. Where religious affiliation was known, Baptist, Catholic, and fundamentalist sects were mentioned most often.

This sample was composed predominantly of Caucasians who hold fundamentalist religious beliefs. When the information is organized in chart form, some interesting trends emerge related to age, education, and income. Physical child abusers tended to be younger, less educated, and of the lower income levels than the other abusers. Sexual child abusers tended to be the best educated and in the higher income levels.

| Factor | Child Abuse | Spouse Abuse | Sex Abuse |
|---|---|---|---|
| Age | late teens–mid-20's | late 20's–early 30's | Mid-30's |
| Ethnicity | Caucasian, black | Caucasian | Caucasian |
| Education | Did not graduate high school | Graduated high school | High school grads plus college |
| Income | Lower to blue collar | Blue collar to middle | Middle |
| Religion | Fundamentalist | Insufficient data | Fundamentalist |

# PERSONALITY PROFILE

**Child Abusers**   The words that most often characterized physical child abusers were isolation, depression, low self-esteem, and hopelessness. They entered parenthood unprepared, either emotionally or educationally, to assume the parenting role. Their deficiency in child development information led them to hold inappropriate expectations for their children. They suffered early deprivation from battering and neglectful relatives. Many lacked consistent parenting figures, having grown up in foster homes and institutions. Some sacrificed their childhood in order to parent their parents. Said one child care specialist, "They have huge dependency needs and no place to put them."

They lack the basic communication skills to ask for what they need and consequently wind up with very little that is gratifying. "They don't like themselves very much," remarked a psychologist. "They feel like losers and every failure reinforces their sense of worthlessness and hopelessness." In a way, they set themselves up for failure—sometimes through their impulsive behavior and sometimes by making themselves unattractive through their hostile and rejecting actions.

All too often they become involved in negative and emotionally unsatisfying relationships in which they are the victims. They find

themselves alone, with no support system, and with multiple problems (financial, marital, alcohol) that place additional stress on their
parenting abilities. One New York worker summarized their plight
by saying: "They are too young, have too many children, too little
money, and too few resources. It's like having 500 pounds of Jell-O
sitting in the middle of the living room." They feel overwhelmed and
powerless to change their lives, a feeling that leads to a "why bother"
attitude. "They have been angry all their lives and now they are angry at home," said a Washington counselor. Their anger masks a deep
depression. According to many counselors, child abusers were depressed and lonely children. They don't know how to have fun or
enjoy themselves. It's as though they are saying, "I am having a rot-
ten time as a parent, so don't expect me to enjoy life."

**Spouse Abusers** Counselors described spouse abusers as pos-
sessive, controlling, impulsive, and insecure. They deal with stress
poorly and have a low frustration threshold. "It seems as though any
challenge leads to chaos," said one worker. "Their wife is the one
link that holds them together." They have few friends outside of the
family. "For many of them," noted a counselor in Boston, "the family
is everything and the wife forms the center of their universe." Individuation or any type of separation is threatening. "They are so tied
to the relationship that they have no sense of the wife as a separate
entity," explained a counselor affiliated with a Colorado program. If
the wife leaves, it is like losing a part of themselves; they become
desperate. They attempt to isolate the woman in the home, cut her
off from friends or family. Jealousy colors their thoughts and fills
their minds with suspicions of what she is doing when he is not at
home. They hold traditional and stereotypic views of male–female
relationships and are concerned with maintaining a masculine image.
The men set rigid expectations. "They build their own reality about
what people should be doing, and if people act differently everything
falls apart," commented a counselor in California. A family referral
service in Canada reported some typical situations that lead to
spousal violence. In one of those cases a woman related, "Usually my
husband has been drinking and comes home looking for a fight. He
wants his dinner even though it may be four o'clock in the morning
or he wants me to go to bed with him. If I don't do what he wants
immediately, he starts hitting me." The abusers are not only impulsive, some are compulsive. "There is a compulsive quality to their
behavior," said a program director in Minnesota, "which shows up in

their setting many rules at home, being performance oriented, and placing high demands on themselves."

A large percentage were raised in homes in which they were physically abused or witnessed abuse directed against their mothers or siblings. Because of their poor communication skills they seem underdeveloped behaviorally, their actions reminiscent of an adolescent rebellion. They often display other impulse and dependency disorders such as alcohol, drugs, and management problems in jobs. According to a counselor in Boston, they carry such a low level of self-esteem that when asked to tell something they like about themselves, many can't think of a thing.

Many spouse abusers never learned to deal with emotional closeness and nonsexual intimacy. They are not in touch with their feelings. "At some level they are vulnerable to their wives in a way that they haven't been to anyone else since childhood," contends a worker in Minnesota. Some counselors believe the men's ambivalence toward dependency comes out in anger and that violence helps the men avoid intimacy. In fact, counselors reported that most emotions, especially sadness, become improperly labeled or responded to inaccurately and are translated into anger.

**Sexual Abusers**   Rigid, domineering, isolated, high expectations, and low self-esteem were some of the words used in describing sexual child abusers. Although some men present themselves as weak and dominated, the majority of men who sexually abuse their children are perceived by counselors as domineering and controlling not only toward the child but toward all family members. "Some see it as a parental right to use and abuse their children," said a worker in a Washington abuse project. "They hold a very macho attitude, they are the law in their home." Even though sexual abusers tend to appear more integrated into work and other socially approved activities than do other types of family violence perpetrators, they do not have the security to meet their need to feel liked, valuable, or in control outside of the family. Some physically abuse their children and spouses as well. "They may be controlling, but they are not responsible people so there is no leadership in the family," reflected a program director in Minnesota. Despite their ability to function on the job, they are passive in the pursuit of dependency needs. They have problems giving or getting nurturing. Many nurturant needs are camouflaged by macho behavior. The issue is the use of power to inappropriately meet their dependency needs. They use incest in the service of other needs—and they do so at the expense of the feelings and needs of other family members. Narcissism and the inability to empathize are also traits that many counselors notice among incest abusers.

Whether through dominating or passive-aggressive behavior, sexual abusers abdicate their parental roles. Not only do parent–child roles become blurred as children meet adult needs, there is often an unclear or distorted perception of the victim's identity. Personnel in a Philadelphia agency can recall instances of men who have sexually abused their young (e.g., 7- or 10-year-old) daughters and then seriously talked about marrying the girls when they are older. "They are also better than average self-deceivers," commented one psychologist who specializes in the treatment of sexual offenders. They rationalize, minimize, and outright deny any wrongdoing on their part. From adolescent sex offenders to middle-aged men, abusers almost always blame the victim for the assault. Some even convince themselves that they feel close to their daughters and the daughters approve of and accept their sexual advances, despite evidence to the contrary. Alcohol use and long-term marital problems often provide the rationale the men need to excuse the sexual acting out which, once begun, is addictive in nature and tends to escalate. Sometimes the incest desire is so strongly entrenched in the subconscious that it will repeat in another setting. A Denver psychologist remembers a case of a divorced incest abuser who met the divorced mother of an incest victim. They began living together and soon could see the potential for abuse because the man started to seek attention from the woman's adolescent child.

Sexual abusers often report having been sexually or physically victimized by relatives (usually male) when they were growing up. They hold high expectations for their own performance, which they find difficult to live up to. They enter adulthood with low self-esteem and unresolved conflicts surrounding masculinity/femininity issues, unable to express resentment or deal assertively with women. They are socially isolated and the fact of incest serves to isolate the entire family. They develop communication problems with their spouses and are not in touch with their own or others' feelings. People with low self-esteem are angry, disillusioned, and powerless and feel they have little to lose.

What emerges from these descriptions of three types of abusers are general characteristics that apply to people who engage in family violence:

- social isolation
- rigid and high expectations
- low self-esteem
- controlling, domineering behavior
- lack of touch with feelings
- high dependency needs
- poor communication skills
- minimizing, denying, deceiving attitude
- feeling of powerlessness to change life
- poor impulse control

Abusers seem to gain very little satisfaction from any aspect of their lives. Their jobs bring few ego gratifications. Financial and relationship problems produce stress. They seem to lack either social or spiritual supports. Many seem to say, "I can't take it any more" when they turn to alcohol and violence. Their social isolation increases the importance of the family, causing the family to occupy a central role in their lives as it becomes the arena in which the abusers expect to meet a greater number of their needs. It also becomes the arena in which they vent most of their frustrations. They can impose on their family, and especially on the victims of their violence, a sense of power and control that they possess nowhere else in their world. They cling to that one vestige of power. The family becomes an extension of themselves and any attempt made by the victims to assert their own individuality is perceived as a threat to the self-structure, a rebellion which must be squelched. The enormity of their own needs blinds them to the needs and wishes of their victims. Self-preservation takes precedence over the wishes of others. Violence is a way to ensure that abusers' needs are met without having to give too much emotionally in return.

# 4
# TREATMENT METHODS AND ISSUES

It matters little what type of program agencies develop if the interventions used by the line staff do not obtain the desired results. What body of practice wisdom exists concerning family violence perpetrators? Do certain techniques work better than others? What problems and issues confront people who work with the abusers? The research project tapped some of the answers to those questions, and the amount of consensus was surprising. Repeatedly, program personnel identified similar strategies or behaviors which they incorporated as part of their repertoire, similar techniques that seemed counterproductive, and similar frustrations they encountered in their work with this type of clientele. In addition, certain issues and rationales which should be part of treatment consideration emerged around such matters as treatment modality, the length of treatment, and the nature of client participation.

The concept of treatment method extends beyond psychological counseling. Treatment methods constitute a broad range of interventions which may be used directly with, or on behalf of, the client or client system. However, prerequisite to the use of any method is an environment conducive to change and growth. Counselors found that their techniques were more effective if they first created an environment that encourages client trust and participation. Acceptance, nurturance, and a nonjudgmental attitude form the foundation for that type of environment. "A client needs to feel accepted as a person," said one worker, "and not as a mean person." Counselors believed that the best way to approach abusers was to convey the idea that they were worthwhile people who had something very valuable to offer their families and the world. They took the position that violence was interfering with their clients' ability to enjoy life and relationships with others. Most counselors warned against the temptation to label the abusers as bad or pathological in the same way that others in society do. They tried to reduce defensiveness in their clients by distinguishing between the person and the person's actions. "Probably the main thing I learned," commented a child abuse specialist, "was to control my own tendency to criticize and be judgmental toward my clients. As soon as I was able to listen to them without moralizing or thinking to myself, 'Ugh, how could you have done that? You must be a terrible person,' I noticed a change in the way they responded to me."

Counselors often allow abusers as much time as needed to tell their story as they see it. However, that does not mean that counselors accept the person's viewpoint as justification for the violent behavior. They do not. Counselors were adamant that the abuse had to stop, but they tried not to condemn the abusers for the feelings of anger, sadness, or fear that might have led to the abuse. They found that criticisms and moralizing generate client resistance whereas acceptance and empathy pave the way for change. "If you can see the clients as people trapped in a pattern of behavior they don't know how to escape," said a private practitioner who works with spouse abusers, "then you are in a position to show them a way out. That way you are not in opposition to their goals, you are aligned with them. And they realize that you care about them because you believe they can change."

## TECHNIQUES THAT WORK

Within that attitudinal framework, the survey respondents mentioned several techniques that they incorporated in their work with the perpetrators of family violence. However, before we describe those that seem applicable to all forms of family violence, a word of caution: Not every abuser feels disturbed about his or her violent behavior. Some believe violence is a legitimate option and that its use is justified. Others enjoy the sense of power violence gives. They equate violence with the self-image of an assertive and capable person—an image not easily cast aside. Therefore, the following techniques will not have the same effect on everyone. They work best when the abuser sees some (even a little) value in eliminating the violence.

**Supportive Confrontation**   Confrontations are used whenever counselors encounter client resistance, or when they see discrepancies between client statements and behaviors, or when outside statements and reports conflict with client statements. Some workers are reluctant to engage in confrontations because they perceive them as head-on collisions between worker and client. Some avoid confrontations because they believe that clients regard any confrontation, no matter how gentle, as negative criticism. However, most people who work with physical and sexual abusers find that confrontations are essential in their efforts to decrease client denial and promote client responsibility, especially concerning the seriousness of the abuse. They are not afraid to discuss the problem, no matter how severe it is, but they suggest that confrontations be supportive. They say to the client: "We know this is difficult to talk about. We are not here to prosecute you, but we need to know what happened." Counselors warn against aggressive, accusative confrontations which have a punitive intent and which tear clients apart emotionally. "Stay in your role as helping person, not accuser," they advise. Timing is important. A few say that confrontations should wait until clients establish some trust with the worker. For the majority of workers, however, confrontations usually take place after the abusers have had the opportunity to describe their perceptions and express their feelings. Sometimes that occurs during the first interview, sometimes much later.

**Enhancement of Self-Esteem**   Many abusers hold themselves in low regard. They believe that they are failures, unable to exert a positive impact on their lives. People who nurture feelings of inadequacy sometimes resort to violence as a bluff of strength to cover their low self-esteem. Batterers need someone to share their pain, to point out their strengths, and to make them feel as though they are valued members of the human race. Counselors work on building clients' self-esteem by validating their feelings and experiences, by looking for positive personal attributes, and by giving positive feedback when clients display desired behavior. "Point to anything that says to them, 'you are important' and makes them feel more competent," suggested one worker. Abusers often either fail to recognize their abilities or discount them. Counselors counteract these distortions by helping the abusers make realistic self-appraisals. "We try not to go overboard in our praise because many of our clients find that phony and hard to accept, but we do make an effort to call to their attention those skills and knowledge they show us which indicate their common sense, their ability to control their temper or manage their daily activities, and their capacity to see more than their own view of a situation."

**Problem Solving**   Perhaps the one skill that enables abusers to cope better with life is the ability to solve problems constructively rather than find solutions through violence. Counselors help abusers avoid being backed into life's corners by encouraging them to find alternatives and to think of options. Some advocate a descriptive problem-solving approach, e.g., describe what you see, what you feel, what needs to be done. Some workers suggest offering behavioral alternatives, such as tearing Kleenex instead of hitting. Others help their clients anticipate the consequences of interpersonal interactions or of expressing anger. Many maintain a here and now focus on particular problems; they suggest the use of clearly spelled out decision-making steps and the use of specific assignments to increase awareness of thoughts and feelings. The goal is to give abusers a plan of action they can apply to future situations.

**Structure**   Abusers need boundaries to help them maintain control over their emotions and behaviors. Counselors use a variety of methods to establish structure and devise points of reference for their clients. "The key here is consistency," claimed one worker. "I have them keep a written daily schedule to give them a sense of clarity and purpose and reduce the chaos in their lives." Other counselors build in structure through the use of specific tasks or homework assignments. Many counselors find that contracts with the abusers provide the necessary structure by clarifying expectations and setting limits that prevent impulsive outbreaks. For instance, they contract with abusers regarding the number of sessions or classes they will attend, or contract with them to call the hotline whenever they feel like hitting. Many programs incorporate impulse control training for the abusers. However, one counselor who works with battering spouses warns that batterers are very controlling people and that by teaching only impulse control counselors merely may be substituting one form of control for another. "Therapists need to go beyond impulse control and explore the fears the abusers have that make the need to control necessary."

**Honesty**  Abusers are skeptical of offers to help them and are ready to bolt at the first sign of betrayal. Commented one worker, "If you hope to gain the cooperation and trust of physical abusers then you have to be open and honest in your dealings with them, especially about reports written for the courts and their likely consequences." The abusers' fear of entrapment inhibits the type and amount of information they confide to their counselors. One worker advised, "Make a commitment to them about talking straight, and stick to it." The need for honesty exists in all areas of worker–client interaction, not only concerning the uses made of information. "Sometimes we are their main link with reality," remarked a therapist in a mental health setting. "We need to be honest with them about how we see them, how they are functioning, and what they can expect from the agency. Sometimes sharing with them an insight about themselves is perceived as a wonderful gift that helps them make sense out of their behavior."

**Modeling**  "We act as role models for our clients," said a parent aide. "We show them by our behavior toward them that there are other ways to interact with people than the ways they have been doing." Clients learn through observation how to transact effective communications. Even more than that, they learn how another person reacts to frustrations, disappointments, and stress. "They are exposed to a whole different way of thinking about the world and to life's events," said a homemaking assistant. "I remember one woman saying, 'In my family, whenever anything went wrong my dad always started drinking and my mom started hollering. Drinking and hollering, that's the way they went through life. I'm glad to know it doesn't have to be that way for me.'"

**Role Playing**  Role playing is a skill development technique that requires active participation by the client. This technique allows clients to try out new ways of behaving without worrying about negative repercussions. Abusers practice what they can do and say in various situations. One program asks abusers to emulate, with members of their families, an interaction demonstrated by the worker until it becomes part of a comfortable behavior pattern. Because role plays are so visible, they are subject to immediate feedback and modification. Many workers help abusers develop empathy for others by putting them in the role of the victim. "Most abusers never see beyond their own point of view, never realize how it must feel to see that hand coming at you. We put them in the role of the victim so they get to see things from a different perspective." Some have also found role playing useful for helping abusers deal with criticisms and perceived rejections. "We teach them how to check out their perceptions before jumping to conclusions. They practice it with us and then they take that skill and practice it with the people at home and at work."

**Buddy System**   Some counselors who operate group sessions advocate the use of a buddy system as part of a self-help endeavor among abusers. Clients select another group member to telephone during times of tension, anger, or loneliness and talk about their feelings instead of bursting into violent action. Having another person available reduces the abusers' dependency level on family members to meet so many of their needs and trains abusers to reach out in times of need. Not only does it divert tension, the buddy system teaches abusers how to be a friend to someone else. They experience both the sense of "being there" for another person and of sharing a personal closeness. Counselors find that the buddy system operates best after the abusers have developed a sense of trust in the group process and have embraced the principles of violence control advocated by the program. Initiating a buddy system too soon may cause the idea to backfire as one abusive individual identifies with and reinforces the anger or paranoia being expressed by another.

**Empty Chair Technique**   The empty chair technique, borrowed from Gestalt therapy, is widely used among people who work with physical abusers. The idea is to generate a fuller understanding and expression of feeling toward another person or toward another part of oneself by asking the same person to play both roles, him or herself and the other person or aspect of self. The individual sits in one chair and speaks to an imagined person in the empty chair opposite. Then the person exchanges chairs and responds as he or she believes the imagined person might. "We find it useful for helping people confront the ghosts from their past," commented a counselor. "They say things that they have been carrying around inside, sometimes for years. And once they hear the 'response' given from the imagined person, they find themselves much more able to deal with it than they had believed. It gives them an insight into the way they see the other people in their lives, or the other parts of themselves, and the fears they have allowed to build up."

# TECHNIQUES TO AVOID

Just as the survey respondents were able to identify the techniques they found to be most effective in their work with the perpetrators of family violence, they also identified the techniques that were unsuccessful. Generally, the techniques to avoid are not opposites of the effective techniques; they are separate entities and they seem to apply to all forms of family violence.

**Coercion** It is good counseling practice to inform clients of the consequences for continued abuse, but counselors warn against the misuse of authority. Coercing clients to comply with your wishes is counterproductive. "Everybody loses when you get into a power struggle with the client," said a counselor who works with both physical and sexual child abusers. "So avoid giving ultimatums like, 'You have to use our service or we will take your child away.' It only makes clients dislike and distrust you more. Their compliance is superficial and they will find ways to undermine your treatment efforts." Some counselors confuse the use of threats with the setting of limits. "We have to let them know who is boss," seems to be their attitude. However, unlike limit setting, which provides boundaries, the use of threats keeps clients in the "one-down" position and reinforces their feeling of powerlessness and hopelessness.

**Rescuing** Clients sometimes are very needy. They are alone. They seem inept in their interpersonal dealings. They are overwhelmed by the most elemental situations. They do not know how to initiate the procedures that will be most beneficial to them and they do not follow through on suggestions. They just don't seem to have their act together. Their lack of knowledge and skill makes it tempting for workers to give advice and even to take over some of the functions that belong to their clients. "I remember one of our new workers running all over town picking up medication for clients, getting clients' belongings out of storage, filling out forms for them," said one program director. "It was a disaster. Instead of teaching them how to negotiate with the system, the worker was going through the system for them. The clients were just sitting there passively receiving all the good things the worker was bringing them. All they ever learned from the worker was how to be more and more dependent." When advocacy goes beyond creating opportunities for clients, and counselors take over activities the clients should be doing on their own behalf, workers limit the problem-solving skills that clients need to develop if they are to cope with future situations.

**Insight and Client-Centered Therapies**  Many counselors avoid both the psychodynamically insight-oriented and the Rogerian client-centered therapeutic approaches with this type of clientele. They find the insight-oriented approach too intellectual and time-consuming and the Rogerian approach too passive. Counselors seem to prefer behaviorally oriented methods with physical abusers. "Stay away from the 'Uh-hum, tell me about it' school of practice," said one therapist. "It encourages rationalizations. The first thing we have to do is stop the abuse and that takes more direct action." Insight may be interesting but it does not necessarily translate into nonviolence. "Many of our clients are better able to use concrete services than psychological services," claims a program administrator. "In fact, many are not psychologically disturbed, they are merely handling interpersonal situations in the way they learned to in their own families." Teaching clients new ways of responding to situations is more efficient and more long-lasting.

**Overexpectation**  Not only do counselors want abusers to stop their physically or sexually abusive behavior, they expect their clients to make significant changes in many aspects of their lives. Some of the expectations held by workers for their clients include learning new ways of communicating, upgrading job skills, giving up alcohol or drug use, and developing socialization skills. The tendency is to push too fast and to expect too much. Workers (often inadvertently) assume the role of a critical parent. When clients are unable to live up to the expectations held for them, the counselors become one more in a string of people whom they have disappointed. Not only does it diminish their already low sense of self-esteem, it may trigger the depression and suicidal ideation that is so common among abusers. In response, the clients either move away from the counseling situation or act out destructively.

**Ruminating**  Clients need the opportunity to vent their feelings, but there is a danger when ventilations are allowed to deteriorate into endless griping or ruminating about past situations.

---

Ruminations are repeated thoughts about situations that usually involve real or imagined slights or rejections. As abusers go over the situations in their minds, they perpetuate the hurt and anger that have led them to become violent. "The more often stated, the more likely believed," said a therapist in a spouse abuse program. "And much of their anger is unreasonable by objective standards. So we limit ruminations as much as possible to prevent continued agitation." Ruminating also interferes with constructive work in other ways. It keeps clients' past focused and takes the locus of control out of their hands. They continue to feel like victims of circumstance and reactors to life's events.

**Identification with the Victim**   Everyone who works with family violence cases has to be concerned with the victim. Even when counselors have no direct contact with the victims their concerns must be for the safety of the victim. However, counselors warn against focusing so much attention on the way the victims are feeling and managing that it leaves the abusers believing no one cares about their feelings or concerns. "As much as possible we try to avoid playing favorites," said a child welfare specialist. "It would be easy to identify with the hurt child. But, if we are ever going to change things, we have to realize that the parents hurt also and need our help every bit as much as the children do." Abusers are very sensitive to criticism and to the belief that people are against them and want to punish them.

**Emotive Techniques**   In an attempt to help clients divert their angry feelings into less harmful channels, counselors sometimes suggest to clients that they should hit objects rather then people. However, many counselors in this survey have found that anger release through physical acting out, such as pounding on pillows, reinforced the very behavior they were trying to eliminate. "I used to tell my clients to hit a punching bag," said a therapist who works with battering spouses, "but I stopped that when I discovered they couldn't tell where the punching bag ended and their wife began." Such hitting does not inhibit or change the physical response; it repeats the physical action used in the violent encounter. However, some counselors do find that a regular program of physical exercise such as jogging, swimming, or calisthenics, combined with relaxation techniques, can help prevent the buildup of tension.

# OTHER TECHNIQUES TO AVOID

Some counselors suggested techniques to avoid that apply mainly to one form of family violence and are not generalizable to all forms of abuse. For example, counselors who work in spouse abuse programs frequently warned not to see both the man and the woman together during the initial session. "We have found that each uses the time to blame the other and justify his or her own behavior. Then they expect the therapist to take sides. There is so much arguing during those first sessions that it isn't possible to accomplish much." Counselors also report that the abusers can be so intimidating that the victims feel afraid to say what they are actually thinking. Some counselors have found the situation more manageable if they see the man and woman separately for a session or two before bringing them together, and some counselors insist that it is better to wait until the abuse has stopped or is under control before they see the couple together.

Most counselors advocate the use of groups with physical abusers because it provides additional support, boundaries, and a sharing quality. Sometimes, though, people who work with child abusers find that their clients are too needy emotionally to participate effectively as group members. The group process requires the ability to give and take. Many child abusers do not feel they have something to offer anyone else. "They are like hungry children," said one group leader. "They want you all to themselves. They feel so impoverished that they can't imagine having a thought or a feeling that anyone else would find useful." In those cases, counselors suggest working with the abuser individually to raise the level of self-esteem with the subsequent goal of placing the client in a group.

People who work with sexual abusers caution against encouraging family members to engage in physical touching until they are well along into the program. "Touching has become sexualized in these families," explained a therapist in a sexual abuse program. "They have learned to be suspicious of the motives behind touching. They need to relearn how to touch appropriately."

# CLIENT REACTIONS

Experience has taught practitioners that physical abusers typically exhibit certain reactions toward them and the service they offer which must be satisfactorily dealt with if treatment goals are to be reached. Among the most typical reactions are those related to denial, lack of motivation, anger, and mistrust. Although not all clients display these behaviors, helping personnel need to be prepared to cope with them should they arise.

**Denial**   Following several therapy sessions, one incest offender told his counselor, "I want you to know that I realize now how badly I ruined my daughter's life and how I hurt my wife." Some clients arrive for service aware of the damage their violence has caused but, for most, like the man in the illustration above, that realization comes only after considerable involvement in a program. The most common initial reaction to an accusation of assault is to minimize or deny that it happened. "I only shoved him." "I only slapped her." "They're lying, I didn't touch him. He fell down the stairs. It was an accident." It is difficult for some people to acknowledge the physical and emotional harm they cause, but that is precisely what they must do according to most counselors. Without acknowledging the role they played in the violent episodes, abusers cannot attain a primary treatment goal: taking responsibility for their own behavior. Accountability for future actions rests on their ability to accept responsibility for their past behaviors, both constructive and destructive.

However, although it is necessary that abusers own up to the problem and to their behavior, it is not necessary that workers wring confessions from their clients or insist on a recital of all the vivid details. Clients may grudgingly admit they sometimes lose their temper or may acknowledge an occasional sexual encounter with a young child; at the beginning that may be enough for the worker to realize that the client accepts some responsibility for his or her behavior. Later on, when the client feels more at ease in the program, it is frequently necessary to go over the circumstances under which the violence occurs and the progression of events so that the client can recognize the signs of impending rage or sexual desire before it reaches the out-of-control stage. According to the counselors, persistent deniers will not respond to treatment and some counselors refuse to continue therapeutic contact if client denial persists for more than five sessions.

**Motivation**   The majority of abusers come for service only under duress. They may fear jail, the rmoval of a child from the home, or the loss of a spouse. They are angry about having to be there and often participate halfheartedly in the program, sometimes on a superficial "in body only" level, sometimes keeping appointments on a hit-or-miss basis. Prominent also are the "two-timers": those people who keep their first two appointments to demonstrate to their spouse, family, or probation officer that they are sincere in their desire to change their behavior—and then never return again.

People who make the best use of a program do so because they see that their violence prevents them from maintaining important relationships. Such was the case of the man who said: "I lost two wives because of my rages. They divorced me and I can't say that I blame them. I have to do something about my temper; it is ruining my life." Or they realize that they have progressively less control over their actions. People who call hotlines, for example, frequently say: "It's getting worse every day. I seem to snap at every little thing they do. I'm hitting them harder. I'm afraid that one day I will really hurt them."

To counteract poor motivation, counselors attempt to demonstrate how the program can create immediate changes for the better in the lives of their clients. Some, for instance, point to the legal consequences of violence that may be prevented by the knowledge offered in the program. Others teach concrete skills that can be implemented in difficult situations that might otherwise lead to violence. Still other counselors rely on the release of tension that comes with the opportunity to ventilate in a supportive environment. It probably never is truly possible to motivate a person who is too threatened or too indifferent to the idea of change, but it may well be possible to sway the thinking of a person who holds ambivalent feelings about his or her violent behavior. Generally, a client who stays with a program for more than five sessions will elect to remain in the program.

**Hostility**   Abusers are well aware of the negative way that society views them, and they in turn direct their anger toward the people who represent the punishing system. Defusing client hostility often is one of the first tasks that confront workers. "I've had to listen to a barrage of swearing leveled at the police, at our agency, at nosey neighbors, at the world, before I could even get a word in," said a protective services worker. However, considering the circumstances, hostility is a perfectly reasonable client response. "Who can blame them for being hostile," said one worker. "If I were in their position I think I would be hostile, too. All they see are people ready to lay on the blame and punishment. They have a side of the story to tell, but it doesn't look like anybody is interested in hearing it." Client hostility may arise from a justifiable indignation at being maligned, but it may also arise from other motives. Sometimes anger masks underlying fears such as the fear of criticism, of failure, of being rejected, at being punished, of losing control. Understanding that the abuser's anger serves a protective function may help workers react less defensively to it. It is also important for the client to realize that workers are there to investigate rather than to blame.

One way counselors defuse hostility is to identify and to empathize with the abuser's pain. They look beyond the accusations and find the underlying feelings. Advised one therapist: "When working with the abuser, focus on his fear rather than on the violence. Learn why he controls and what he is running from." Another way counselors defuse hostility is to avoid defending the system or agency. Even though it is difficult to convey the sense of wanting fairness for the abuser as much as for the victim, especially when the worker represents the criminal justice system or protective services, that is what breaks through the anger and defensiveness. "As soon as you defend the system," noted one worker, "you set up an us versus you situation. The only logical thing a client can do in that case is to keep his anger focused at us, the enemy."

**Dependency**  In most therapeutic situations counselors are advised to discourage the development of dependency among their clients. However, family violence abusers often present a facade of pseudoindependence, forced on them by isolation or by rejecting or inconsistent early relationships, which keeps them from accepting supportive or counseling services. Violence erupts, in part, because of the abuser's inability to develop an effective support network which can be used to alleviate the feeling of being overburdened. Learning to trust the people in their environment, to believe that someone will be there when they call out for help, is a major therapeutic task. "We tell our clients to call us when they feel the urge to use violence," said one administrator. "We want them to turn to us as an external support agent because we feel that it is important for them to experience consistency and trust in the people around them."

Perhaps the best way to build trust is by being available and responsive when clients do call. "We want them to know that they can rely on us until they are able to assume effective functioning on their own," explained the administrator. However, it takes time to correct distortions produced by isolation and limited feedback, to develop accurate reality testing, and to teach the skills of impulse identification and management. To avoid encouraging overdependence, counselors follow the principle of "doing with" rather than "doing for" their clients. For instance, they assist the client with their money management problems by teaching them how to budget instead of telling them what to buy.

# TREATMENT ISSUES

The choice of effective treatment methods is related to the successful resolution of important therapeutic issues such as the length of treatment, the type of treatment modality offered, and the voluntary or involuntary nature of the service. For example, some treatment techniques may be more appropriate for use in an eight-week program than in a twelve-month program. This section discusses some of the treatment issues that the research participants believed held important implications for the success or failure of their work with clients.

**Mandatory vs Voluntary Treatment** Mandatory treatment forces a person to attend a particular program. Forced attendance usually results from court sentencing and may be imposed in conjunction with incarceration or as a condition of probation. Fewer than 10 percent of the programs surveyed were composed of clientele whose participation was entirely mandatory. However, many respondents mentioned that even though they considered their programs to be voluntary, several of their clients applied because of pressure placed on them by community agencies or the criminal justice system. These people could be considered "semivoluntary" or, as some counselors referred to them, "forced voluntary" clients. They had to enter some program in order to regain custody of their children or to avoid going to jail. The choice of program was left to the client, but the need to be in a program was externally imposed. Only about one-third of the respondents said that their clients were there on a voluntary basis. A large percentage of programs contained both voluntary and involuntary clients. (See Appendix B.)

Arguments were strong on both sides of the mandatory–voluntary issue. Counselors who advocated a program that was entirely voluntary linked their preference to client motivation and involvement.

"We don't want to spend our energies battling with resistant clients," said a counselor whose agency provided service only to clients who entered voluntarily. "We know that clients who enter our program do so because they are disturbed by their inability to control their anger. They are looking for alternatives and are ready to accept our suggestions." Those who favored mandatory participation cited leverage as the most important advantage to the therapist. It gives therapists some authority they might lack otherwise. "It is a trade-off, really," said a counselor affiliated with a mandatory program. "We have to deal with high levels of hostility at first, but we also avoid the high dropout rates that are so common in work with abusers. In fact, I think that we have an edge over voluntary programs because our clients have to stay with the program even when the topics we discuss are disturbing to them. So we have a better chance to help them work through the unpleasant or disruptive feelings."

Some problems may arise when types of clients are mixed. People who work with both voluntary and involuntary clients noticed a difference in the type and degree of participation. Those who attended voluntarily were more likely to complete the program and less likely to resume abusive behavior. However, counselors also point out that some involuntary clients can be positively influenced to remain in the program by other clients, especially those clients who have been with the program long enough to internalize the rules and act as role models.

**Active vs Passive Intervention**   Traditional therapists wait for the client to call for an appointment, close the case records of clients who do not keep their appointments, refrain from giving advice to clients, and talk to clients about behavior rather than demonstrate it. Counselors who work with physical abusers advocate a much more active approach. "We have to make contact right away or we are liable to lose them as clients," said one counselor. "If we waited until they kept an appointment, we would spend a lot of time just sitting around," said another. "You need a different mindset with this type of client. You have to do a lot more reaching out." Many counselors find that they spend more time out of the office making home visits than they might with their other clients. They are more persistent and insistent about maintaining ongoing appointments. When clients do not keep appointments, their counselors telephone immediately, or go to the clients' home, or arrange transportation for clients. "We have even paid the cab fare so that our clients could keep their appointments with us," remarked a counselor in a child abuse program. "We want them to know that these appointments are important and that we expect them to be here." Counselors may see clients more than once a week. They suggest specific ways of behaving. They prefer treatment methods that require both client and worker participation, such as those associated with experiential, behavioral, and problem-solving approaches. As one administrator summarized, "We intrude a lot in their lives because we want to change their usual patterns of behaving." The most likely way for that to occur is through active intervention.

**Structured vs Unstructured Treatment**  Closely related to active and passive intervention is the issue of how tightly structured the program should be. Structure is most often accomplished through the use of contracts, theme-centered discussions, and skill training. Structure lends focus to worker client interaction. Some program personnel make no attempt to focus client discussions. "We leave it to the client (or group members) to decide what they want to talk about at the beginning of each session." However, most counselors advocate a more structured approach. "Our clients have a hard time restraining themselves. We give them the boundaries they can't always give themselves. The more we structure, the safer they feel." Maintaining a clear focus encourages greater depth in client thinking and discussing. Problems can be partialized so they seem less overwhelming. "We get more accomplished and they leave feeling a greater sense of mastery," said a therapist affiliated with a skill training program. Of equal importance, structuring the program gives clients fewer places to hide from unpleasant feelings. Sometimes client concerns are smoke screens sent up to keep counselors from exploring more frightening areas. "We changed to a more theme-centered approach because we found that our clients consistently avoided certain subjects like intimacy." Counselors are careful to avoid structuring programs in ways that constrict or prevent client participation. Within the program structure counselors are sensitive to the clients' immediate concerns as well as to feelings and situations that may have been triggered by material from past sessions.

**Individual vs Group Treatment**  With most forms of clinical problems the favored method is a one-to-one approach with clients, but with physical abusers groups represent the modality of choice by far. Although most programs continue to offer individual counseling as an option or adjunct to other forms of treatment, program developers and counselors find the advantages of group interaction highly compelling. Administrators prefer groups because they make better use of human resources. Groups enable fewer trained personnel to provide service to a greater number of clients. Counselors, or group facilitators, prefer groups for many other reasons. "It is faster and a more efficient use of my time to disseminate information to groups rather than to individuals," commented the leader of an educational group. "It saves me hours of having to repeat essentially the same material." Speed is not the only, or even the main, reason, however. Many counselors find that group process reduces problems with client resistance to authority figures and improves their ability to cut through to important material. "The group is a wonderful source of support for both the client and therapist," said one group counselor. "Clients find a built-in support network not otherwise available to them, and I find that clients are less dependent on me for solutions to their problems *and* that I do not have to be the limit setter all the time because the group exerts its own pressure on clients who break the rules."

Although groups may be the treatment of choice in general, work with individuals continues to have its place and most programs incorporate it as part of the service offered. For instance, even though families and couples represent types of groups, therapists mentioned that the overflow of angry feelings or threats expressed in family treatment sometimes intimidates the children or the spouse, and they suggest that these types of groups be used after the threat of abuse has been controlled. Some program personnel routinely see new clients individually for a few times to assess the person's readiness for group and to acquaint the person with the program and its guidelines.

**Long-Term vs Short-Term Treatment**   "We are prepared to see clients for as long as they are willing to see us," said a program director. "The problem is, they aren't all that willing to see us." The majority of programs offer long-term service, ranging from one year to an indefinite period. Unfortunately, clients do not share the professional's enthusiasm for long-term programs. Unless they are mandated to participate, most clients remain in family violence programs for less than one year, with a high percentage of those attending less than six months. (See Appendix B.) The programs that seem best able to maintain long-term connectedness with clients are those that offer supportive service, such as parent aides. These programs provide concrete service as well as in-home service to clients. Nonmandatory programs that operate only from the mindset of long-term treatment run the risk of losing client motivation and client participation. To remain viable some agencies have developed programs that combine both long-term and short-term components. One program, for example, offers both a twelve-week group for individuals and an eighteen-month counseling program for couples or families. Another program combines a five- to six-week program for individuals with a group experience that lasts one year. Indications are that high-impact, short-term (between three and six months) programs that engage clients more than once a week promote greater client ego investment and connectedness with the program. Programs can be extended for those clients who would benefit from continued service. For example, one program offers its service in twelve-week segments. Clients contract for the initial twelve-week phase and then are free to continue in the program for as long as they wish at twelve-week intervals.

# PART TWO

# Profiles of Programs for Abusers

This section provides in-depth descriptions of six programs which offer services to family violence abusers within unique and nontraditional service delivery formats. In addition to an overview of the program components, each chapter presents the major administrative issues involved in the development and ongoing operation of the program, the treatment issues confronted by line staff, and a detailed case example which illustrates the program's operation.

# Introduction
# to Part Two

The study which supplied the information for this book began in the late 1970's—a time of great expectations for program planners and direct service practitioners who sought to stem the tide of family violence. Social scientists had verified the widespread existence of violence among family members, new laws were enacted that protected the victims and held the assaulters accountable for their actions, state and federal funds were being earmarked to support programs that would intervene in family violence, and the 1980 White House Conference on Families reaffirmed the need to raise the quality of family life by removing those forces, including violence, which contributed to its breakdown. The problem of family violence seemed to be finally and irrevocably out in the open, and the means for controlling it were close at hand.

However, that optimism proved premature in the face of a deepening economic recession in the early 80's. Double digit inflation, rising unemployment, Reaganomics, and the new federalism took their toll on family life and the programs designed to protect family members. At the federal level, the commitment to fight family violence weakened. The Office of Domestic Violence, which began during the Carter administration, was demolished by personnel and budget cuts during the early years of the Reagan administration. With it went all federal programs to prevent spouse abuse. The National Child Abuse and Neglect office suffered a 30 percent budget cut as well as a reduction in the size of its staff. The budget cuts reduced the number of demonstration projects it could sponsor throughout the country and necessitated that it withdraw the special attention previously given to sexual child abuse. A government moratorium on printing began to inhibit the future dissemination of information derived from the programs in progress.

Some of the people who participated in the original study were recontacted in late 1982 to find out what impact the economy had on the incidence of family violence in their communities and on their work with violent family members. They reported that unemployment and rising costs had increased the level of stress under which families must operate. People were unable to pay for the basic services, such as heat, electricity, and rent, needed to ensure their survival. Unemployment had forced some families to move to more affordable housing. In some cases, the experience of uprooting themselves heightened family stress by increasing their level of isolation. At the same time, the number and types of community resources designed to relieve family stress decreased.

Program directors also noted an increase in the number of family violence cases, especially those of more severe abuse, that were being referred to their programs. Several administrators reported that their workers were operating at maximum, instead of minimum, caseload levels. Because of caseload sizes, they were unable to accept all the cases referred to them and workers in the referring agencies were forced to cope with client problems in the best ways they could.

The need for knowledge about family violence and its treatment has not diminished as a result of the economic situation. Rather, it has heightened as helping personnel are confronted by families who have depleted their resources and discovered that their usual coping methods are inadequate to handle the accompanying emotional strains. With fewer referral options available, it becomes increasingly important to prepare line staff to contend with client crises that result in violence. The sharing of practice wisdom developed by people who have implemented programs that focus on family violence intervention now holds even greater value for administrators and practitioners who encounter client problems that involve family violence.

Among the many programs that were contacted during the survey, several operated their services within unique formats and program structures. A general description of the newer formats was given in Chapter 2. Part 2 provides indepth descriptions of programs that illustrate some of the newer formats so that administrators and line staff who wish to develop interventive programs for family violence perpetrators can more fully appreciate what they and their clients might encounter. Although the administrators expressed satisfaction with the success of their programs, no attempt has been made to evaluate the quality of these programs or to compare their effectiveness in preventing abuse with programs that operate within more traditional formats.

Each chapter in Part 2 describes a program that illustrates a specific format: community consortium, residential program, in-home service, counseling/education program, guided self-help program, and family camp. To maintain consistency, each chapter leads the reader through the following progression: a) the needs, philosophy, and struggles that led to the creation of the program; b) the components of the program and the type of personnel and staff training needed; c) the presentation of a typical case from intake to termination; d) the resolution of recurring treatment issues; e) the on-going administrative issues essential to program operation; and f) the key elements needed to ensure the success of the program.

Experience and economics have led to changes in many of the programs. In the face of funding reductions the staff of the Family Crisis Center, a residential program, was reorganized in the direction of greater expertise. Two house supervisory positions were replaced by one social work position. The administrator has found that, by upgrading the position, the same amount of work could be accomplished, as well as before or better, by one person.

The staff of the Family Training Program, an in-home service, which merged with an existing community agency in the hopes of decreasing the program's overhead expenses and generating a more consistent financial base, eventually left the auspices of the agency when state funding was reduced. The budget cut reduced the staff of the Family Training Program from five people to two before the director of the program decided to convert it to a nonprofit organization so that the program would be eligible for community financial support. The move enabled them to develop contracts with the state Social Services department and with Community Corrections and to refill one of the positions that had been vacated. They are in the process of increasing the size of the program.

The director of the counseling/educational program, the Domestic Abuse Project, retained most of the program's content, but restructured the program to better meet the needs of its clients. She instituted a two-phase progression in order to reduce the waiting period from time of admission to the program until entry into the structured group therapy aspect of the program. The original plan, reported in Chapter 8, called for entry into a self-help group for several weeks until a structured therapy group began a new eight-week cycle. Once clients completed group therapy they were eligible to join couples groups and multiple family groups. Now clients immediately enter Phase 1, the structured group therapy portion twice a week for eight weeks, followed by Phase 2, a sixteen-week process group held once a week that includes couples and families. The program also includes more individual sessions with clients. Self-help groups located throughout the community provide support for clients both during and following completion of the program.

The Sex Offender Program, which operates within a guided self-help format, remains basically unchanged. Because the program is located in a state hospital, it is funded as part of the hospital's budget. Although the state has decreased its funding to some programs, the Sex Offender Program has suffered no cutbacks. And the administrator anticipates no cutbacks because of the large number of prisoners who are awaiting entry into the program.

At the time of the original survey the family camp project, developed as part of the Family Life Educational Program, had already lost its funding. The program coordinator modified the program, but even the funds for the modified version soon were depleted. The coordinator has applied for state funds and hopes that money will be available to reinstitute the program, if not in its entirety then at least in the form of a retreat for families. According to the coordinator, the plan for a family camp has not been abandoned, it is merely "on hold."

# 5

# COMMUNITY CONSORTIUM: Project F.I.N.D.

Project F.I.N.D. (Families Involved in New Directions) addresses the problems of physical abuse or neglect and sexual abuse to children in Louisville, Kentucky, and the surrounding area. It operates under the auspices of the Jefferson County Child Abuse Authority, which represents the integrated efforts of a twenty-member-agency consortium. Each member of the consortium contributes staff, facilities, operating budget, expertise, and consultation to it. Project F.I.N.D. offers three major components:
• A treatment program for parents and families
• A therapeutic program for children (including a 24-hour crisis nursery)
• Inpatient hospitalization for children

In addition, Project F.I.N.D. staff provide community agencies with assessments of families in which child abuse or neglect occurs and also investigate all cases of suspected child abuse/neglect that are referred by the local children's hospital. They also offer community education and consultation to professional and lay persons. All services are free.

## DEVELOPING THE CONSORTIUM

Project F.I.N.D. is an outgrowth of a federally funded project called Project PACT, which began in 1975 and ran for two years until the funds were depleted. The person who directed Project PACT was wise enough to realize that the program would collapse unless the community contributed the funds needed for its survival. She publicized the impending demise of the program in an effort to make everyone aware of the loss to the community if there were no child abuse and neglect treatment program. The extensive media coverage of the issue aroused the interest of many community leaders, ten of whom formed the consortium known as the Jefferson County Child Abuse Authority (JCCAA). These leaders were knowledgeable agency officials who understood how to organize the community and who were committed to maintaining a community service for abused children. They did not draft extensive written agreements or even a statement of purpose. Initially their interest was for action, not rhetoric. Each pledged to contribute what they felt their agencies could provide in the way of personnel and physical facilities as well as money.

Once the commitment was made, they hired a project coordinator, Madeline Reno, to design the program in order to determine exactly what they would need to supply. The program that emerged consisted of two treatment teams, a nursery, and child hospitalization. In subsequent years a greater emphasis on prevention through community education was added to the basic service delivery design. Although the program began in the summer of 1977, it was not until November 1979 that JCCAA articulated a mission statement for itself. Their mission includes:

- Developing an annual comprehensive and coordinated plan for the delivery of services for the prevention and treatment of child abuse and neglect.
- Developing operational definitions of abuse and neglect to serve as the basis for local intervention strategies.
- Establishing a multidisciplinary child abuse/neglect case consultation team.
- Ensuring that training is provided to local community service systems personnel.
- Encouraging the identification and reporting of child abuse/neglect by implementing community education and awareness campaigns.
- Participating in or initiating its own research evaluation efforts in order to gain knowledge of the community's effectiveness in child protection.

Figure 5.1 presents an overview of the original JCCAA and organizational structure of Project F.I.N.D. Each of the ten-member organizations contributes either funding, staff, facilities, or consultation. Many of them contribute more than one.

---

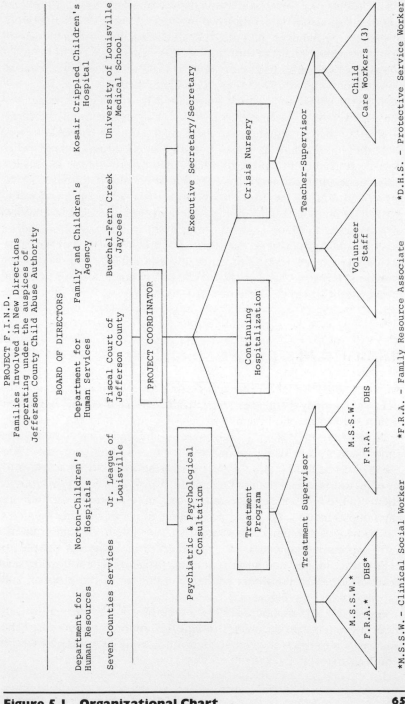

**PROJECT F.I.N.D.**
Families Involved in New Directions
operating under the auspices of
Jefferson County Child Abuse Authority

**BOARD OF DIRECTORS**

| | | | |
|---|---|---|---|
| Department for Human Resources | Norton-Children's Hospitals | Department for Human Services | Family and Children's Agency | Kosair Crippled Children's Hospital |
| Seven Counties Services | Jr. League of Louisville | Fiscal Court of Jefferson County | Buechel-Fern Creek Jaycees | University of Louisville Medical School |

PROJECT COORDINATOR

Executive Secretary/Secretary

Psychiatric & Psychological Consultation

Treatment Program

Continuing Hospitalization

Crisis Nursery

Treatment Supervisor

Teacher-Supervisor

M.S.S.W.*    DHS*
F.R.A.*

M.S.S.W.    DHS
F.R.A.

Volunteer Staff

Child Care Workers (3)

*M.S.S.W. - Clinical Social Worker    *F.R.A. - Family Resource Associate    *D.H.S. - Protective Service Worker

**Figure 5.1  Organizational Chart**

The JCCAA was, and still remains, a voluntary association. Any member can drop out at its own volition. However, all members agreed that, whenever possible, the chief executive of each agency would sit on the board of directors to ensure that the board be composed of people who had the power to make decisions and financial arrangements that affected their individual agencies.

Project F.I.N.D., the agency maintained by JCCAA, has never replaced, excluded, duplicated, or in any way undermined the functioning of other community agencies. In fact, once it was established, the other community agencies breathed a collective sigh of relief because it gave them a place to which they can refer their clients for assessment and treatment. Since its inception, the JCCAA has added several advisory committees to provide broader scope. It has expanded its membership to include twenty other appropriate community agencies and individuals. In June 1980, the JCCAA modified its organizational structure so that Project F.I.N.D.'s current program director, Betty Levy, reports to a steering committee composed of six members of the JCCAA that contribute direct financial support to the project rather than to the entire JCCAA board.

## PROGRAM DESIGN

Project F.I.N.D.'s goals are to reduce or prevent child abuse and neglect, to remedy problems experienced by abused or neglected children, to intervene in family crises that might lead to child abuse or neglect by providing a safe environment/emergency shelter for children, and to provide training to other community agencies. The agency accomplishes these goals by offering a variety of services to families and other community agencies. It provides direct services to clients in the form of a crisis nursery, case investigations, and individual, couple, family, and group counseling. Services to other agencies are provided through case assessment, consultation, staff training, and community education. A volunteer program trains people to help in the nursery and adult treatment program. The following section will focus on the direct service component of the program and its personnel. (See Figure 5.2.)

Project F.I.N.D. is housed in two facilities. Adult and family services are offered in an office building in downtown Louisville. The children's nursery is located several miles away in a wing of Kosair Children's Hospital.

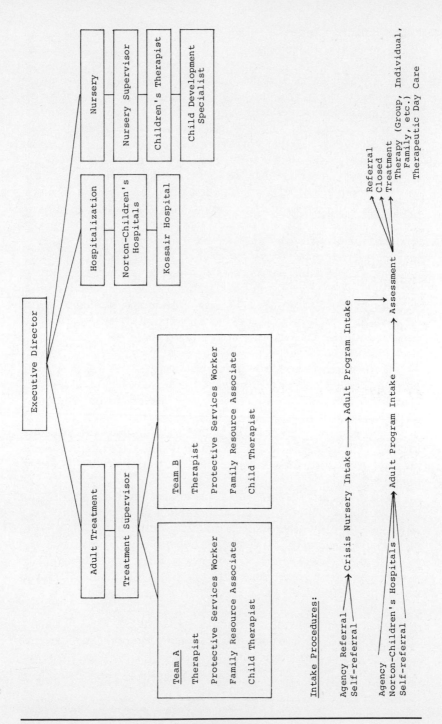

**Figure 5.2  Direct Service Structure**

67

**Treatment Teams** Direct service to adults is provided by members of a treatment team from 8:15 A.M. to 5:15 P.M., with evening hours available. A treatment team consists of a clinical social worker (M.S.W.) who provides individual, couple, family, and group counseling; a family resource associate (B.A. or B.S.W.) who offers concrete, supportive services such as transportation, food stamps, and home visiting and who also leads the women's group, a weekly socialization group for clients; a protective services investigator (M.A. or B.A.) who conducts the initial investigations on medically referred cases; and a child therapist (M.A.). Project F.I.N.D. utilizes two treatment teams which are overseen by one treatment supervisor (M.S.W.). Each team takes responsibility for gathering and synthesizing information about a family and determining an appropriate treatment plan. Each team member takes primary responsibility for a specific referral source—hospital, agency, or self. Team meetings are held once a week to discuss cases that are in various stages of the assessment or treatment process. Caseloads vary; each clinical social worker carries 25 to 30 cases; the investigators may see ten to fifteen new referrals each month; and the resource associate provides assistance to about 25 families on an ongoing basis.

Investigations of suspected abuse or neglect cases by Project F.I.N.D. protective service workers are confined to those referred through Kosair Children's Hospital. All other investigations are handled directly by county protective service workers. Just as other protective service workers, Project F.I.N.D. investigators must report every abuse situation to both the police and the state. The investigator talks with doctors or nurses to obtain detailed information, examines the child for visible injuries, and contacts the parents for an interview.

People who are accepted into the counseling program are not given an option about the type of counseling they can receive. Very often the clinical worker will start off with either individual or couple therapy once a week. Eventually the worker tries to involve the whole family. However, because so many of the cases they receive involve children who are under the age of 6, total family therapy is not always conducted. Ongoing cases are generally seen for at least six months.

In addition to individual and couple counseling, Project F.I.N.D. also maintains several groups. These include parenting skills groups, a women's club (activity group), and groups for the adolescent victims of sexual abuse. At other times, groups for physical and sexual abusers have been conducted. All therapy group leaders are professionally trained at the master's or doctoral level.

The women's club differs from the usual group format in that it is an activity rather than a therapy group. It provides a support network for the women as well as recreation and is a needed service because most of the female clients are very isolated. Group activities have included tours of factories, picnics, ice-skating parties, and presentations by speakers on topics such as assertiveness and parenting. The club meets weekly for three hours and is co-led by the two resource associates. Attendance averages six to eight women per meeting. While the women are participating in the group, their children under the age of 6 are cared for in the nursery.

Progress reviews are held every three to six months, and in court-involved cases (approximately 35 percent of the caseload) the staff has the option of returning to court.

**Nursery and Treatment Program for Children** The nursery provides day care for children whose families are involved with Project F.I.N.D. and temporary crisis care for children from birth to 6 years old. A nursery supervisor (M.A.) is responsible for the smooth functioning of the nursery as well as for writing reports and helping to formulate policy. Additional staff include a child development specialist (B.S.) who does testing and activities; six full- or part-time child care workers who carry out the play activities; volunteers who assist the child care workers; and a children's therapist (M.A.) who offers verbal and play therapy to individuals and groups of children.

The nursery, which began as a crisis facility for infants and young children, currently has three main functions:

1. It provides temporary crisis care to children from birth to 6 years old whose families are in crisis and may be endangering the welfare of their children. The children can be referred by community agencies or by the parents themselves and are eligible to receive around-the-clock care for up to 72 hours. Crisis situations that necessitate nursery care for the children may recur and the children will be provided care. In these recurring situations the nursery staff will refer the family to Project F.I.N.D. so that they may receive counseling and supportive services.

2. It offers preventive services to parents who feel temporarily overwhelmed by child caring responsibilities. Once again these may be agency-referred or self-referred cases and children can receive

care for up to 72 hours. The nursery staff screens out inappropriate referrals. There is no limit to the number of times a parent may request service, although multiple requests would probably indicate some ongoing need or problem that should be dealt with.

3. It provides therapeutic day care for those children whose families are involved in counseling at Project F.I.N.D. These children are assigned to the nursery only if they have special developmental educational or emotional needs.

The nursery also offers a cooperative care aspect as part of the preventive function of its program. It will provide day care for the children of Project F.I.N.D. clients when the counselor has determined that the client, although not in crisis, needs supportive service while he or she takes care of other important business, such as obtaining food stamps or searching for housing.

Day care runs from 9 A.M. to 2 P.M. Monday through Thursday and is available only to children from birth through the age of 6 years. The only children in the nursery after 2:30 P.M. or on weekends are those receiving crisis or co-op services. The nursery is a voluntary program for the parents; no one is forced to use the service, even in crisis cases. It takes only those children for whom it feels it can provide good quality care. Consequently, it does not admit children who have contagious diseases or who are severely physically handicapped or extremely self-destructive.

Even though the child population in the nursery is fluid, it is not unusual to see a child from three months to a year so that long-term planning can be undertaken. Friday afternoons are devoted to reviewing every child's case and making treatment plans. As much objective information as possible about the children is obtained from medical, educational, and psychological sources. Because many of the children who use the nursery facility have noticeable developmental or socialization problems, the nursery administers the Denver Developmental Test. The nursery also uses the services of a children's therapist (M.A.) who uses various therapeutic strategies with the children.

**Inpatient Hospitalization for Children** Children with suspected nonaccidental trauma or neglect may receive inpatient medical attention. The children may continue to receive inpatient care until an investigation has determined whether the home environment can ensure their safety. Staff physicians, nurses, and other medical personnel provide a full range of medical services as needed in each case.

Hospitalization includes observation and assessment. The cases are usually discovered in the emergency room, although cases also may be discovered on one of the children's wards, especially if the child has suffered injuries such as fractured bones or burns that require long-term treatment. While the child is in the hospital, both medical and Project F.I.N.D. (Protective Services Invistigator) personnel are involved. They check to see what kind of visiting patterns the parents set up with their child. When it seems indicated, Project F.I.N.D. investigators might do an assessment on the family to determine whether it is safe for the child to go home again and whether the family should be receiving some form of treatment either from Project F.I.N.D. or another community agency. Investigations usually take several days because the investigator often works on several cases at a time. If the abuse is considered to be mild or if the child has been removed from the home, the investigator writes a report but has no further involvement with the case. Home monitoring via periodic home visits may be initiated.

# STAFF TRAINING

New members of the treatment team receive an orientation that lasts approximately two weeks. During that time the new workers shadow the other workers, go to court to see what the court process is like, visit the emergency room of the hospital, and go on calls to the hospital with the investigator. The treatment supervisor teaches them how to fill out the major forms that are used by the agency.

Staff receive ongoing information from both in-service training sessions and conferences. Every month the agency sets aside a few hours for in-service training in areas that the staff perceive as felt needs, such as how to work with clients who are alcoholic. The staff is also encouraged to attend at least one conference each year. The agency pays for attendance at those conferences.

In the past, a rich source of input came from the monthly inter-agency coffees sponsored by Project F.I.N.D. For an hour each month staff members from another agency were invited to visit Project F.I.N.D. for coffee, doughnuts, fruit, and conversation. Personnel from each agency described its function and structure. These get-to-gethers kept workers aware of the resources in the community and helped to keep lines of communication open.

Volunteers are used extensively in the nursery component of the program. They are expected to make a commitment of at least three months and in return are given a regular schedule plus one full day of training each quarter.

## LINKING CLIENTS AND PROGRAM

Project F.I.N.D. wants to offer its services to those people who might not be able to find help elsewhere in the community. Therefore, it accepts referrals only for assessment rather than for direct treatment. Once the assessment has been made, the staff decides whether Project F.I.N.D. is the appropriate agency for that particular case. This procedure helps to prevent duplication of services in the community.

The program receives its referrals in one of four ways. The first is through the Children's Hospital. The medical personnel request an investigation when they notice bruises on a child or an injury that does not make sense or note that the parents are not visiting a child who required hospitalization. The Project F.I.N.D. DHS workers always take responsibility for investigating these cases. The investigation includes a description of the type and severity of injuries and the age of the child. The injury plus the child's age are important in assessing the home situation of the child. For example, a three-month-old child with a fractured skull would probably be in more danger than a seven-year-old child who had several bruises on his buttocks. The investigator also checks for prior reports of abuse and examines the home situation to assess the physical environment, the condition of the other children in the home, the extent of alcohol or drug use, and the presence of major emotional problems among the family members.

A second means of referral is through another agency, which might request an assessment to help determine whether a child should be sent home or placed in foster care or whether the parents may need the services of Project F.I.N.D.

A third referral source is the crisis nursery, which might refer a family that seems to have ongoing crises and uses the nursery frequently.

A fourth source of referrals is the potential clients themselves. Self-referrals are considered the best source because they often are made before serious harm has come to the child. For instance, a parent might call the agency and say, "I saw your ad on television and I know that could be me in a day or two if things don't change." Self-referrals tend to be short-term cases that can be resolved by provision of information about how to handle conflict situations.

Once the referral has been made, the clients are expected to contact Project F.I.N.D. and arrange for an initial appointment. Only after the clients initiate contact does the assessment process begin. The process includes the filling out of an intake form which asks about the presenting problem, the family composition, a description of the incidents that led to the referral, the child's medical condition, and any history of abuse or neglect. (See Figure 5.3.) Every person is required to make a kinetic family drawing, to complete an Adult-Parenting Inventory, and, if they can read on at least a sixth grade level, to take an MMPI or MCMI. Then the staff does an extensive social history which focuses on the parents' own background and includes any abuse that they may have experienced, how they got along with their own parents, where they came in their family's history, how and what they learned about being a parent. The assessment process also involves obtaining release slips and contacting *every* agency that the family has been involved with for any type of service. Not only does Project F.I.N.D. contact those agencies, it may invite those who have worked with the family to attend the assessment. This helps detect discrepancies or fill in gaps about the family. The data collected during the assessment process, which can take several days or weeks, are summarized on a form that resembles a sociogram depicting the family constellation. (See Figure 5.4.) This diagram concisely presents basic information about each person, such as where they were born, whether they have had any problems with the law, how well they performed in school, the level and source of their income, and the presence of drinking problems. Attached to the sociogram is a Lifeline, which is a chronology of the major events in each person's life. (See Figure 5.5.)

The assessment process culminates in a case presentation given during one of two weekly team meetings. The workers discuss the family needs and appropriate ways of dealing with current problems. For instance, do the parents need to learn parenting skills? Would they fit in parent education courses or would they benefit more from concrete services? Do they require Project F.I.N.D. counseling services or would the problem be better treated by some other agency? Fifty percent of the referrals end at the assessment phase. The information collected is used by the referring source to help personnel understand the family dynamics or determine a treatment plan. The Project F.I.N.D. staff provide service to the remaining cases that they

Project F.I.N.D. Intake Form          By:_____

Date:_____Referral Source:_____

Address:_____Phone:_____

Services Being Requested by Referral Source:_____

_____

Presenting Problem:_____

_____

|                CHILD                |        PARENT(S) OR GUARDIAN        |
|--------------------------------------|------------------------------------|
| Name:_____        | Name:_____         |
| Birthdate/Age:_____       | Address:_____         |
| Sex:_____Race:_____       | County:_____Phone:_____        |
| Present Location:_____        | Occupation:_____         |
| Hospital Number:_____       | _____         |
| Social Security No._____       | Annual Net Income:_____         |
| Medical Card:_____      | Social Security No.:_____         |
| Attending Physician:_____       | Medical Card No.:_____         |
|                                      | Family Doctor:_____         |

HOUSEHOLD COMPOSITION:

Name                              Birthdate     Phone        Role




Significant others in family   Address       Phone        Role



Involved professional workers  Address       Phone        Role

**Figure 5.3   Intake Form**

Descriptions of incident(s) leading to referral:

_____

_____

_____

_____

_____

Description of child's condition upon first examination:

_____

_____

Child's current medical condition:_____

Parents' version of what happened:_____

_____

_____

_____

_____

Medical opinion as to what happened:_____

_____

_____

_____

_____

History of previous abuse/neglect:_____

_____

_____

Cleared through:

DHR (588-4215)_____M.S.S.D. (581-6184)_____

City Police (581-2465)_____County Police (588-2098)_____

P.A.C.T. Cards_____

**Figure 5.3   Intake Form, *continued***                    **75**

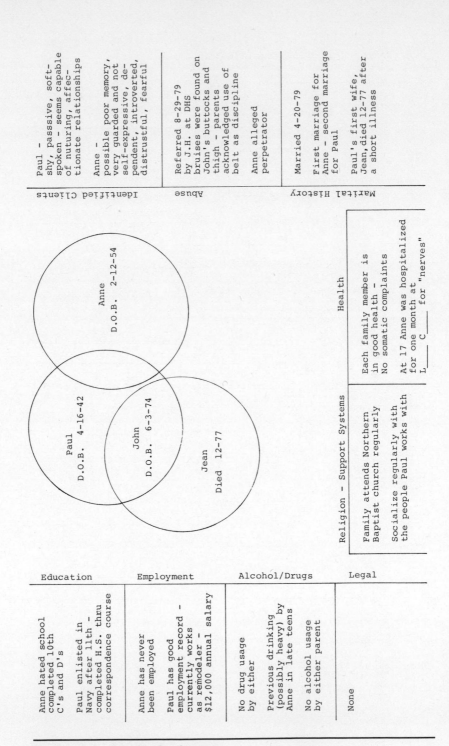

**Figure 5.4 Family Sociogram**

LIFELINE

| Age | PAUL |
|-----|------|
| Birth | Born 4-16-42 in Columbus, oldest of four siblings - Father stationed in Europe until 1945 - mother worked until then so Paul was cared for by his maternal grandmother - described parents, family as close, openly affectionate - father was shy, quiet, "ruled the roost" - mother was sociable, the comforter and the disciplinarian - some spankings with hand and belt but no real abuse |
| 6 | Didn't like school, C average - made friends easily - believed parents' marriage to be very happy - good family life |
| 14 | Continued average grades in high school - had several friends - no major conflicts with parents, sex education learned at school |
| 17 | Started dating - completed eleventh grade |
| 18 | Joined the Navy - traveled extensively |
| 22 | Returned home to live with family |
| 23 | First job - renovating buildings, then with kitchen remodeling company |
| 24 | Met Jean (she was 14) dated for three years |
| 27 | Paul moved with Jean's family to Louisville and lived with them for one year, then he and Jean married - described marriage as "excellent," "very close relationship," "much open affection" |
| 32 | John was born, product of a planned pregnancy - full term - "good baby" - Jean provided most of the child care - Paul enjoyed playing with John |
| 35 | In July 1977 Jean's illness began - she was hospitalized in October (two surgeries) - died in December (blood clot) - Anne started baby-sitting with John in Feb. '78 - Paul and Anne began dating in May '78 (Paul had not dated anyone else) - |
| 37 | Paul and Anne married April 1979 |

**Figure 5.5  Lifeline**

LIFELINE

| Age | ANNE |
|-----|------|
| Birth | Born 2-12-54 in Lafayette, youngest of four girls - father died before Anne was 3 - Anne claims she knows little about her father - "hurts to ask mother about it" - Mother worked at local factory - Anne doesn't remember who watched her while mother worked - says she was close to mother and sisters - affectionate family |
| 6 | "Hated every minute" of first grade - repeated first and third grades - poor academic performance - received spankings from mother when teachers sent notes home from school - raised Baptist, mother was strict though Anne says she was not abusive - "it hurt me not to have had a dad" |
| 14 | Attended Northern High School - "school was worse" - had few friends |
| 17 | Started skipping school in tenth grade, dated some, finally dropped out of school - started drinking, hanging around the "wrong crowd" - no drugs - hospitalized for one month - would give little information about this except to say, "I thought everybody hated me" - "nerves" - returned home to live, earned some money baby-sitting |
| 24 | Met Paul, began baby-sitting for his son John who was 3 years old - started dating Paul "before his wife died" (contradictory info) |
| 25 | Married Paul in March '79 - Anne doesn't like housework - she seems to be lonely and bored and though she claims she has close friends in her neighborhood - she is ambivalent about having another child which Paul wants - she does claim to have difficulty getting John to mind her at times |

**Figure 5.5   Lifeline,** *continued*

have assessed. With these clients the staff develop a Goal Attainment Scale. (See Figure 5.6.)

Treatment begins during assessment procedures and may include some counseling for the parents in addition to the gathering of information. Once a family has been accepted into the program, however, a more formal treatment plan is worked out. Staff decides which services family members should receive. While the family might receive only monitoring for a few months, most of the people accepted for service enter some type of counseling—individual, marital, family, or group. Individual counseling is done with single parents. Couple therapy is the usual treatment undertaken if the parents are willing to participate.

The issues most frequently discussed are the marital relationship and differences of opinion related to child rearing. Parents discuss the conflicts in their relationship, how they deal with problems that arise with the children, what they do as a family, and what new activities they can try together. Ongoing cases generally are seen for at least six months. Although they adhere to no formal plan, the therapists usually focus on the abuse and the circumstances under which it occurred. They also give attention to the parents' sexual relationship, their backgrounds, and the roles they assume in the family; in addition they teach them how to support each other in child-rearing matters. Family therapy is conducted where appropriate and feasible. In an attempt to maintain continuity, the family is assigned to the same treatment team that had conducted the assessment.

## CASE EXAMPLE

**Presenting Problem**  On a court referral, the parents, Susan, 40 years old, and Danny, 50, contacted Project F.I.N.D. Danny had whipped Susan's two children, Carol and Dennis, ages 8 and 5, with a belt and had left bruises. The parents separated for a brief time. Susan agreed to a reconciliation if Danny would agree to counseling. Later, Susan found Danny molesting Carol. This led to another separation following the Protective Services worker's investigation. Susan insisted on counseling as a condition of reconciliation. Danny is employed at a local company; Susan is not employed outside the home.

**Background Information**  After Danny's mother died when he was 2 years old, he and several of his siblings were placed in an orphanage. Danny was 9 when he rejoined his father, who had re-

| I. Marital/Couple Relationship | II. Child/Parent Relationship | IV. Family Management | V. Personal Competence |
|---|---|---|---|
| a) Lack of agreement about methods of discipline<br>b) Poor communication between couple<br>c) Couple presents united front facade<br>d) Substance abuse | a) Refusal to acknowledge problem<br>b) Role reversal<br>c) Lack of parenting skills, knowledge of children<br>d) Inappropriate discipline of children<br>e) Inappropriate expectations of child<br>f) Eliminate abusive behavior toward children - decrease frequency of abuse by parent<br>g) Protect child from out of family abuse<br>h) Inability to demonstrate appropriate caring for child<br>i) Substance abuse by parent(s) | a) Changing crisis life-style<br>b) Knowledge of and ability to use community resources related to needs of family<br>c) Improving home management abilities | a) Substance abuse<br>b) Develop self-nurturing behaviors<br>c) Improve education and/or employment<br>d) Recognize and stop self-defeating and/or destructive behaviors<br>e) Ability to establish and maintain a positive one-to-one relationship |
| II. Social Relationship<br>a) Resolving conflicts with family of origin<br>b) Enmeshment with family of origin<br>c) Isolation<br>d) Poor/inadequate interactional skills | | | |
| Problem 1 III-D Date: 7/30/81 | Problem 2 III-D Date: | Problem 3 Date: | Problem 4 Date: |
| Ms. B punishes daughter (5) by hitting her with a belt when child disobeys. | Ms. B expects daughter (5) to keep the house clean - sweep floor and do dishes - as well as picking up after younger siblings. | | |
| Ms. B sends daughter to her room when child disobeys. | Ms. B expects daughter (5) to make her bed, pick up her clothes, take her own bath, and get her own sandwiches. | | |

**Figure 5.6  Goal Attainment Scale**

married. Though he seemed to idolize his father, in some respects there is little indication that they had a close relationship. His relationship with his stepmother was characterized by resentment and hostility. Danny entered his first marriage when he was 19. This union brought four children. He left his wife eleven years later when he discovered that she was having an affair. Despite this fact, he claimed the marriage had been perfect until the wife's affair and he denied the existence of any marital problems. Danny was 30 when his first marriage ended, and he spent the next eight years living with his parents and maintaining rather superficial relationships with women and friends. A year after his father died, Danny married Susan, whom he had been dating for several months. He felt ambivalent about this marriage and admitted conflicts had been present from the beginning in regard to such matters as the children, the use of discipline, Susan's employment, and their in-laws.

Susan came from a violent background. Her father was alcoholic and physically abusive to his wife and children. Susan recalls only minimal nurturing from her mother. Susan left home at 17. She soon became pregnant and married the child's father, who began being abusive toward her. After the birth of her second child, she left her husband and children. Within the next year she moved in with a boyfriend, whom she later discovered to be alcoholic and a violent-tempered man. Carol and Dennis were born from this relationship. Four years later Susan left the relationship after learning that her sister was having an affair with her husband. Susan moved in with another man, also an alcoholic, and this relationship too ended with Susan's sister becoming involved. Susan attempted suicide at this point. A year later she married Danny. Her rationale was, "I didn't really love him when I married him; I did it for security." Susan seems moderately anxious and depressed, emotionally immature, and dependent, and she shows poor judgment in choosing men who reinforce her negative self-concept. She does recognize that she has difficulty with interpersonal relationships and has shown a willingness to seek treatment.

Danny presents a distant, rigid, and resistive profile. He is distrustful and has trouble relating on any but superficial levels. His rigidity and defensiveness seem to mask underlying unmet dependency needs as well as feelings of insecurity and inferiority. His rigidity and denial make him difficult to work with in treatment.

**Treatment Plan**   There are many problems this couple needs to work on. One is poor communication, another is difficulty taking each other seriously, a third is a lack of problem-solving skills, a fourth is an unrealistic view of children, a fifth is a poor sexual relationship, and a sixth is discord regarding parenting. The treatment plan for all of those problems includes marital therapy and family therapy.

## Progress Notes

*July 26:* Last week Danny hit Carol and Dennis with a belt as a means of discipline. He left bruises on the back of their thighs. Susan was not present at the time. Both admitted serious disagreements about the children and methods of discipline. The couple separated for a few days but have since reconciled. Susan has insisted on counseling and Danny is agreeable.

*July 31:* Session with Susan to complete social history. Susan was obviously upset. Yesterday she found Danny sitting in the bedroom with Carol on his lap. He had his hand inside Carol's panties and was fondling her. This stopped when Susan walked in. Later Susan talked to Danny privately and learned that he had done that before on several occasions, but he refused to discuss it. Danny did tell Susan that no genital penetration had occurred. Susan also talked with Carol in private and she has confirmed this. Susan reported the incident to DHS and demanded that Danny move out.

*August 11:* Obtained social history from Danny. He was very anxious and defensive when discussing sexual activity with Carol. He denied ever penetrating her but stated he did fondle her on several occasions. He said he did not remember when his behavior first began and he was generally resistant to discussing the matter.

*August 18:* The couple cancelled today's appointment.

*August 25:* The case was assessed and it was decided that the couple would be seen in marital therapy. On 8-24 there was a conjoint session. Danny stated that he considered his sexual molestation of Carol over and done with and saw no need for further counseling. I explained my legal responsibility to report the abuse and the necessity for their continued involvement in therapy. Both agreed there were numerous other marital conflicts.

*Summary of appointments from September 1 to September 15:* They cancelled an appointment on the 12th. Hostility escalates in this family because Susan and Danny are negatively enmeshed. There seems to be little security, individuality, or freedom in this marriage. Danny does not want Susan to have a job, restricts visitation with friends and relatives, and often complains if she leaves the home at all without him. Susan chooses to nag and complain rather than assert herself. Focused on differentiating their individual lives from their life as a couple. Susan needs a lot of support in asserting herself. Danny withdraws in sullen anger or spouts ultimatums to defend against changes being made. He is very unaware of his own feelings and has even more difficulty relating them. Susan allows herself to be hooked into hostile arguments and is still determined to change Danny and force his approval for things she wants to do. No apparent progress from this pattern so I will discuss it in team supervision.

*October 26:* The couple did not keep their appointment.

*November 3:* A conjoint session: It was mutually agreed that they were not making progress in current treatment. I suggested that they join group and they agreed to attend.

*November 16:* Couple's first group session: Both were very quiet but seemed interested in what others were saying. Danny quietly admitted sexual abuse of his daughter but seemed very shy and would not elaborate. At the end of the session Susan said that she now felt better than she has in a long time after hearing that other people with the same problem were getting help.

*November 23:* Both were quiet again tonight, but very interested. Susan did support the therapist in the idea that the daughter's welfare was paramount.

*November 30:* Danny reacted to the talk on children being placed out of their home, telling how he was taken from his family at an early age and raised in a succession of foster homes and finally landed in a children's village.

*December 7:* Danny was still pretty quiet but was able to relate fairly well when asked to directly by the therapist. Again he was able to relate to idea of children being taken from the parents' home and seems to have deep feelings about this but has a hard time expressing feelings. Susan was also quiet but did talk briefly about her anger at Danny for relating sexually to her daughter instead of to her.

*December 14:* Attended group tonight but nothing new to report.

*December 21:* Susan shared her jealousy experiences with the group and related how she now handles such situations. She also was able to give some good comments to another couple about how she viewed their situation as acted out by their role playing. Danny was also able to relate to coping with a jealousy situation and, for the first time, even talked without being asked.

*December 28:* They had a hard time getting serious about goals for the new year. Susan would like Danny to do specific things right away when asked rather than putting things off until Susan becomes angry. Danny would like Susan to pick up dirty coffee cups and put them in the trash instead of leaving them in his car. More generally, both seem to "enjoy" not doing little things that rub each other.

*January 4:* Danny was quiet again except to relate his early life as a foster child and the rejection in his family. Susan was active in responding to other group members' work. No work was done tonight on her own situation.

*January 11:* Susan talked a lot tonight about problems that she is having with her alcoholic father. She related feeling caught in the middle between her mother, who voices wanting the father to stop drinking but who has been joining him more and more for drinks, and her father, who becomes mean and nasty under the influence. Susan received lots of support from other group members, particularly from a couple who were both reformed alcoholics themselves.

*January 18:* Danny reported much more contact with his stepson during the past week and Susan sees a big improvement in her son's mood. Danny seemed to feel good about the contact and received lots of support from other group members about what he has done with Dennis. Danny may be developing some positive feelings about his parental responsibilities.

*January 25:* Couple attended group but nothing new to report.

*February 1:* Danny continues to feel better about his relationship with the children. He is spending more time with them, especially Dennis, and is enjoying them more than ever before. He and Susan are more coordinated in their discipline of their children. Danny needs at some point to discuss the abuse of Carol. But to this point he has come a long way in opening up in group and should not be rushed. Susan is concerned with chronic, episodic drinking binges by her father, who lives next door. She was given Alcoholics Anonymous and Al-Anon information by other group members.

*February 8:* Couple attended group; nothing new to report.

*February 15:* Danny and Susan talked a little about Danny's abuse of Carol. Danny was very embarrassed and could not, or would not, recall any of his feelings related to the abuse. The pressure at the time of the abuse was a paternity suit against Danny filed by a previous girlfriend. This had upset both Susan and Danny quite a bit. Danny continues to do well in dealing with the children.

*February 22:* Tonight's group focused on another couple who had surprising developments in their family situation. Both Susan and Danny were able to give positive feedback to this couple and were able to offer helpful suggestions in terms of dealing with their situation. No work was done on their own situation, however.

*March 1:* Couple attended group; nothing new to report.

*March 8:* Couple attended group; nothing new to report.

*March 15:* Couple was absent from group. Did not call to say they would be absent.

*March 22:* Susan and Danny said they were absent last week because Carol was in a play at school and they wanted to attend. Since there was only one other couple in attendance and since the atmosphere was trusting and confidential, therapist broached the discussion of the abuse. Susan described catching Danny manipulating Carol in the bedroom one Sunday when she (Susan) was supposedly asleep. This was after several months of vague feelings that something untold was happening between Danny and Carol, especially when Carol complained of her "pee-pee" hurting. Danny attempted to deny the abuse at first but admitted it when Susan pressed him. It had been going on for several months and Danny said that he knew he would be caught eventually. His open manner of abusing at the time suggests he was unconsciously setting it up to be caught. The couple separated at Susan's demand, only to be reunited two weeks later when Danny agreed to continue counseling and not to abuse again. In the interaction in group it became obvious they were displaying the usual pattern of unresolved chronic problems between husband and wife, with husband acting out in anger through the abuse. Danny had a very passive-aggressive style with Susan and she mothers him a great deal of the time. He was petulant and placed some of his irritation toward Susan on the children. He behaves almost as a sibling at times to the children. A lot of attention was directed to specific patterns of communication between Susan and Danny, and between Danny and the children. We need to help him become more of a parent and less of a child, and Susan to be more of a wife and less of a mother to Danny. We can see improvement by Danny's reaction to a recent incident in which the children were throwing rocks at each other. Instead of punishing them physically, Danny asked each of them to select his or her own punishment, a creative and effective way of disciplining.

*March 29:* A new couple attended group tonight. Both Susan and Danny were excellent in welcoming them and giving them support. Danny, who was extremely shy and quiet during his initial sessions, talked fluently and easily about how he had felt and how he helped himself become more talkative. Both Susan and Danny reported that they had spent an excellent last five days being able to talk, express feelings, and just relating appropriately to each other. They had attended a dinner dance on Saturday night and Susan stated that Danny had danced with her and with some other women, had talked and laughed with everyone, and in general had had a fun time. Danny seemed to behave more like a father to the kids this week and the children had seemed more like wanting to relate to him than they had in the past.

*April 5:* Susan and Danny report having another good week with each other. They both appeared to be very happy and were working together on any problems with the children. Susan happily reported that Danny seems to be doing extremely well in his relationship with them.

*April 12:* Both were able to offer some helpful insights and suggestions tonight to another couple who were on the verge of separating because of the man's immaturity. Susan could relate well to the other member's constant need for affection as this had been a problem for her in the past, always needing reassurance from Danny that he loved her. Susan offered several insights into what might make a person need that constant attention and also gave some ways that she had been able to overcome the problem. She talked a good bit about self-image and seemed to give other group members several good issues to talk about.

*April 19:* Danny shared quite openly with the group his feelings about his stepmother being hospitalized this week with a possible terminal illness. The stepmother had been a central nurturing figure in Danny's life since he was 12 years old. He stated that he was probably closer to her than to his real father. He also talked about problems with his oldest son, whom he feels has been spoiled terribly by his ex-wife. His two sons had visited with Susan and him. Danny has come a long way in being able to share his feelings openly and in his ability to trust the group to give him support and feedback. Susan seemed rather happy tonight. She and Danny seemed to feel much more comfortable in their relationship with one another. It appears that they may be ready shortly to terminate from the group.

*April 26:* Discussed the possibility of Susan and Danny leaving the group in the near future. Both of them, the other group members, and the therapist feel they have come a long way in their relationship with themselves and their children. Danny seems much more relaxed and sure of himself with both children now. Susan reports how good this has been for the children. The couple have agreed to attend several more group meetings before termination and after that will be placed on one-year follow-up.

## TREATMENT ISSUES

A major barrier that workers face is the one imposed by the clients' denial and hostility to the allegation that they abuse or neglect their children. All team members, no matter what their function, contend with these client attitudes. According to one worker, "It can be frustrating to be met by that all the time. You have to keep reminding yourself what your goal is in order not to be put off by the person's initial anger."

Building a relationship is time consuming because the worker is often seen as an enemy. According to one therapist, "Most of our clients are poor people and poor people have multiple problems, not just abuse. Sometimes it is difficult to come in as another agency whom they view is going to interrupt their life. So you have to be prepared to deal with people's hostility. I expect it to be there and I can understand it without personalizing it.

"There is a lot of resistance to change. The most difficult clients are not always the most obviously resistant. They come in smiling and agreeable and say, 'Yes, we have had difficulties but. . . .' These are the people who will not be open to looking at their situation. Sometimes it is easier to deal with a person who is openly hostile. I remember a woman who would not talk to me during the first session and just gave me a Sonny Liston stare. At first I tried to come across as warm and understanding so that she would express some of her own feelings—surely she must be a little hurt or angry that she was being forced to come here? No response. I became more insistent about her need to communicate and she muttered that I was meddling in her business and that she did not have anything to say to me. I told her that I was going to stick with her and one way or another we were going to get through to each other. After two or three equally frustrating sessions in which the woman grudgingly said a few things, I suggested a home visit to which she agreed. Just prior to the home visit she had to make another court appearance and came within a hair's breadth of having her child taken away from her. At her home she once again became like a statue and we reached an impasse very quickly. So I said, 'Look, let me tell you something. I have had problems with my own son. He is a little bit like your son, he's rambunctious. Sometimes he does things before he thinks about them.' I talked about my son for about fifteen minutes and all of a sudden she was smiling and saying, 'I thought none of you people up there had any children of your own and were talking out of books.' Eventually she became one of my most open and cherished clients."

Not all treatment problems occur because of internally motivated feelings. Some are related to very real concrete problems. One of the biggest is transportation to the office. Most clients are seen in the downtown office and must rely on bus service or their own cars to keep their appointments. The agency van is used only to take children and mothers to the nursery. Some clients are forced to cancel their appointments when they do not have enough money to buy gasoline, and in cold weather it is difficult to find clients who are willing to wait on street corners for the buses that will bring them downtown.

These factors produce one of the most frustrating aspects of the job for workers, that clients do not keep their appointments. Estimates indicate that 35 to 40 percent of all scheduled appointments are not kept. Of those, half have been cancelled and the other half have not. Workers try to avoid the high no-show rate by calling clients to remind them of their appointments. Making home visits is not always a solution either, because clients may not be home at the time of the appointment. Workers try to confront the issue by asking clients to discuss what they don't like about the service that is being provided or about the behavior of the worker so that they don't drop out. However, if the client refuses treatment, the worker has little recourse except to refer him or her back to court, if it is a court-mandated case, and let the judge settle the dispute. About one case in ten may involve people who attend once or twice and then drop out.

Although Project F.I.N.D. is a small agency, its clients are scattered throughout Jefferson County. The physical distance that must be covered is a special problem for the resource associate, whose job entails a high percentage of visits to clients' homes. The resource associates try to keep things manageable by grouping visits to clients who live in the same general vicinity, but sometimes they may be with a client who lives 20 miles out of town and when they phone the office for their messages they discover that a client at the other end of town is in the midst of a crisis and needs their immediate attention.

Investigators on the team are faced with a different pressure. They have to make rapid decisions about people which can have serious repercussions on the individual and the family. In some cases these are life and death decisions that affect the child, and in some cases they are decisions that can cause the breakup of the family unit. By the end of their investigation they must decide whether to remove the child from the home or ask that charges be filed against the parents. There is always the fear that their decision might be wrong, that they overreacted or underreacted to the information they collected. With several investigations to conduct in a short time, the sense of responsibility and pressure often seem overwhelming.

Being a member of a team reduces some of the pressure. Workers report a kind of family spirit that develops which helps them through the times when they feel depressed, incompetent, or overloaded. They have learned to trust each other and to draw on each other's strengths. Team membership provides built-in consultation during difficult assessments or when cases reach a plateau.

One of the problems posed by housing services in two different facilities is that team members are separated from the personnel who work in the child care component of the program, reducing the amount of direct contact and consequently the amount of immediate support and feedback. For example, it would be easier if the person working with the child could walk down the hall and say to the person working with the parents: "This child has withdrawn very suddenly. Is there anything going on in the family that might account for the change?" Even though that type of interchange can occur over the telephone, it would be more effective if members of the treatment and nursery staffs were able to participate in direct, continuous consultation. Ensuring that all workers in the program derive the benefits of mutual support requires active planning for ongoing communication and interaction.

# ADMINISTRATIVE ISSUES

**Liaison with the Board**   Perhaps the most important skill a program coordinator needs is the ability to walk a tightrope while balancing several objects. Even though the board may be agreed on its basic mission, there is not always consensus about the details. The director must answer to twenty different board members each of whom may have different ideas and interests regarding various aspects of the program. (This process has become easier since the shift to a six-member steering committee that meets with the director.) She has to balance and integrate these interests and also oversee the program. The job requires the ability to respond not only to the directives that the board makes concerning the program but also to the directives the board issues regarding the functioning of the board itself. To do this necessitates close interaction with many board committees. In addition to meeting with the steering committee each month, the director sits on ten board committees.

**Funding**   The budget for Project F.I.N.D. in 1982 was close to $370,000 in personnel, facilities, and money. Not all agencies contribute equal amounts of money to the operating budget. The director prepares a budget and then must ask each agency in the consortium to contribute certain items. For instance, she asks one agency, "Would you give X amount in consultation funds this year?" and another agency, "Would you contribute X amount toward operating expenses?" Sometimes she asks them for in-kind items such as a van, or driver, or secretary. One of the realities of this type of organization is having to deal with problems around the equitable distribution of resources. The director might ask for an additional staff person such as an intake worker and be turned down by all the agencies. In cases where they have to go without a needed person, the director tries to protect staff by setting standards, such as caseload size, that will allow the program to continue to give quality service. However, that practice can also create tension because it might mean that they cannot accept all the cases that are referred by one of the agencies in the consortium.

**Merging**   Because this type of program is dependent on the cooperation of several agencies, it is especially vulnerable to major shifts that might occur within the consortium. For example, at some point it is possible that two members of the consortium might merge to form one large agency. That can jeopardize the program in several ways related to funding, personnel, and facilities. The tendency would be for the newly created agency to say, "Now that we are one large agency, Project F.I.N.D. will not receive as much money from us as they did when we were two separate agencies." The newly merged agencies might consolidate staff and not be able to provide the type or number of personnel it once did. It might even close down one of its buildings and no longer have the space to house one of the program components provided by Project F.I.N.D. It is the director's responsibility to anticipate the consequences of changes among consortium members and do the planning needed to keep the program viable.

**Personnel Practices** All staff are contributed to Project F.I.N.D. by the various members of the consortium. Some agencies make the position available and allow the Project F.I.N.D. director to hire the person she would like to fill it. Other agencies select the people who will work in the program. In some cases the Project F.I.N.D. staff may interview the candidates but the final determination is made by the contributing agency. Unless an agreement is formulated with the contributing agency in advance, problems can be created if the person does not work well in the Project F.I.N.D. program. Also, Project F.I.N.D. does not have its own payroll. Each person who works in the program is subject to the personnel policies and practices of the contributing agencies, including salary levels, sick leave, insurance programs, and vacation periods. Disparities and inequities between the policies of the various agencies can undermine staff motivation.

# ELEMENTS FOR SUCCESS

The agency relies on the community for its referrals. Therefore, it is important for the director and the staff to become fully involved in the community in order to maintain visibility. It is also important for the program to possess a high degree of visibility among the members of the consortium so that the consortium can feel that it is continuing to make a worthwhile investment. Even though there may be disadvantages to having services housed in two separate facilities, it does provide better public relations for the program because the funding sources feel more invested in the program when they can see Project F.I.N.D. offices or personnel in their buildings.

The director believes that successful operation depends on the provision of needed services rather than duplicating services that are available elsewhere in the community. By filling gaps in service provision, the program stands a better chance of being accepted and used by both lay and professional groups. Furthermore, the service provided must be of high quality in order to maintain program credibility. High-caliber service is more likely to meet program goals, produce client satisfaction, and generate continued referrals from local agencies.

# 6

# RESIDENTIAL PROGRAM: Family Crisis Center

The Family Crisis Center deals with the problems of family violence by offering residential care to all members of the families in which violence occurs. Developed and operated by Child and Family Services at Knox County, Inc., it is available to residents in and around Knoxville, Tennessee, who have need of both shelter and counseling to help cope with crises that periodically arise in the family. The program consists of two major components:
• Shelter for adults and their children
• Counseling for the shelter residents and family members

Because of its crisis orientation, the program is short-term, with shelter given for a maximum of two weeks and counseling for no longer than three months, including a 60-day follow-up period. All services are free.

## DEVELOPING THE CENTER

Although the program began in January 1978, the idea for it originated many years before when the current director of Child and Family Services, Charles Gentry, was still in private practice. He could recall being in clients' homes in which there was a gun lying on the table and knowing that it was only a matter of time before one spouse would shoot the other or him or herself. "They had reached their wits' end and viewed killing as the only way out. I was frustrated because clients were unable to get the services they needed in the community. The programs just were not there." Because it would be impractical to send a therapist to a family's house every time there was a family crisis, it became clear that the whole family needed some place to go where someone would take over and help them get organized.

Once he became the executive director of Child and Family Services, Mr. Gentry established group homes for children who were emotionally or physically abused and whose parents needed counseling as well. When those proved successful, the agency began thinking about establishing the residential crisis center. Here, they could have both spouses under one roof, or have one person in the residential center and reach out to the other, and help them start to communicate in such a way that they could decide on a more constructive course of action for their lives. During 1977 the idea was sounded out with various individuals and groups. At first it met with considerable community resistance: some groups maintained that it was not proper to interfere in the family's business, others believed that such a program would force the adults to stay together, and still others believed that it was too dangerous to house both the abuser and the abused under the same roof. To counteract those attitudes, a meeting was called of community groups that had some interest in child and spouse abuse. That meeting uncovered a divergence of viewpoints about how family problems should best be treated. People who were interested in child abuse tended to favor removing the children from the home and letting the courts deal with the parents, and people who were interested in spouse abuse favored removing the woman from the situation and letting the criminal justice system deal with the man. The main task at the meeting was to convince both of the groups that total family involvement would be therapeutically more effective and financially more efficient. For example, if the child was being abused and the parents seemed to have the potential for dealing with the child in a more constructive way, then it would be possible to have them all stay in the residential center and literally teach them a different way of interacting. Or, in spouse abuse cases it might be appropriate to meet the dependency needs of both partners through residential treatment and teach them to relate in nonabusive ways so they could decide whether to remain together or to separate. It was necessary to convince the group that by ignoring the violent person they would be minimizing the worth of that person and, as a consequence, the person was likely to become more violent. It was also necessary to point out to community leaders that the funds of this country are controlled by men—in Congress, state legislatures, United Way organizations, for example—and that by taking a total family approach they would be helping the men also. That proved to be a popular and conciliatory notion.

The most convincing argument, however, was proof that the center was needed. After an unsuccessful attempt to convince a member of the United Way board to become an advocate for funding the Family Crisis Center, Mr. Gentry received a call from the same board member the following day: "Charlie, one of my employees was beaten by her husband last night. Can you help her?" The reply: "If we had that Family Crisis Center I was talking to you about, we could help her a lot." The board member told that story at some of the United Way campaign meetings and ultimately the United Way appropriated $15,000 to help initiate the project.

By 1977 the Tennessee state legislature had already begun to appropriate funds to establish shelters in the major urban areas of Tennessee. The Child and Family Services agency, having met with the opposition groups and deciding to continue with the Family Crisis Center project, applied for those funds and received $35,000 for the first six-month period of 1978. During fiscal 1978–1979 the state allocated $70,000 to their program.

The next step was to acquire a residence. The agency had already documented that other community agencies that offered shelter, such as the Salvation Army, Volunteers of America, and the Y groups, did not want to initiate a service for violent families. The question for the agency board of directors was whether to rent or purchase a residential facility. Purchase seemed the better alternative because landlords might be reluctant to rent their property when they learned that some of the people who used the facility could be violent. One of the board members was prepared to underwrite a down payment of $10,000 for the property. Several local banks were consulted to determine which would require the least down payment, charge the lowest interest, and give the longest period to pay the mortgage. Because the agency was known to be financially responsible, they found a bank willing to finance the entire $48,000 purchase price. The residence they purchased was a two-story duplex in a blue-collar neighborhood. The residence, called the Kent C. Withers Family Crisis Center, in honor of the man who had provided a

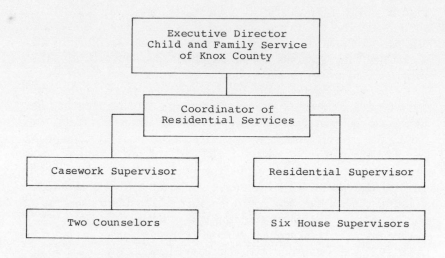

**Figure 6.1    Organizational Chart**

$10,000 stock certificate as a guarantee toward payment of the mort-gage, houses two separate residential programs operated by the agency. The downstairs portion offers shelter to runaway youth and the upstairs portion serves adults and their children who need shel-ter and counseling to cope with a family crisis. Figure 6.1 shows the organizational structure of the program.

## PROGRAM DESIGN

The major activities at the Family Crisis Center stem from the pro-gram's objective to provide short-term shelter care to families who also have a counseling need. However, another goal is to strengthen both families and individuals by helping clients learn new behaviors so they have alternate ways of acting and reacting. The program de-sign reflects the belief that learning new behaviors occurs best when the family members are in a less frightening environment. This sec-tion will focus on the residential and counseling elements of the program, which is administered by the coordinator of residential services (M.S.W.) whose job functions include supervision of all the residential programs offered by the agency.

**Residential Component** The residence offers food, shelter, and, when necessary, clothing for the adults and their children. The residence is staffed by one residential supervisor (B.A.) and six house supervisors (high school or B.A.), four full time and two part time. They function as house parents and are responsible for the safety of the house, the implementation of routines, and the development of a comfortable atmosphere that is conducive to counseling. They help the residents keep medical and agency appointments. In addition, one house supervisor is consistently assigned to plan the menus and purchase the food for the residents. One of the house supervisors works from 7 A.M. to 3 P.M. Monday through Friday; the others work twelve-hour shifts from 7 A.M. to 7 P.M. or from 7 P.M. to 7 A.M. with five days on and five days off. There is 24-hour house supervision daily.

The residence consists of a living room (which can be converted into a sleeping area), dining room, kitchen, bath, and two bedrooms. The facility contains nine beds and during a three-year period has housed 875 people from 420 families for at least one night. The average length of stay is eleven days. All residents are involved in keeping the house clean and preparing meals. Everyone, including the children, is expected to sign a chore list (Figure 6.2) and carry out those chores. Regular routines are maintained as much as possible. For example, breakfast has to end by 9 o'clock and the dishes have to be washed. Lunch is served at about noon and dinner somewhere between 5:30 and 6:30. On a rotating basis one or two residents take responsibility for the meal preparation for all the residents. Everyone usually eats together.

Maintaining cleanliness and routines are considered important parts of the residential experience. They are designed to replace chaos with order and teach people to be more considerate of others. In addition, there are general house rules which all residents must follow if they wish to remain in the facility. (See Figure 6.3.)

School-aged children who are in residence remain enrolled in the school they had been attending. The residential facility provides for their transportation to school. Younger children are supervised by house staff or by other residents when parents have to be away dur-

|  | Sun. | Mon. | Tues. | Wed. | Thurs. | Fri. | Sat. |
|---|---|---|---|---|---|---|---|
| **KITCHEN A.M.**<br>__Wash Dishes<br>__Scrub Counters<br>__Mop Floor<br>__Put Away Food |  |  |  |  |  |  |  |
| **BEDROOMS**<br>__Sweep, Pick Up<br>__Make Beds<br>__Hang/Fold Clothes |  |  |  |  |  |  |  |
| **BATHROOMS**<br>__Tub __Sink<br>__Toilet<br>__Mop Floor/Sweep<br>__Diaper Pail |  |  |  |  |  |  |  |
| **LUNCH HELP**<br>__Plan/Cook<br>__Set Table |  |  |  |  |  |  |  |
| **KITCHEN NOON**<br>__Wash Dishes<br>__Counters __Table<br>__Put Away Food<br>__Sweep |  |  |  |  |  |  |  |
| **DINNER HELP**<br>__Plan/Cook<br>__Set Table<br>(Plan the Night<br>Before) | (2) | (2) | (2) | (2) | (2) | (2) | (2) |
| **KITCHEN P.M.**<br>__Wash Dishes<br>__Counters __Table<br>__Put Away Food<br>__Sweep | (2) | (2) | (2) | (2) | (2) | (2) | (2) |
| **DINING ROOM**<br>__Pick Up __Dust<br>__Ashtrays __Sweep |  |  |  |  |  |  |  |
| **LIVING ROOM**<br>__Pick Up __Dust<br>__Ashtrays __Sweep |  |  |  |  |  |  |  |

**Figure 6.2   Chore List**

| | Sun. | Mon. | Tues. | Wed. | Thurs. | Fri. | Sat. |
|---|---|---|---|---|---|---|---|
| | (2) | (2) | (2) | (2) | (2) | (2) | (2) |
| LAUNDRY*<br>__Gather & Wash<br>__Dry & Fold<br>__Put in Closet<br>__Return to Owner<br>*Finish Before 1 P.M. | | | | | | | |
| FRONT PORCH<br>__Sweep/Mop<br>__Dishes<br>__Pick Up Toys | | | | | | | |
| TRASH<br>__Bathroom<br>__Office<br>__Kitchen<br>__Lids on Cans? | | | | | | | |
| STAIRWELLS<br>__Remove Objects<br>__Sweep/Mop<br>__Downstairs En-<br>   trance Swept<br>__Front Landing<br>   Swept | | | | | | | |
| BACK PORCH<br>__Sweep/Mop<br>__Dust Shelf | | | | | | | |
| YARD: FRONT & BACK<br>__Pick up Trash<br>__Sweep Steps &<br>   Walk<br>__Sweep Porch | | | | | | | |
| MOW LAWN/SHOVEL SNOW | | | | | | | |
| OTHER | | | | | | | |

* LAUNDRY PROCEDURE: Small laundry hampers are located in the bathroom and in each bedroom, including the living room area set aside for sleeping. Dirty laundry must be placed in these hampers, not on the floor or around the bathtub. Residents assigned to the laundry chore are responsible for gathering up dirty laundry from hampers, sorting by color and fabric, laundering, drying, folding, putting away, and distributing clothing.

---

**Figure 6.2   Chore List,** *continued*

GENERAL RULES

1. Each resident is expected to obey all federal, state, and local laws.

2. The possession and use of alcoholic beverages, street drugs, narcotics, nonprescribed drugs, and weapons are prohibited. Residence may be denied to anyone in an intoxicated or drugged state.

3. Physical fighting or any display of violence or abuse will not be tolerated. Spanking or other kinds of physical punishment will not be tolerated in the Center.

4. All residents will participate in treatment planning and a counseling program established with the Center staff.

5. All capable residents will be required to perform household chores which will be outlined with them by Center staff. If chores are not done, privileges may be withheld for 24 hours.

6. Residents will attend school, job training, or employment, unless appropriately excused. If school attendance is impossible, arrangements must be made to get assignments from teachers. On each school day, at least two hours must be spent in studies or related activities.

7. All residents must inform staff when they are leaving and when they expect to return. They must sign in and out at the desk, indicate where they are going, and leave a phone number where they can be reached in case of emergency.

8. A resident is automatically discharged from the Center if he or she stays out all night.

9. Residents must be at the Center by 6 P.M. unless appropriately excused.

10. For the first 48 hours that a person aged 12 to 18 is in residence at the Center without parent or legal guardian, he/she will be able to go out only under the direct supervision of a staff member. After that time the privilege may be allowed depending on behavior and with the permission of the staff.

**Figure 6.3  General Rules**

11.  Each resident will respect the rights and privacy of the other residents.  Residents can enter another's living space only with permission.

12.  Children under 12 must never be left unattended. Children 12 and over must be supervised.

13.  Phone calls may be made from the Center phone with permission of the staff.  Calls must be limited to five minutes.

14.  All residents will observe health rules and submit to a physical exam and other medical care if this is considered necessary by Center staff.

15.  No smoking will be allowed in eating or sleeping areas.

16.  Front and back doors should be closed at all times. Only staff members may answer these doors.

17.  No residents of Family Crisis Center may enter the Runaway Shelter without permission of both staffs.

18.  If any rule is broken, a meeting of residents and staff will be held to decide how to deal with the offender.  Residents who break a rule may be asked to leave after such a meeting.

**Figure 6.3   General Rules, *continued***

ing the day for job interviews, legal or medical appointments, or other necessary business.

**Counseling Program**   Counseling staff are housed at the residential center. The counseling staff consists of three people, a casework supervisor and two counselors, all of whom hold Master's degrees. The casework supervisor provides consultation to counseling staff and maintains a client load. The counselors are responsible for individual and group counseling, developing a treatment plan, and supervising the house supervisors. Like house supervisors, the counseling staff work a twelve-hour shift, from 1 P.M. to 1 A.M. with five days on and five days off. Counselors make contacts with community agencies during the afternoon, provide counseling to clients from 5 to 10 P.M., and consult with house supervisors and do case dictation and record keeping from 10 P.M. to the end of their shift.

The counselors meet with each resident individually every day for varying lengths of time to determine whether treatment goals are being met. In addition, group meetings with residents are held every evening for an hour and a half. The group meetings usually include the adults and their teenaged children who are in residence, the family members not in residence, visitors, and former clients who attend group meetings for support. Groups for younger children are also instituted when sufficient numbers are in the residence.

If only part of the family unit requests assistance and is housed at the residential facility, it is the counselor's responsibility to reach out to the other family members and arrange for a meeting with the rest of the family. Whenever possible the counselors set up marital and family sessions. The number and length of sessions vary depending on the nature of the problem and the willingness of the other family members to participate in the program.

Because the program is short-term, it is important for the clients to become knowledgeable about the various community programs that can provide ongoing assistance. They might need to apply for public assistance, housing assistance, or vocational training, and usually it is necessary to arrange for long-term counseling when the family leaves the residence. Although the counselors assist in directing residents to the appropriate community agencies, it is the clients' responsibility to obtain the care they will need on a longer term basis. Clients are provided with bus fare or transportation. When necessary a volunteer or staff person will accompany the client to the other agencies.

Clients are entitled to assistance from the counseling staff for 60 days following their exit from the residence. This usually takes the form of individual, marital, or family counseling. Former residents may also participate in the evening groups held at the residence. Sometimes follow-up services involve additional linkage to community services or advocacy on behalf of the client. Very often the problems that surface during the residential experience cannot be adequately dealt with on a short-term basis and the case is transferred to other counseling programs at Child and Family Services or to another counseling agency once the follow-up period ends.

# STAFF TRAINING

The program offers one to two hours of orientation to incoming staff. Most staff have had some previous classroom or on-site training for dealing with violence in families. Additionally, each new social worker receives one-to-one supervision from the casework supervisor and from the coordinator of residential treatment. Each new house supervisor receives one-to-one supervision from the residential supervisor. All new employees receive a policies and procedures manual and a job description which detail the FCC daily routine and the specific duties for employees and clients. New employees also receive specific articles or reading materials which assist them in understanding family systems, violence, dependency, the needs of the children and the adults, and the holistic approach used at the Family Crisis Center.

House supervisors receive approximately twelve hours of information about child care issues from a local child care association at sessions that are held two or three times a year. Both house supervisors and counselors may attend the twice monthly in-service training programs sponsored by the parent agency, Child and Family Services. Each staff member also receives a total of 40 hours a year of conference time. They are free to go anywhere they want but must document their activities and share the information they receive with the other staff members.

The coordinator of the Family Crisis Center sometimes offers in-service training around specific problems that crop up in the residence. These training sessions are handled by the staff and often involve role-play techniques as well as discussion about the best ways to deal with a particular problem. In addition, staff meetings are held every other week to discuss administrative policies and procedures as well as case situations. Also there are many informal exchanges of ideas among staff that occur during the quieter moments.

Volunteers, recruited mainly from among the ranks of local college students, are screened by FCC staff or the director of volunteers for Child and Family Services. During an orientation of one or two hours they are given information about the program and the needs of the clients. They are assigned to specific supervisors according to their background and FCC function. Some volunteers are called on when needed for specific activities; others are placed on a set schedule. Many of the volunteers receive training in the college classroom as provided by Child and Family Services staff. Professional training is emphasized with both paid staff and volunteers, and many of the latter have gone on to earn advanced degrees.

## LINKING CLIENTS AND PROGRAM

Referrals to the Family Crisis Center may come from several sources including hospitals, lawyers, doctors, social security office, social service agencies, police departments, or the potential clients themselves. The majority of referrals, however, come from the Department of Human Services and the Community Action Committee (a local agency that sponsors youth and adult programs). Requirements for entry into the program are kept to a minimum and include (1) being a resident of Knox County and (2) being in need of both shelter and counseling. A person who needs only a place to stay would not be considered an appropriate client for this program. However, people who are having family problems or personal adjustment problems and have no place to go or people who fear for their safety because of a family situation would be eligible for service at the Family Crisis Center. Although they are prepared to handle all types of family and personal problems, staff most often deal with family violence situations.

If, after the initial telephone consultation, it is determined that the situation fits the criteria for service, the person is asked to come to the Center. When the person is in a dangerous situation, the Center might ask the police to bring the person to the facility. When transportation is a problem, the Center will arrange for it. Ordinarily, only part of the family is present at intake. The first step is to help the clients relax and feel comfortable. The counselor offers them a cup of coffee, talks about general things, and shows them where to put their belongings. Then the counselor conducts an initial interview that lasts from fifteen minutes to an hour depending on the person's willingness or ability to talk. The counselor reviews with the client the forms that are used in the program which need to be completed at some point, although not necessarily during the initial interview. They include an intake information form, medical forms, permission forms to take children on recreational outings or treat the children for medical emergencies if the parent is not there, and forms that allow the release of information from other agencies. One item that is discussed during the first interview is the rules that govern living at the residence. The counselor asks the client to sign an agreement to abide by those rules.

Most intakes can be completed within an hour and include the clients' background and childhood experiences as well as the circumstances that brought the family to the Center. Usually during the intake interview the counselors ask the clients to think about what they wish to accomplish while they are in residence. At the following session (usually the next day) clients are asked to complete a goal attainment scale. (See Figure 6.4.) All goals are set up in behaviorally measurable terms. The goal areas most dealt with are medical, housing, finances, decision making, and outreach to other family members. The scale asks the person to identify progressive behavioral stages that range from the most unfavorable treatment outcome in relation to a specific goal to the best anticipated treatment success. For example, if the goal concerns employment, the progression of stages may include person does nothing, person talks about wanting a job, person explores interest and options, person goes on interviews, person obtains employment. The counselor places a check mark at the stage of the continuum at which the person enters the program and an asterisk at the level at which he or she leaves.

After the goals have been established, the adult residents are placed in the ongoing groups that operate each evening. Young children who are in residence are seen in a separate group. Adolescents who have been involved in the family conflicts are invited to participate in the adult group. There is no set format for the hour and a half daily group. Discussions are determined by the immediate needs of the group members and can involve anything from general household complaining to very intense therapy sessions. When the problem involves an abusive parent, the group sessions might be used to

Level at Intake ✓
Level at Follow-up *

| Check whether or not the scale has been mutually negotiated between client and interviewer | Yes___ No___ | Yes___ No___ | SCALE HEADINGS Yes___ No___ | Yes___ No___ | Yes___ No___ |
|---|---|---|---|---|---|
| Scale Attainment Levels | Scale 1 Employment | Scale 2 Housing | Scale 3 Decision making | Scale 4 Medical | Scale 5 Self-esteem |
| a. Most unfavorable treatment outcome thought likely | Does nothing | Has no plans | Feels confused | Needs a physical examination | Withdrawn, depressed, hopeless |
| b. Less than expected treatment success | Talks about wanting a job | Explores options | Can prioritize needs | Explores options | Many negative self statements |
| c. Expected level of treatment success | Explores interests & options | Applies for assistance or temporary shelter | Can list pros and cons | Makes an appointment | Few negative self statements |
| d. More than expected treatment success | Goes on interviews | Gets a roommate | Makes a tentative decision | Has an examination | Some positive self statements |
| e. Best anticipated success with treatment | Gets a job | Finds permanent housing | Action steps taken as planned | Plans for follow-up medical care | Many positive self statements |

**Figure 6.4   Goal Attainment Scale**

discuss child-rearing problems and techniques for dealing with children. The group sessions are also used to provide assertiveness training, relaxation techniques, guided imagery, and role playing of particular behaviors such as job-seeking skills.

Because of the program flexibility, the counselors are expected to tailor the treatment modalities they offer to the needs of the clients. For example, one situation involved a husband and wife in residence, with no children involved. It was the second marriage for the woman; her children were living with the first husband in another city. Although she had not been married to the current husband for too long, they had been involved in several knock-down, drag-out fights. They stayed in residence for two weeks during which time they participated in couples counseling, group counseling, and occasional individual sessions. While in the program the man learned that as a husband he did not have to make all the decisions and hold all the control. He became aware of his use of sex and violence as means to assert his masculinity. Since both partners held poor opinions of themselves, they were taught to bring out their individual strengths. The husband was helped to allow his wife to find outside employment without perceiving it as a threat to the relationship. They left the program better able to identify and communicate their needs.

In cases where only part of the family unit seeks help from the Family Crisis Center, the situation is handled differently. The adult is informed about the Center's policy of contacting the spouse who is not in residence. The person in residence is not required to meet with the spouse. However, the counselor reaches out several times and offers to meet with the spouse on the assumption that the spouse is feeling angry and hurt and is going through his or her own crisis. Not all spouses care to participate. Some believe that the resident is the person with the problem and do not feel the need for counseling for themselves. However, many are happy for the opportunity to talk things over with the counselor. Depending on the circumstances—the fear felt by the resident, the dangerousness of the spouse, or the wish by the resident for a separation—the counselor may meet with the spouse away from the residence or in one of the offices located on the first floor of the building. More than one meeting with a spouse may occur while the other adult member of the family remains in residence.

# CASE EXAMPLE

Mrs. B called the Kent C. Withers Family Crisis Center (FCC) at 8 o'clock on Tuesday evening. It was difficult for her to talk because she was crying. Her husband had beaten her. She had taken their baby and run to a neighbor's house. She had seen a program about the FCC on television and she wondered if she could stay at the FCC for a few days while deciding what to do next. Her neighbor could bring her to the FCC. She was given the address of the Center and the name of the person to ask for when she arrived. She was told that a room was available for her and her child and that a counselor would talk with her. Twenty minutes later Mrs. B arrived at the Center carrying her eleven-month-old son. All she had with her were the clothes that she was wearing and a few baby things that her neighbor had given her.

Upon arrival at the FCC, Mrs. B was tremulous and pale. Obviously, she had been crying. There were multiple bruises on her face and arms. During the initial interview her baby (Jim) was clinging to her. An FCC volunteer stood nearby, trying to make friends with little Jim. Mrs. B needed help with Jim, who was coughing and appeared to have an elevated temperature. Since he was so tense, no immediate attempt was made to take his temperature. His clothing and over-all appearance suggested marginal care, possibly neglect. Abuse would need to be ruled out.

Mrs. B said she was four months pregnant and worried because she had been experiencing abdominal pains ever since her husband hit her earlier that evening. It was decided that the first order of business was to get Mrs. B and Jim to a physician. After signing the appropriate FCC release forms and emergency medical care forms for herself and Jim, Mrs. B agreed to go to the hospital emergency room. By this time she had begun to spot.

About three hours later Mrs. B, Jim, and one of the FCC house supervisors returned from the hospital. Mrs. B was put to bed and told that she needed to follow physician's orders. Rest was most important. She would be able to make some plans in the morning. Meantime, staff would help her care for Jim's bronchitis during the night.

The house supervisor and the FCC counselor sat down to discuss the B's' family situation. Since the house supervisor had just spent several hours with Mrs. B, she knew a great deal about her. Mrs. B was 19 years old. The B's had been married for three years. Mr. B had a good job as an apprentice construction worker. He always brought his pay check home. He loved Jim and Mrs. B knew that he loved her too. He drank a lot and at first she thought he hit her just when he had been drinking because he didn't know what he was doing. Later, however, he began to beat her when he was sober. The beatings had gotten more frequent and more severe, especially since she became pregnant for the second time.

Actually, the first beating occurred during Mrs. B's first pregnancy. She had tried hard to be a good wife, but Mr. B never seemed satisfied. This evening he had come home early from work, and when he discovered that Mrs. B had been visiting a neighbor and had not begun to prepare dinner, he exploded. He hit her several times with his fists, pushed her down, and kicked her. She threw an ashtray at him. He was startled but kept after her. She crawled to the bedroom, got Jim out of his crib, and ran out the back door. Mr. B called after her, saying he was sorry. She kept running until she came to a friend's home. By this time Mr. B was nowhere to be seen.

During the trip to the emergency room Mrs. B confided that she still felt some love for her husband and knew he would be worried about her. He used to be so passionate and sometimes still was. It all puzzled her, because she was certain that Mr. B loved her. After all, Mr. B had been married before, was ten years older than Mrs. B, and seemed so loving and protective before they married. After she saw the doctor, Mrs. B called her husband and told him a counselor would be calling him the next day to arrange an appointment. She also told him she wasn't sure what she was going to do except that she needed some time away from home to think things over.

Mrs. B agreed to meet with her husband and the counselor, but not the next day. She did call him, however, and he said he was so sorry and promised her that he would never hit her again. Mrs. B had heard that many times before and she agreed with the counselor that she needed more than his promise. She wanted to try counseling but was not willing to attend counseling sessions with Mr. B until he agreed to ongoing contacts with a counselor.

On the second day a male counselor arranged to see Mr. B at his home. Mr. B agreed to the counseling, saying that he would not be able to work until Mrs. B returned to him and, besides, he "loves" her. He promised to pursue counseling help but denied that he had ever hurt her physically. They did argue a lot, he admitted, and he guessed they needed help, but he wasn't sure that counseling would be the answer. If she would just come home, everything would be fine. They could work it out.

By the third day Mrs. B was feeling better. She had expressed an interest in doing some of the housework or in doing something "to keep busy." The house supervisor reminded her of the doctor's instructions and arranged a program of activities that was within the limitations outlined by the doctor. Mrs. B was surprised at the food she saw the other children at the Center eating and decided to try giving little Jim some fresh fruits and vegetables. She also experimented with letting him drink from a glass. Mrs. B began to enjoy this and expressed pleasure at having learned something new already. She seemed less willing to talk, however, and wasn't sure she really needed counseling. She just wanted to stay until she could decide what she was going to do. Meantime, she did participate in floor games with Jim, the other parents, and their small children.

Mr. B called frequently during the third day. Mrs. B finally agreed to see him even though the staff told her that she could wait if she wanted. A meeting was arranged with the two of them and the counselor. Before the meeting, Jim visited with his father but was somewhat reserved. Staff recognized, however, that this could be age-appropriate behavior for a child who has been separated from a parent. During the counseling session that evening Mr. B was extremely anxious. He talked about not wanting to "go on" without his wife and son. He just wanted to take Mrs. B home, but the counselor pointed out that things had been serious at home. It was suggested that Mr. B become a resident of the Family Crisis Center so that some joint planning could occur. FCC staff, with their extensive experience, could help the B's understand each other and help them get more emotional, social, sexual, and job satisfaction. Staff could help them with Jim and some of their disagreements about him. For instance staff could offer more help with his nutrition and discipline. Mr. B was encouraged to return to work. With Mrs. B's support and approval Mr. B decided to move into the Center. He stayed for the FCC group meeting and the assignment of chores for the next day. He then went home to get clothes for all three B's.

For the next few days Mr. B went to work every day. Mrs. B's and Jim's health continued to improve. Jim was becoming more energetic. Mrs. B spent much time getting herself organized and seemed to depend on the structure imposed by the schedule of activities at the Center. She did some reading and talked to the staff about child care, infant stimulation, normal childhood development and health care, particularly prenatal problems. She even attempted to reduce her smoking because she feared that it might affect her unborn baby. She became very involved in the afternoon activity groups and worked with one of the counselors to prepare a program on nutrition for toddlers. The Bs were seen in conjoint counseling and attended the FCC group meetings every evening.

There were still many problems between the B's. For instance, Mr. B seemed to become angry every time Mrs. B made an independent decision. He became anxious about the "new things" Mrs. B was learning and expressed this in the joint counseling session by saying, "She won't like her house after being here." Mrs. B reassured him about this, but reminded him that things could never be the way they were before because she wouldn't stay with him under those circumstances. Mrs. B said that just as she had learned not to spank little Jim since she had been at the FCC, Mr. B would have to learn not to hit her. Mr. B was able to talk about his fears and frustrations. He soon began to see how threatened he felt by Mrs. B's attempts to "grow up." He admitted that he needed her dependency on him, but he had trouble recognizing that he was dependent on her. Talking about his feelings was very difficult for him. When discussing alternatives to violence, he liked the idea of jogging when he felt he was getting upset. He guessed he could even get himself into another room to calm down when he was ready to blow up. He actually did this on two later occasions while he was at the FCC. There were no episodes of physical abuse at the FCC.

Mrs. B recognized how much she had learned about her own needs and those of her husband and child. She also recognized that she was very dependent because she did not have much confidence in her ability to do anything. While she was at the FCC she began to talk about completing her G.E.D. (high school equivalency examination). Mrs. B thinks that after her baby arrives she might get involved in school again.

Mrs. B began to recognize that she thought abuse between family members was normal. Both her parents and Mr. B's parents were abusive to each other. It had only vaguely occurred to her that in some marriages husbands and wives do not beat each other. She decided to look at her own methods of handling frustration and anger. Her approach to child discipline could stand examination. Communicating openly seemed impossible to her, but she could recognize the importance of being able to do this.

As Jim became more alert and enthusiastic, he explored the FCC, giving Mrs. B and the staff many opportunities to use new disciplinary techniques such as diversion of attention, floor games, and removal of any dangerous or breakable objects from his "territory." Mrs. B had never realized that children had to explore as part of their development and that later Jim would be able to learn, without being spanked, that some objects are breakable or dangerous.

After ten days at the FCC the B's expressed interest in keeping their family together. They felt that they had accomplished a great deal during their stay at the FCC, wanted to continue counseling, but resisted a transfer to a counselor at the main office of Child and Family Services (CFS). Consequently, follow-up counseling by one of the counselors at the FCC was scheduled for the next 60 days with the understanding that a CFS counselor would become involved during that time.

At first, upon returning to their home, the B's were elated, but within 24 hours they obviously missed the protective structure of the FCC. Mrs. B made several calls to the FCC, needing support and reassurance. During the next four weeks a male counselor from CFS began working with the B's and their FCC counselor. Arrangements were made for entry into a couples group and the CFS counselor began taking over management of the case.

Together with their counselors, the B's recognized that having another child would place more stress on their budget and on their needs for attention from each other. Yes, Mrs. B had felt depressed after Jim was born, and maybe she would need a counselor to give her some encouragement and some pointers on coping with depression.

Mr. B did well at work but did have some drinking episodes during the next few months. His denial was hard to overcome, but Mrs. B and the counselor insisted on open communication about all family problems. The counselor spent part of every session pointing out at least one strength each that Mr. and Mrs. B showed. He kept focusing them on one problem at a time, rather than allowing them to criticize each other or themselves about a multitude of problems. At the same time, the counselor made occasional home visits, arranged for baby-sitting for Jim during counseling sessions at CFS, involved the B's in some prenatal care and basic child care courses, and assisted both Mr. and Mrs. B in learning to assert themselves without violence. Mr. B was able to talk about some of his feeling of sexual inadequacy and jealousy and his tendency to accuse his wife of being interested in other men. Sexual fantasies and tendencies to project fantasies or actions were discussed. Both of the B's learned a lot about their sexual inhibitions and how these had frustrated them and made them jealous.

Eventually, another son was born. Again, Mrs. B was depressed, but the counselor capitalized on the truth that the depression had passed before and it would pass again. A friend, whom Mrs. B met in couples group, stayed with her the first day home from the hospital. Mrs. B's mother came for three days and some neighbors helped out. Mrs. B was amazed that her new friendships offered such a helpful support system.

Within six months, counseling had been decreased to twice monthly and the B's were ready to support and be supported by their broadening group of friends.

## TREATMENT ISSUES

Prolonged conflict in the family produces stresses and strains that can promote emotional disintegration even among the healthiest of individuals. Eventually their actions begin to reflect their inner tur- moil and disorganized state of mind. A major treatment support is to structure the Family Crisis Center so that the residents can start to pull themselves together. Scheduling when to go to bed, when to get up, when to have family or group meetings becomes an important external support mechanism. Sometimes the staff have to teach basic housekeeping skills such as cooking, cleaning, or laundering so that the family environment can be more organized and satisfying. Ac- cording to the director: "When you look at some of the reasons why the family has had arguments, you can see that the food has been terrible, or the house is a mess, or the husband does not make any money. Everybody is angry with everybody else because they just have not met each other's needs. They did not have consistency when they were children and they do not have consistency now that they are adults. They become scared, depressed, anxious, or fearful, and then they strike out at other people. Our philosophy has been that if you can structure the place so that they do not have all those fears and do not feel frightened that they or their spouse or children are going to fall apart, then they will begin to relax. And it works beautifully."

Treatment expectations must be tailored to the short-term nature of the service provided. If the whole family is in residence, then it is possible to work on communication skills, point out certain attitudes and behaviors, or link people to concrete services. When only the mother and children are in residence, then it is possible to work on interactions between the adult and the children but it may not be possible to arrange for more than one total family session during the two or three weeks they are there. Counselors feel acutely aware of the time pressures and even during the intake process are considering the elements that will be needed for termination. They need to pace their activities so that neither they nor their clients will develop unrealistic expectations about what can be accomplished during their stay and the follow-up period once they leave.

The most common factor that needs to be dealt with is the low self-esteem that is so characteristic of the clients who use the Center. Groups help to overcome that feeling because the clients are more likely to perceive themselves, rather than other people, as being worthless. One exercise the counselors use is to ask each person to write on a piece of paper one characteristic about herself that she likes. Then that paper is pinned to her back and everyone has to go around the room and write something positive, something he or she likes, about each person. When they unpin the paper, the clients are often surprised to find the worthwhile traits that others see in them. It becomes a powerful validating experience which can counteract some of the negative self-impressions the client has formed about him or herself. One counselor commented: "That paper becomes a valuable item for our clients. Many of them hang it on the wall over their bed or take it with them when they leave the Center."

The children who are in residence present many behavior problems both at the Center and at school. They may ignore their parents' orders, hit other children, evidence sleep disturbances because of nightmares or fear of ghosts, or act out to gain attention because they do not feel that people listen to them. Even though children love to receive counseling for themselves, and some is provided to them, the counselors believe it is more productive to work with the parents so that they learn to respond more directly to their children's needs. The staff realize that the parents themselves may be in such a state of crisis that they are too emotionally drained to give the children the attention they need and so prefer to ignore them. The Center provides day care service so that the quality of the time parents spend with their children improves. Using a group process with mothers of infants and young children, counselors arrange for mother–child activities in the form of games that enhance touching

**Profiles of Programs for Abusers**

and bonding. One such game is to have the mothers pretend to make gingerbread cookies out of their children. The child is the dough and the mother has to knead the dough gently. Another regular activity occurs after the evening chores are finished and the children are bathed. The parents are expected to read their children a bedtime story. Counselors also encourage parent–child weekend outings, such as an excursion to the local zoo.

The two biggest problems counselors experience with spouse abusers are cutting through the stereotypes the men hold about themselves as breadwinners and motivating them to continue in a counseling program. Most spouse abusers feel worthless because they cannot support their families as they would like. Many of the men work two jobs, creating marital and family problems. Sometimes the initial gains that were made at the Family Crisis Center are wiped out when the family leaves because the abusers think that as soon as the family is together again, the problem no longer exists. They may refuse to continue counseling at another agency.

It is difficult for the counselors to plan for a "regular" program of group or conjoint activities because the clientele in the program changes so often. They never know whether they will have intact or partial families, whether there will be several adult couples or only mothers and children, whether most children will fall into the same age categories, whether the problems encountered will be universal and have relevance to the other residents or will be so diverse that there will not be much common ground in group meetings. Because of the unpredictability of the client population, not all treatment modalities can be used with clients and the counselors must be prepared to offer the best program that can be arranged within the given circumstances, even if it falls short of the ideal.

The most frustrating aspect of the job is having to work within the confines of limited community resources. Many people who seek help at the Center need concrete services in the form of housing, employment, or public assistance. However, it takes time to get the necessary approval of the forms and, even when assistance is given, the dollar amount is too low to permit the clients to find affordable housing.

Because residence staff and counselors work a twelve-hour shift for five days and then are off for five days, there is a question about the continuity of service and the ability for the residents to develop trust and confidence in the workers. However, according to the workers, no problem exists because the personnel are fairly complementary in their approaches and they hold a complete briefing with the oncoming workers before going off duty. The staff perceive this type of scheduling as beneficial for a number of reasons: they can give their full attention to the clients, they are less likely to be manipulated, and they reduce burnout by having sufficient time to themselves on their days off. Although there are clients who might find it easier to talk with one worker than with another, in general clients are given an opportunity to see that they are able to form relationships with more than one person. Ultimately, this experience enhances the clients' sense of personal power as they realize that they do not have to rely on only one person to obtain the things that are needed.

## ADMINISTRATIVE ISSUES

**Personnel** The board of directors of Child and Family Services delegates to the executive director the responsibility for hiring staff for the Family Crisis Center. He hires the coordinator. Together they hire the personnel to fill positions that require a Master's degree. The program coordinator has the responsibility to hire those positions that require a B.A. or less. Because all staff are dealing with day-to-day crises, it is important that they relate well to the coordinator as well as to the clients and to their co-workers. To develop the best functioning staff possible, the director believes that the coordinator should be able to choose the people who work in the program. The main characteristic they look for in all the staff who work at the Center is flexibility. According to the program coordinator: "You have to have a person who can roll with the punches, one who is not going to become psychotic because a house supervisor did not show up. We want someone who is well enough integrated personally to be able to say 'no' when necessary but not one who is a slave to the rules. You have to eliminate those who are too disorganized or too rigid. But, if I had to rule anybody out it would be the person who was too rigid." They also look for people who have a work history that demonstrates their reliability and who can function independently with a minimum of supervision, people who are self-starters. People with the least training require the most supervision. Not only do they need constant guidance about what to do, they also do not handle crises as well as a better educated person does. The program is moving more toward hiring people who hold at least a B.A. degree for all its house supervisor positions.

**Funding**  It costs approximately $120,000 a year to operate the Family Crisis Center. More than half of the operating expenses come from the state's general funds and are administered through the Department of Human Services. The administrator and the board of directors realize that they cannot wait until the program is already cut from the state budget and then try to reinstate it. They must anticipate when a cut might happen and alert legislators to the possibility so that it can be prevented. The executive director of Child and Family Services makes it a point to appear before the state's legislative delegation several times a year to remind the legislators of the program and warn them of the temptation for some state administrator or committee to cut the program from the budget. The program also receives funds from United Way, Knox County government, and private foundations for varying periods of time (e.g., one or two years). Thus the administrator is constantly searching for funds, a task that necessitates the ongoing and time-consuming activity of writing and rewriting grant proposals.

**Community Contacts**  The agency issues periodic media releases to inform the general public about the program and what it offers. However, the day-to-day operation of the program relies heavily on referrals to and from community resources. For example, even though the program is not restricted to taking referrals from the Department of Human Services (DHS), most people who are admitted to the Family Crisis Center are either referred by DHS to the Center or are referred by the Center staff to DHS. The same applies to those community agencies that deal with housing, employment, vocational rehabilitation, alcoholism, or counseling. It is not enough to have good relationships at the top; it is important to maintain contacts on at least three levels—administration, supervision, and line worker—to permit the smooth back and forth flow between the programs.

**Open Residence**  Issues of family violence that most frequently come to the attention of the Family Crisis Center involve spouse abuse. Consequently, as part of its function, the Center serves as a shelter for battered women. Unlike most shelters that protect and hide the whereabouts of the facility, the location of the Center is open and known. This was a conscious administrative decision which was made prior to the opening of the facility. According to the executive director: "We let photographers and television reporters take pictures of the facility because I wanted to make certain there was nothing secret about this place. A lot of times violence comes out of paranoid feelings, and the more secretive we are the more we might be setting up a paranoid person to try to seek us out. It would become a game to try to find us. And, quite frankly, since we have only 319,000 people in the whole county, we would not be that difficult to find. The word would soon get around. What were we supposed to do, move to a new location every six months? So we decided to leave the doors open. People were welcome to come here and we would deal with them when they got here." The agency has maintained close ties with the police, who can be called on to provide workers or clients with protection when they are faced with a violent spouse, but so far there have been no serious problems.

## ELEMENTS FOR SUCCESS

Ideally, a Family Crisis Center should be one of a gamut of services for the treatment of violence in families. This can be arranged by making a pact between agencies and/or by housing the program within a larger umbrella agency. Successful operations of a holistic family crisis center requires broad community support and continuing involvement, along with diversified program funding. Such involvement is assured by active public awareness campaigns which inform the community about the intergenerational, interrelated nature of all forms of violence in families.

An FCC program needs to develop specific house rules and program structure, combined with a flexibility on the part of the staff. The program personnel must respect each child, man, and woman, and must believe that each member has the potential for change. Every family situation is different, so a differential approach to diagnosis and treatment is required. Staff must be well-trained, particularly in family dynamics. Staff are needed who subscribe to a family systems, community systems treatment approach; who have been desensitized so that they do not identify with either the victim or the aggressor; and who are supervised by highly knowledgeable and experienced staff. Staff must maintain good relationships with housing,

**Profiles of Programs for Abusers**

employment, legal, health, social services, educational, and other community resources so that clients can gain access to those services as needed. When access is restricted and when services are limited, advocacy must be a strong component of the family crisis center program.

# 7

# IN-HOME SERVICE: Family Training Program

The Family Training Program (FTP) reduces parent–child violence among families that reside in the Kansas City area in the states of both Kansas and Missouri). It began as an independent service but currently operates under the auspices of the Jewish Family and Children Services (JFCS). Family Training Program gives service to families in which there is known child abuse/neglect or in which the potential for such behavior is high. It offers one main component:
• Home-based parent skill training
This is an intensive program, based on behavior modification principles and techniques, that assesses parenting skills and teaches effective child management and parent–child interaction skills. Included as parts of the service are client advocacy and around-the-clock worker availability. All services are provided free of charge.

## DEVELOPING THE IN-HOME PROGRAM

The programming format used by the Family Training program has evolved from a model known as the Achievement Place Research Group originally developed at Kansas University in 1968 for use with delinquent children. That model operates on the premise that delinquent children can be helped to change if they are taken out of their homes and placed in a group home setting, where they receive behavioral therapy by a professionally trained husband–wife team. In 1972 another group at the university tried a modification of that model with families who sought help at the outpatient pediatric clinic with complaints that seemed related more to behavioral than to medical problems. Instead of removing the children from the home, the group worked with the children and their parents in the family setting.

The next modification came when the current director of the Family Training Program, Barbara Kuehn, and her husband decided to apply the in-home concept to abusive families. They spoke with people in Juvenile Court and Protective Services to determine whether there was a need for the service. Both agencies agreed to endorse a proposal for that type of program. In 1975 they applied for a Title XX purchase of service contract with the state of Kansas to give home-based training to abusive parents who were referred to them from SRS (Social and Rehabilitation Services), the state agency that provides protective services for children. At the same time they went to funders in the community and obtained the necessary 25 percent matching funds from a private foundation, a church, and two individuals.

The state funded the program at $20,000 for the first year. Although the project originators envisioned the program as a husband–wife team effort, it took so long for the funding to begin that the co-writer of the grant obtained other employment to ensure that the couple could survive economically. Ultimately he opted out of the program and another person, Joe Grinstead, replaced him as the male therapist. The two ran the program alone for the first three years and obtained consultation on an as-needed basis from the person who had adapted the model for use with pediatric cases.

Because the program was funded under Title XX, the monies could be sent only to a nonprofit organization, so the grant was administered through a local church. Within a few years it became clear that foundation funds might not always be easy to obtain. The foundations strongly suggested that the group become a member of the United Way or affiliate with an existing agency if they hoped for long-term survival. At first the group approached the United Way. However, merely to qualify for United Way consideration required that they become a nonprofit agency. That is, they would have to adopt by-laws, develop a board of directors, and implement an organizational structure which, considering the size of the program, seemed too complicated. Instead, they canvassed the community looking for an agency affiliation which would welcome the type of service they offered but would allow them maximum autonomy in running the program. They selected the Jewish Family and Children Services agency because staff there seemed more concerned with quality than with quantity. "In our interviews at other places," commented the project director, "the push was for numbers. Their concern was with the number of clients we handled in a year—keep them going, drop that family, pick up another. To provide this service you simply cannot have that attitude." Because the program with its behavioral approach was so different from the psychodynamic and psychosocial approach usually offered by the agency, it was not easy to convince the JFCS Board of Directors that they should incorporate the program within its structure. However, Executive Director Lee Kalik was able to point to both the low-risk financial burden of the program and the high rate of client success the program had demonstrated in its first three years of operation, and in August 1978 the Family Training Program became part of Jewish Family and Children Services.

During most of its operation the Family Training Program provided its services to residents of Johnson County, Kansas. Since joining Jewish Family and Children Services, however, it has received a special grant to operate a program in Jackson County, Missouri, and also has increased its staff by three therapists. Figure 7.1 illustrates the organizational arrangement of the program.

## PROGRAM DESIGN

The Family Training Program is designed to assist families who come into contact with the protective service unit of the State Social Rehabilitation Services. The program attempts to maintain the family as a unit. According to one therapist, "We would like to see children who are having difficulties with their parents stay in the home. However, we would like to see that environment much less violent and destructive to the family. That's our goal. The way we do that is to teach the parents alternative parenting skills, alternatives to the things they were doing that brought them to the attention of the state agency." The underlying premise is that working with the family can be more successful if the work is done in the environment where the problems occur and at the time the problems occur.

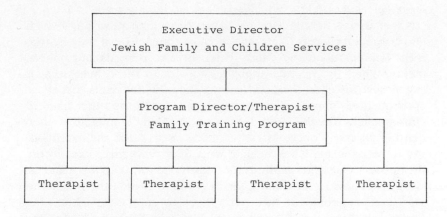

**Figure 7.1   Organizational Chart**

**In-Home Treatment Model**   The program operates from referrals made by the protective services workers and accepts as its
first priorities those cases in which the child would be removed from
the home if this service were not available. Service is provided to
families in which the identified child is aged 10 years or younger.
The program offers service to its clients 24 hours daily. Program
headquarters are located in a small satellite office of the parent
agency on the Kansas side of the state border, but the program therapists prefer to operate from their homes or cars via an answering
service and a beeper system which allows them to maintain close
contact with their clients and each other.

   The Family Training Program is administered by a program director (M.A.) who carries a half-time caseload in addition to her administrative responsibilities. The program director is responsible for the
four full-time therapists (M.A. and M.Ed.) who ae affiliated with the
program. All therapists have a strong theoretical background in behavioral psychology. Four therapists carry cases in the Kansas City,
Kansas, area where the program originated, and one therapist carries
primary responsibility for cases in the Kansas City, Missouri, vicinity.
Full-time therapists are expected to carry an ongoing caseload of six
to eight active cases, work with sixteen to twenty families a year, and

provide seven-day-a-week, 24-hour-a-day on-call availability to their clients. To prevent burnout, therapists rotate their on-call time on weekends and holidays, with each person taking a turn.

All of the techniques are based on behavioral principles which encourage the parents to arrange the consequences that the environment imposes upon the child's behavior into rewards and punishments. When the parents apply reinforcers to those behaviors or events that the child likes and enjoys, then the behaviors that those consequences follow will occur more often. On the other hand, if consequences that the child does not particularly enjoy follow, then that behavior will occur less often. "We try to teach the parents to use those concepts when dealing with their problems," explain the therapists. "Our interventions are fairly uniform across families. When we come to mealtimes, for example, we teach the parents to set up an environment that encourages appropriate mealtime behavior and discourages inappropriate mealtime behavior." Often the therapists use a token system to structure the parents' interactions with their children. The tokens may be poker chips or paper and pencil marks that can be accumulated and traded for something the child considers valuable, such as a certain amount of television viewing time. This tool is used to monitor both positive and negative interactions and the consistency with which the parents are utilizing positive and negative consequences.

The program addresses the two most basic problems in parent—child interactions: noncompliance on the part of the child and inconsistency on the part of the parents. The aim is to teach the parents how to maintain control so that they do not have to attempt to reestablish it through the use of physical force.

The program stresses uniformity and consistency among the therapists also, and all of them use the same basic methods when working with the parents and the children. Usually one therapist works with everyone in the family who is involved in the situation. Co-therapists are used only occasionally, primarily to underscore the techniques that are being applied or in situations in which one of the adults in the family might feel more comfortable learning from a person of the same sex. Regular appointments are set with the families for home visits. However, clients are encouraged to telephone their therapist when problems arise so that the therapist may take them through the steps of each procedure on the telephone.

Generally, changes in the family are established within 60 therapy hours or approximately three to four months. Therapist interaction with the family is most frequent (two or three times a week) during the first month, when they are teaching the parents the new model and helping them change nonproductive patterns. When parents can use the procedures without assistance from the therapists, home visits decrease to once a week and problems that crop up between visits can be dealt with on the telephone. Where counseling is indicated, the families may be referred to the parent agency, Jewish Family and Children Services. Once parents have learned to implement the model fairly consistently, they may be removed from active status and placed in the monitoring portion of the program. Monitoring lasts for three to four months during which time the therapists maintain monthly contact with the family and continue to be available either for telephone or home visit consultation if the situation should begin to deteriorate.

## STAFF TRAINING

When a new member is added to the staff, he or she is chosen on the basis of extensive knowledge of, or experience with, behavioral principles. The skills that are taught to the families have been broken into separate components. "The new worker goes through the specifics in much the same way that we teach parents. We model, then we ask our new therapists to role-play, and after we have given them feedback several times they reach a level where they understand what we expect, what we want them to get parents to do. It takes three or four hour-long sessions in the office. Then they spend time learning the rationales we have developed so they understand why to use specific procedures, what the new ways of interacting will teach the children, why parents should call when they are having a hard time, and what to say when they *do* call."

The new person accompanies an experienced worker on the job. They double up on families until the new worker is ready to work independently. Depending on the needs of the individual, the veteran therapists sometimes do additional in-home, on-site supervision with the person. One therapist recalled the process she had followed when she joined the FTP staff. "Barbara and Joe asked me to do some initial reading on child abuse. Then I started out with them to observe. At one point they said, 'Okay, we're going to start with this family and you will be doing the introduction.' They sat back and it would look as if I were going to be the primary therapist. Afterward, we talked about it and they pointed out what I had done well and what information I had left out." For at least the first month all home visits are made with an experienced therapist. They meet at a common point, go together, and return together. In this way they have time on the way to help the new therapist determine what to focus on during the visit or how to achieve the goals set for the visit, and on their return they discuss how things went, what was accomplished, and what failed.

The agency has been very supportive of the workers' receiving new input from outside sources and will pay for staff attendance to one or two conferences during the year. In the past the agency has paid for their attendance at meetings held at the Menninger Clinic as well as behavioral therapy conferences in New York. There also are regular in-service training opportunities sponsored by the agency around topics which the staff has identified as areas of particular interest.

Because workers are paid on an hourly basis rather than receiving a monthly salary, they are able, within certain limits, to control their own time. For instance, a therapist may work twelve hours one day and choose not to schedule appointments for the next day. By using this system, they have been able to prevent burnout and decrease worker turnover.

## LINKING CLIENTS AND PROGRAM

Referrals for service are not accepted from the community at large but are funneled through two primary agencies, Social Rehabilitation Services (state protective services) and Jewish Family and Children Services. Because Title XX is its major funding source, the program obtains most of its referrals from protective services. Self-referrals are possible but cannot be made directly to the program. Instead, these requests first are assessed by a worker at protective services to determine the appropriateness of the referral. In general, cases of greater severity are referred to the program because the in-home service helps to keep families together. Approximately 70 percent of the referrals involve women who are single parents. Most referred cases are accepted for treatment. However, FTP tends to refuse cases in which the parents are involved with heavy, ongoing drug or alcohol use. The therapists have found that those parents are not sufficiently stable to retain the information that is being passed on to them.

Members of Jewish Family and Children Services staff may refer clients directly to the program, and these referrals are taken when workers have room on their caseloads. The JFCS clients pay for the service according to a sliding scale; however, the contract with SRS stipulates that the program may not provide service to a private family at a lesser rate than the state is charged.

The program director assigns referred cases to each therapist. They, in turn, conduct an initial interview with the parents to explain the program and to offer the parents an opportunity to participate. Although the program is voluntary, many clients are forced by court order to seek counseling or parent education training from a community-based program such as FTP. The therapist describes the program's purpose and program components, the working agreement in regard to expectations held for the parents, and what they are prepared to provide for the parents. Expectations for the families include: focusing their entire attention on the training program, using the procedures they are taught between home visits, calling to ask for assistance when they have a problem implementing a technique, confronting the therapist or notifying their protective services worker when they have a problem understanding or feeling comfortable with what they are being asked to do in the program.

If the parents consent to participate in the program, they are asked to identify the traits or behaviors the child exhibits that they do not like or ways they would like to see their child behave. That information is listed on the Parent Evaluation Sheet (Figure 7.2). Therapists use this Parent Evaluation Sheet to identify the parents' concerns and establish those as the treatment goals toward which they will work. Parents keep a daily record of these target behaviors so that they may determine to what extent changes are moving in the desired direction.

During the first two weeks workers expect to be involved intensely, making at least two to four home visits plus telephone contacts the first week and two to three visits plus phone contacts the second week. Most visits last at least an hour. Only family members may attend the sessions; friends and neighbors are excluded. All people who have any parenting responsibility are asked to be present. As one therapist expressed it, "If there is a grandmother or aunt living in the home, we want her to be involved in all the sessions because when the parent is out of the home the relative will be doing the same things we are asking the parent to do. If they don't use the same technique as the parent, the program probably will not work." Interruptions are kept to a minimum while the therapist is in the

Instructions: Consider your child's behavior during the past 24 hours. Mark an X in the True (T) column if the behavior occurred at least once. Mark an X in the False (F) column if the behavior has <u>not</u> occurred at least once during the past 24 hours.

Name: _____  Date_____ to_____

Parent: _____

| BEHAVIOR | Sun. | | Mon. | | Tues. | | Wed. | | Thurs. | | Fri. | | Sat. | |
|---|---|---|---|---|---|---|---|---|---|---|---|---|---|---|
| Example Behaviors | T | F | T | F | T | F | T | F | T | F | T | F | T | F |
| Did he comply with first request? | | | | | | | | | | | | | | |
| Did he talk back? | | | | | | | | | | | | | | |
| Did he go to bed without a fuss? | | | | | | | | | | | | | | |
| Did he fight over bath time? | | | | | | | | | | | | | | |
| Did he take bath right away? | | | | | | | | | | | | | | |
| Did he fight with sister? | | | | | | | | | | | | | | |
| Did he fight with friends? | | | | | | | | | | | | | | |
| Did he argue with Mom? | | | | | | | | | | | | | | |
| Did he wait for Dad's help? | | | | | | | | | | | | | | |
| | | | | | | | | | | | | | | |
| | | | | | | | | | | | | | | |
| | | | | | | | | | | | | | | |
| | | | | | | | | | | | | | | |

**Figure 7.2   Parent Evaluation Sheet**

home; visitors who come to the door during that time are asked to come back another time and phone calls that come in are returned later. If clients cannot keep the appointment, they are expected to cancel at least an hour in advance to prevent the worker from making an unnecessary trip. Two or more cancellations in a row indicate resistance, which is confronted by the therapist and reported to the protective services worker. If it continues, the case is terminated. Only one in ten referrals presents that type of problem. According to one staff member, "Those are usually the people who play the 'welfare game.' They agree to accept services and then don't do anything. That gets the social worker off their back."

At the second visit the parents and therapist fill out the required forms, which include consent forms, an intake sheet, child's history, and school information. (See Figure 7.3.) The parents are asked to complete a standardized test which measures their perception of the child's behavior. (They will complete this instrument again before the case is terminated.) During that visit the therapist explores the support systems that are available to the family and also the parents' perceptions of their in-home and community relationships.

The intervention system is introduced at the third visit. The program revolves around a central model of behavioral change which begins by teaching the parents how to praise their children. This is followed by an explanation of the way parents should give and receive tokens. Then the children are taught how to receive and return tokens. The parents and children learn the timeout technique which is then used when the child is being especially resistant. During timeout, which usually lasts less than five minutes, the child is placed in a nonstimulating environment, such as on a chair that faces a blank wall. The timeout period gives both the parent and the child an opportunity to think things over. Throughout the sessions the therapists explain their reasons for what is being taught and answer all questions the parents ask. If one area, such as bedtime, is of particular concern, then the therapists give the parents additional instruction about the use of tokens or other strategies for that situation.

The therapists follow a similar format for teaching each interaction skill, explaining each procedure before introducing it and then demonstrating what is expected of the parent and child. The parent and child practice what was demonstrated, and the therapists give feedback about the practice and answer any questions. Also they tell why the procedure will improve parent–child interactions and parent control. It may take two to four trials across a number of visits for parents or children to be able to use a procedure correctly.

Family Training Program

Consent Form to Gather Supplemental Information


     I have been told that an Evaluation Program is being
conducted through the Family Training Program, which is
trying to evaluate several approaches to working with
families referred to the local Protective Service Unit.
As a part of this project, I will be asked to respond to
several tests of my child's behavior and to maintain a
daily record of his behavior for approximately one week
with each test series.

     I have been told that any information gathered will
be held strictly confidential.  I understand that this
information cannot be released to any agency or individual
without my first signing a Release of Information Form for
each agency requesting information.  Any communication of
this information for purpose unrelated to the specific
program will be done anonymously.  I understand that there
is no risk involved and I am willing to spend the short
time required to provide the information.

     I have also been told that I may refuse to participate
with this information gathering program at any time without
in any way jeopardizing our status with the Protective
Service Unit.  In giving my consent, I acknowledge that my
participation is voluntary and that I may withdraw at any
time.

     The purpose of this information gathering program was

explained to me by: _____


Youth's Name:_____

Parent's Name:_____

Parent's Signature:_____

Youth's Signature:_____Date:_____

**Figure 7.3   Family Training Program**

```
JEWISH FAMILY AND CHILDREN SERVICES - INTAKE           CASE 1
NAME_____ MAIDEN NAME_____ STATUS_____
ADDRESS_____ TEL._____
CITY, STATE, ZIP_____ COUNTY_____
```

Intake worker _____
Date of contact _____
Assigned worker _____
Date of first contact _____
Date of first interview ____

For which person(s) is service
requested _____
_____

Who first contacted agency
_____
_____

Situation of Intake Contact

_____Office drop in
_____Out of office
_____Telephone
_____Correspondence
_____Other

Source of referral or
knowledge of agency_____
_____
_____

Current marital status_____

Incoming Status

_____New to agency
_____Service terminated prior yr.
_____Service terminated this yr.
Cross references_____
_____

Date of marriage _____

Previous marriage
_____

Race      Religion
_____    _____

| Seen in interview | Name of Family Members | Sex | Relationship to family head | Birth-date | School, grade, occupation, whereabouts if away |
|---|---|---|---|---|---|
| ____ 1 | | | | | |
| ____ 2 | | | | | |
| ____ 3 | | | | | |
| ____ 4 | | | | | |
| ____ 5 | | | | | |
| ____ 6 | | | | | |
| ____ 7 | (others involved) | | | | |
| ____ 8 | | | | | |

| Education & Occupation | Family Head | Spouse |
|---|---|---|
| Highest school grade completed | | |
| Name of business or industry where employed | | |
| Business telephones | | |

Gross family income
_____/wk., mo., year
Source _____
Fee scheduled _____
Date established _____
_____Weekly
_____Billed

Previous counseling experience ___yes ___no
Specify _____
When? _____

Medical insurance company
_____
Policy number _____

**Figure 7.3   Family Training Program, *continued***                    131

| PROBLEMS PRESENTED OR OBSERVED | SERVICES REQUESTED |
|---|---|
| (Place initials by all problems reported by any family member and all noted by worker) | (Place initials by all requested even if not provided by agency) |

| Type of Problem | PROBLEMS SEEN BY: Family | Worker |
|---|---|---|
| **Family Relationships:** | | |
| Marital . . . . . . . | _____ | _____ |
| Parent-child (child under 18) . . . . . | _____ | _____ |
| Total family relation- ships . . . . . . | _____ | _____ |
| Other (Specify _____) | _____ | _____ |
| | | |
| **Individual Personality Adjustment:** | | |
| Child (under 13) . . | _____ | _____ |
| Adolescent or youth (13 thru 17) . . . | _____ | _____ |
| Adult (18 thru 59) . . | _____ | _____ |
| Aged person (60 & over) | _____ | _____ |
| | | |
| **Other Problems:** | | |
| Child rearing/child care practices . . | _____ | _____ |
| Management of home. . | _____ | _____ |
| Management of money, budgeting, etc. . . | _____ | _____ |
| Problems in social contracts or use of leisure time . . . | _____ | _____ |
| Inadequate income for basic needs . . . . | _____ | _____ |
| Job-related concerns | _____ | _____ |
| Housing problems . . | _____ | _____ |
| Unwed parenthood . . | _____ | _____ |
| Legal problems . . . | _____ | _____ |
| School-related concerns | _____ | _____ |
| Drinking problems . . | _____ | _____ |
| Acting-out behavior . | _____ | _____ |
| Health problems . . . | _____ | _____ |
| Medications . . . . . | _____ | _____ |
| Other (Specify _____) | _____ | _____ |

**SERVICES REQUESTED**

Counseling about:
____Marital problems
____Parent-child problems (child under 18)
____Other family relationship problems
____Individual adjustment
____Educational problems
____Unwed parenthood
____Debt or credit problems
____Vocational or employment problems
____Problems of newcomers
____Other
(What? _____)

Care-Taking Services:
____Home care services
____Day care services
____Foster care services
____Group home services
____Institutional care
____Protective services
____Friendly visiting
____Telephone service
____Kosher meals
____Transportation

Other Services:
____Direct financial assistance
____Groups (Include family life educ., therapy groups)
(Type? _____)
____Health clinic services
____Psychological services
(What? _____)
____Adoption
____Other (What? _____)

____Referral
Type_____

DISPOSITION
(at end of first interview)
____Further services planned
____Referral Place_____
____Case closed
____Date_____

OTHER COMMENTS

---

**Figure 7.3  Family Training Program,** *continued*

Primary Focus of Service

I   Family and individual relationships
    1.  _____ Marital relationships
    2.  _____ Parent-child relationship or relationship of individual
              child under 18
    3.  _____ Other family relationships or relationships of
              individual adults
    4.  _____ Total family relationships

II  Environmental or situational conditions
    5.  _____ Financial difficulty
    6.  _____ Physical illness or handicap
    7.  _____ Mental illness
    8.  _____ Intellectual retardation
    9.  _____ Arrangements for physical care of family member
    10. _____ Other environmental or situational condition

III Other
    11. _____ Report given on terminated service
    12. _____ Inquiry made for out-of-town agency


Reason for Termination

I   Tel. or corr. only with family or contact on behalf of family
    1.  _____ Family did not follow through
    2.  _____ Referred elsewhere
    3.  _____ Presenting request or need met by agency
    4.  _____ Report given on terminated service
    5.  _____ Inquiry made for out-of-town agency
    6.  _____ Service not available

II  In-person interview(s) with family
    7.  _____ Referred elsewhere
    8.  _____ Service terminated by casework plan
    9.  _____ Family withdrew or terminated service
    10. _____ Further service not possible


FINANCIAL ASSISTANCE GIVE

_____ yes _____ no

Amount_____


Date Terminated
          CATEGORY OF SERVICE AT TERMINATION

_____ Tel. or corr. only with fam.          )   THRU
_____ One in-pers. interview with fam.      )   CONTACT
_____ 2-5 in-pers. int. with fam.           )   WITH
_____ 6 or more in-pers. int. with fam.     )   FAMILY
_____ Thru contact on behalf of family


**Figure 7.3   Family Training Program, *continued***

Ninety percent of the program is aimed toward having parents, rearrange the consequences for the child's behavior. For example, a typical scenario:

MOTHER: John, clean your room. It's a mess.
JOHN: Not now, Mom, the guys are waiting for me.
MOTHER: You're not leaving this house until you clean your room!
John throws a tantrum. Mother hits him. John runs screaming from the room.

The sequence of events is different when the Family Training model is implemented. If Mother asks John to clean his room and he does, then John receives Mother's praise and some tokens. If he does not, the Mother takes back some of the tokens John has previously received. If John continues to refuse to comply with Mother's request, he is instructed to enter timeout as a disciplinary action. If John has been compliant in the timeout setting, Mother praises him for calming down and then reinstructs John to clean his room. If he still refuses then he is put in timeout again to see how boring it is when he is not following directions. When he follows the parents' instructions, however, he receives reinforcement through more positive interaction with Mother and from the receipt of additional tokens.

Once the parents have learned the three basic skills of praise, tokens, and timeout, the therapists teach them procedures for handling special problems. The most common special problem areas include mealtime, bedtime, how to gain compliance, toilet or bedwetting problems, restaurant and store behavior, school problems, peer relations, sibling rivalry, lying, stealing, tantrums, and talking back. When necessary, therapists will go out to the home when the special problem occurs to teach the appropriate procedure. Usually, that does not happen until the parents have mastered some of the basics. That is not always the case, though. In one case a mother who was scheduled to see the therapist for the introductory session called and told the therapist that she did not want to see her children (ages 3 and 2 years) anymore; she could not stand them. The night before, they had gotten the Rice Krispies and chocolate syrup out of the cupboard and spread them all over the living room. They never seemed to listen to her, but bedtime was the worst. They simply would not go to bed before midnight and then would get up several times during the night. The woman was a single parent and a working mother who had to get up at 6 A.M. The goal was to have the children in bed by 10 P.M. so the mother could have some time for herself. The therapist arrived that evening about 8:30 and helped the mother establish a routine in which she would take care of all the bathroom needs, glasses of water, and other excuses children use when they want to get out of bed. Then the children were put to bed. When either child got up, he or she was given one swat on the behind and told to go back to bed. No other interaction with them took place. Although that first night the children tested out the limits many times, the mother was thrilled because the children were asleep before midnight. The therapist spent several evenings in a row working with the mother until the problem was under control.

The therapists find that the child needs to learn how to be a child as much as the parents need to learn how to parent. "Typically, abusing parents do not assume the authority role in the family system. They tend to use their child as an equal, a peer, to share the problems and the weights of their worries and concerns. So the child responds in a very peerlike manner. We try to turn that around, which means that we not only have to teach the parent 'This is what you do to take authority,' but also teach the child 'This is what you do to be a child.' We teach them the appropriate ways to raise questions or objections."

The use of a telephone is so integral to the reinforcement and guidance therapists give to their clients that access to a telephone is almost a condition for acceptance in the program. Clients are encouraged to call whenever they have questions or difficulties. As parents learn to implement the behavioral procedures, therapists rely more on telephone instructions than home visits to help the parents cope. Parents are asked for details about what interaction is happening with the child, what they said, and what they did. Also, parents are given instructions about what to say and do that will change the situation. The parents carry through the directions and then telephone the therapists afterward to discuss how well the child responded.

Therapists write periodic notes about the family's progress within the specific areas they hope to change. (See Figure 7.4) The staff will consider a change for the family from active intervention to monitoring status when parents are able to use the procedures they have been taught without therapist prompting. Monitoring is also indicated when the topics originally listed on the Parent Evaluation Sheet have all been addressed and the parents are reporting that those are no longer problem areas. Before placing the family on monitoring status, the Family Training Program therapists teach the par-

PROGRESS NOTE

Family name_____ Date_____

Introduction_____ Intake_____ First home visit_____

Demonstrate = 1   Practice = 2   Rationale = 3   Feedback = 4   Reinforce = 5

| Mealtime | Bedtime | Other |
|---|---|---|
| _____ Stay at table | _____ Procrastination | _____ Marital _____ Social |
| _____ Refuse to eat | _____ Out of bed | _____ Familial _____ System- |
| _____ Playing with food | _____ Verbal behavior | welfare |
| _____ Taking too long | _____ Potty stop | |

Tokens
_____ Giving
_____ Taking
_____ Getting
_____ Losing
_____ Use of praise
_____ Extra jobs
_____ Loss of privileges
_____ Out of chips

Timeout
_____ Set rules
_____ Demonstrate
_____ Practice
_____ Rationale
_____ Feedback

Nontoken Contingencies
_____ Differential reinforcement
_____ Positive practice
_____ Redirecting

Situations
(1)_____
(2)_____
(3)_____

Situations:_____

_____

_____

_____

_____

_____

_____

_____

_____

_____

_____

Parental
_____ Compliance with therapist
_____ Follow through between home visits
_____ Prompted praise
_____ Unprompted praise
_____ Process unclear
_____ Define limits
_____ Make limits known
_____ Use appropriate process
_____ Practice fines
_____ Cooperation during home visit
_____ Consistent parenting during home visit

Social Interactions
_____ Saying "No"
_____ Talk back and argue
_____ Affect
_____ Parents
_____ Siblings
_____ Peers
_____ Teachers

School
_____ Off task
_____ Incomplete work
_____ Talking
_____ Out of seat
_____ Pestering others
_____ Noncompliance

Problem Solving
_____ Define problem
_____ Options
_____ Consequences of options
_____ Plan of attack
_____ Follow through

COMMENTS:  ON BACK

**Figure 7.4   Progress Note**

ents how to initiate the token system again if things begin to slip. They practice with the parents a few times about how to set up the rules, how to put the tokens back in, what criteria to use for leaving them in, and how to take them back out again.

# CASE EXAMPLE

**General Information**   Stephanie is 24 years old and has been divorced for a year and a half. She is a secretary at a large catalog company and says she likes her job. She has custody of her two children, Roger, 3½, and Carol, 2½. Roger is in a preschool program and Carol is with a baby-sitter during the day. Father has the children for overnight visits once a week and weekend visits once a month. Stephanie reports, however, that he often cancels visits at the last minute.

The referral for suspected child abuse came from a neighbor, who reported a great deal of screaming and yelling and was afraid the mother was out of control. The social worker met with Stephanie and found her to be more than agreeable to work with Family Training. Stephanie admitted that she had no control over the children and at times wanted to give them up and never see them again. The worker reported that Stephanie appeared relieved to know there was help.

**Treatment Goals**   During the first meeting with Stephanie I had her identify as specifically as she could the problem she was having with her children. I wrote down each concern she mentioned. I then asked her to keep track of the children's problem behaviors for five days. At the end of that period we determined which problems were the most frequent and which problems bothered her the most. From that list we set our goals:
1. To have the children get ready for bed when asked and without any talking back or fighting.
2. To have children in bed on time (Carol at 7:30, Roger at 8:00).
3. Once children are in bed, to have them stay there.
4. To increase compliance.
5. To increase independent play.
6. To have children sit at table for length of meal.
7. To decrease children's whining.
8. To decrease children's tantrums.

---

**First Week of Treatment**  Stephanie chose to work on bedtime procedures first since the children were not getting to bed until midnight and therefore she was getting no time to herself and very little sleep. The first evening we determined the bedtime routine and implemented the bedtime procedure. Stephanie followed my instructions and the children were asleep by 10:30. The next two evenings the bedtime procedure was followed and the children were asleep by 9:00. By the third evening Stephanie was following the procedures without any prompts from me.

**Second Week of Treatment**  The second major concern that Stephanie wanted to work on was getting the children to do what she asked. We worked on the important components of compliance teaching. We discussed the importance of praising children when they were behaving appropriately (she had done some praising of the children for following the bedtime procedure) and practiced watching the children every few minutes and praising them when they were being good. Initially, I had to tell her what words to use to praise, but by the end of the second evening she was taking the initiative and praising the children frequently. I taught Stephanie the use of timeout. By the fourth practice she was implementing all the steps. Also, the first time she needed actually to use timeout, she implemented it correctly. In addition to teaching compliance, I observed Stephanie with the children during bedtime. She was continuing to be consistent and had increased her praise statements while implementing the procedures. Carol was in bed by 7:30, Roger by 8:00. Stephanie said that she couldn't believe the change.

**Third Week of Treatment**  There were two visits during this week to observe bedtime (children were going to bed without a fight, going to bed on time, and staying there) and to observe the use of praise and timeout. Stephanie was using timeout when the children did not do what she asked and when they were hitting each other. She was not using it when the children said "no" or talked back. I suggested she begin using it for those behaviors as well. She again told me how much better the children were behaving and said that she almost looked forward to being home.

**Fourth Week of Treatment**  Stephanie had called and said that Roger and Carol had begun to whine a great deal and she couldn't stand it. She had tried timeout, but they sat in the chair and whined even more. We let whining be the focus of our fourth week. We reviewed the importance of praising the children when they were being good and then decided that for behaviors such as whining and pouting the children would be sent to their room until they felt like using their "regular" or "big" voice or having a pleasant expression. Roger immediately chose to use his "big" voice and to not pout instead of having to go to his room. It took Carol five times of being sent to her room before she decided not to whine. Stephanie reported that Carol often would walk toward the bedroom whining and then turn around and walk back to the family smiling. During this fourth week timeout had to be used about once a day. Bedtime was not a problem at all.

**Fifth Week of Treatment**  During the fifth week I taught Stephanie some problem-solving techniques so that she could begin to identify, implement, and evaluate solutions on her own. We used a previous goal of increasing independent play as the first problem she would attempt to solve on her own. At the end of the week we reviewed how the solution she had chosen was working. She had increased Roger's independent play ten minutes and Carol's five. In addition, she had taken the initiative to solve the problem of mealtime and felt that was going well, too. It appeared that she felt comfortable with the procedures, was using them, and was finding them effective. In order to see how well she had met the goals she had identified, I asked her to keep track of the children's behavior again for a week.

**Sixth Week of Treatment**  Stephanie's observation of the children over the last week indicated that she felt there has been a considerable decrease in their inappropriate behavior. She had been extremely cooperative and willing to learn, and practice, the child management procedures I recommended. We decided to keep in telephone contact over the next two weeks so that she would have that time to work on her newly learned skills without my continual support.

**Ninth Week of Treatment**  During our telephone conversations over the last two weeks Stephanie reported that things were still going well. Bedtime was not a problem at all, timeout was used when needed, and she had had to send Carol to her room twice in one day for whining. She said she felt much more in control and even though her children weren't perfect, they were "pretty good." It was then decided, after my talking to the social worker, that this case would be placed on monitoring for the next few months.

**Monitoring**  During this period Stephanie and I talked on the phone four times. She called once to discuss a school-related problem that she was having with Roger. The teachers had reported that he was not listening during group time. We went over the problem-solving steps and she came up with three solutions to discuss with the teachers. The other three conversations were initiated by me to see how the children were doing. Stephanie always reported that the children were doing well as long as she was consistent. She said she noticed that when she let discipline slip and paid less attention to them, the children would push her to the limit. I, of course, agreed with her observation.

**Case Summary**  At the beginning of Family Training's work with the J's case the mother was extremely negative about her children's behavior and her ability ever to have control. She was concerned that she might hurt them or just leave them. She expressed that she did not want to do either. Stephanie was highly motivated to learn the child management skills and that had a great deal to do with her quick success. She always practiced the procedures and used them when I was not there. She took advantage of the 24-hour phone service to get answers to questions or to get help with problems. We met all her goals; the children are more compliant, they play independently, they do not whine or tantrum as often, they stay in their chairs for the length of the meals, and they go to bed without fighting. Stephanie reports that she now enjoys being with them and that she feels much better knowing how to handle their misbehavior. Stephanie has completed the Family Training Program and, as of the date of this report, the case is closed.

# TREATMENT ISSUES

Unlike workers in many other programs that deal with child abuse, Family Training Program workers encounter very little initial resistance or hostility among their clients even though entry into the program is not entirely voluntary. In large measure client acceptance stems from a program designed to deploy therapists to the home when they are most needed and to work on the problems that the parents, rather than the professionals, identify as most difficult to handle. Clients usually perceive the FTP workers as new and welcome resources. Initial reservations diminish as the parents see changes occur rapidly in the way they and their children interact. "Most parents want the help. When they use the techniques that we teach them, they soon realize that they don't have to hit their child. Many are astounded that they don't have to resort to what they had been doing in the past."

The bigger problem for FTP therapists occurs when other family members undermine the program. Therapists encourage participation of, but do not insist on working with, all the adults in the family. Among two-parent families they have dealt with therapists often find that the fathers are less cooperative. "Self-concepts are a key issue. The mother says, 'I can't do a thing with these kids, but he [the father] can.' Usually, that only means that the father hits hard enough and consistently enough to make the child listen. When we enter the scene and teach the mother ways of getting control that don't require hitting, the children start to be responsive to the mother, which suddenly makes the mother less dependent on the husband. He, in turn, will sabotage our system to decrease the mother's effectiveness and restore things to the way they were."

If one parent does not want to participate, workers still believe they can help the family by working with the one parent who is cooperative. This does not mean that therapists ignore the non-cooperative parent, it just means that workers need to take more of their time to work through some of the concerns and difficulties the noncompliant parent has in using the program. When they know that the father is the primary abuser, then therapists put more of their efforts toward convincing the father to participate. For example, they would make certain that visits are scheduled when the father is home and try to integrate him into the sessions.

When working with parents who have a very young child or several children under the age of 5, FTP therapists may spend as much of their time educating parents about the developmental needs of children as they do teaching them child management techniques. They discuss developmental norms, age-appropriate expectations, how to plan schedules, what resources are available and how to use them, and how spouses can support one another. "We teach the parents how to teach. For instance, asking a 6-year-old to clean up her room may mean something different to the child than to the parent.

We teach the parents how to ask the children to perform tasks. We teach them to be specific with the children, to determine whether they can take five instructions at the same time or only two, to monitor the children as they are performing the task and assessing whether they are doing it correctly, to praise all the good things they have done in relation to that task, and to point out what remains to be done or corrected."

Socioeconomic level plays a role in the type of focus that is used. Therapists find that with families in the lower socioeconomic level they must do a lot more demonstration and modeling of behavior to accompany what they say. Generally, it takes longer to complete the program with lower socioeconomic families.

Not all problems that are dealt with in the program are client determined. The concerns listed on the Parent Evaluation Sheet do not necessarily represent the entire range of behaviors the therapists are prepared to handle. For instance, "The parents might not identify fighting between siblings as something of concern to them, but we may see the siblings tearing each other apart while we are in the home. So, we would institute changes in their behavior when we establish the token system." Because inconsistency by the parents and noncompliance by the children are such basic and universal issues, the therapists incorporate training in those areas as part of their own agenda with the family. They ensure inclusion of those skills by asking a broad-based question to which there is usually only one answer, such as Did the child do as you asked the first time? "Nobody ever says yes to that, so it is always an area that can be checked as something to work on." A related therapist agenda item is clarification of expectations. "One of the things we teach parents is that before you can expect the child to do what you want, you have to make your expectations clear. Once the expectation becomes clear, then it comes down to an issue of compliance."

The therapists warn parents not to be deceived by the honeymoon period of initial change. As the novelty wears off the children test the parents and the system and may even say: "Here, I don't want your token. I'm not going to play your game any more." Along with the warning, the therapists give parents guidance for dealing with the situation. "It comes back to stating the expectation by saying to the child, 'I'm sorry, that is not an appropriate way to handle the situation. I want you to pick up the token.' If he does, fine; if not, then he goes into timeout and the criteria for leaving timeout is being ready to pick up the token. So the interaction is right back into the system they are being taught to use." The parents are told to call the therapist when the child tests the system because this is a time when the parents are most likely to revert to their former ways of handling things.

One of the most controversial aspects of the program is the occasional use of physical punishment Family Training Program therapists allow parents to administer to their children as part of a disciplinary measure. Ordinarily, discipline is handled through the techniques of token loss and timeouts. Under certain circumstances, however, parents are allowed to swat the child when he or she is noncompliant. Therapists teach parents to use the least restrictive means that are effective. For example, if the child leaves the timeout situation prematurely, the parent is told to put the child back on the chair without saying anything. If the child leaves again, then the parent can put the child back and hold him or her in the chair until he will stay there on his own. If the child leaves once more, the parent may give the child *one* swat on the bottom and then put him back in the chair. The therapists base their rationale for using physical punishment on the assumption that for abusive parents the use of physical means to handle situations is deeply ingrained and not likely to be totally eliminated merely because the parents are told not to use it. They have tried to structure the use of physical force in a way that is least likely to harm the child. Their rule is that only one swat may be given each time the child leaves timeout too soon.

Disciplinary actions comprise only about one-tenth of the parent–child interactions in the program; the other nine-tenths are task oriented and involve the use of praise. "Timeout and token loss are punishers; they teach only what you don't want the child to do. If you teach him only what you don't want him to do and then you go away, the child doesn't have any new skill to replace that with so he is going to go right back to what he had been doing. So we use the punishers to get rid of the behavior and at the same time use the reinforcers and modeling and intensive teaching process to teach the child more appropriate behaviors." Whenever the child does something well, he or she is praised and given a token or poker chip. For example, "Thank you, Jean. The way you said that was very pleasant. Here is a token." or "Good! You are helping your sister. I like that. Here are five chips." The use of praise is extended to siblings also. The therapists take the time to teach children how to behave with their brothers and sisters. "A lot of that involves problem solving. 'Joe, you want to play with Bobby's toys. What is the best way to do that?' 'I could ask him.' 'Okay, do that and let's see what happens. If Bobby says "yes" then you say "thank you." If he says "no" then that is his choice even though it doesn't make you very happy. So let's talk about what you can do then.' We model this type of procedure three or four times and then ask the parent to take over."

Therapists who enter this field should be prepared to repeat their instructions to the parents over and over again. "The need for repetition is incredible," say the therapists. "We do 30 to 40 repetitions per behavior that we want to teach the parent. For instance, how to attend to the child when he is being appropriate. It takes demonstrating that every time we go out. It requires that parents practice it several times during each home visit. And each time we explain some portion of the rationale behind why it is important to attend to the child when he is acting appropriately. We not only repeat it, we have the parents practice it repeatedly. So they are not just hearing us say it over and over, they are doing it over and over and we are giving them feedback."

## ADMINISTRATIVE ISSUES

**Program Integration** When an already existing program joins an already existing agency, it takes a certain amount of accommodation and compromise on each side to produce a comfortable fit. The situation is even more complicated when the theoretical frameworks used by the program and the agency are not the same, when personnel practices differ, and when the program therapists do not interact with the agency staff on a daily basis. All of those have been factors that needed to be addressed as part of the ongoing efforts to integrate the Family Training Program into the Jewish Family and Children Services agency. According to the executive director of the agency, "We are continually working toward integration at the programmatic level. The unorthodox nature of the treatment approach used in the Family Training Program in which the clients stay at home rather than come to the agency has meant thinking about how the rest of the staff can use that. It has also meant that Family Training Program staff have had to keep in mind that they were part of the Jewish Family and Children Services." The FTP staff are required to attend the agency's weekly staff meetings and to complete the same statistical reports as do the other agency personnel.

Two issues that had to be confronted early were those of dress code and professional jargon. The agency requests that its staff dress professionally when seeing clients. However, the FTP staff find that they are less threatening to their clients if they dress in jeans and other casual clothing. "If we dressed up for our interviews, our dropout rate would be a lot higher. In fact, if for some reason we have to dress up for an agency visit or some other occasion, we might say to the client that we had to be at a meeting and jokingly add that we had to look 'professional.' Otherwise, we would look out of place in their surroundings and make them feel uncomfortable." Differences in professional jargon have interfered with the communication between the agency and the FTP program staffs. "Not only are the concepts and words different," commented the agency director, "it is sometimes a problem understanding where the different professional mindsets are coming from." It has required active discussion to arrive at a working interaction between the behavioral and psychosocial perspectives.

**Funding** The current annual operating budget for the Family Training Program is $85,000. The program is expensive in relation to the number of clients seen, a total of 65 to 70 families during the year. However, it is inexpensive in comparison to the cost of out-of-home placement, which may run as high as $12,000 per person a year. The move to Jewish Family and Children Services did not eliminate the need to find the 25 percent Title XX matching funds. The agency picks up the administrative and secretarial overhead as part of its own budget but obtains the needed matching funds from local foundations. For the most part the program sells itself because of its demonstrated success so there has been no major problem finding outside funding sources. However, if funding ever becomes a problem, the agency is prepared to assume fiscal responsibility for the program. That possibility was inherent in the basic commitment made to the Family Training Program at the time of its incorporation into the agency structure.

**Personnel Practices** In most respects, the Family Training Program staff are subject to the same hiring, firing, and personnel practices established by the agency. However, because of the way the program is funded, the FTP staff are not part of the wage and benefit package offered by the agency. FTP therapists receive an hourly wage rather than a monthly salary. Each worker contracts for providing a certain number of hours per month of therapy, usually an average of 115 hours. The expectation is that the level of billing will allow the therapists to be compensated on a professional level that is commensurate with their experience and education. They must justify all the time they bill for. The pay check varies from month to month depending on the size of the caseload and whether they had taken any vacation time. FTP therapists are free to determine their own hours as long as they provide adequate service to their clients. For example, if they work until 11 P.M. one day, they may work only from 9 to 3 or from 2 to 10 the next day or even decide to take the day off. They also submit bills for staff meetings and other activities required by the agency. The flexibility in work schedules and the amount of money they are paid sometimes create questions among other agency staff. The executive director usually points out that there are both positives and negatives in each plan. Although other agency staff receive less salary, they do receive fringe benefits and they are guaranteed a job at the end of a contract year whereas FTP therapists are dependent on "soft" money for their existence.

## ELEMENTS FOR SUCCESS

This is the type of program that can function independently in a community because of its contractual ties with a large referring agency. However, without constant interaction with the staff of the referring agency or participation within the organizational structure of the community, the program may lose its visibility as a viable and ongoing service. The project director encourages the Family Training therapists to maintain regular contact with the protective services workers so that referral channels are kept open. In addition, the director is a member of various county and city Child Protective Teams as well as a Child Abuse Coalition, which ensures that the program is represented on a countywide and citywide basis.

To develop the Family Training Program format in a more traditional setting requires an administrator who not only can tolerate differences but also can help the line staff and board members understand and appreciate those differences. "Things are not always going to be as structured in this type of program as they are in others," explained the executive director. "An administrator has to keep an open mind and be prepared to ride with a lot of things. You have to allow the therapists to retain their mode of operation and not force them to conform to a different way of working." According to the project director, accessibility to the board is especially vital to ensure their continued support of the program. "If the board members do not understand or feel comfortable with what we are doing, then they will not provide the program advocacy, the strong statements about the necessity of our program, to city and county funding sources. And without that advocacy, the existence of the program is jeopardized."

A prime requisite for success is staff that are well trained, dedicated, and well paid. "It takes people who are well trained in the behavioral approach and who are willing to give a lot of time to their clients. It is difficult to find people who are willing to put the needs of their clients ahead of their own needs and who will work on weekends or holidays, not to mention taking the time to learn about the community and the people in it." The program operates on the premise that if dedication is demanded from staff, then they must be compensated for their investment. "It is not fair to ask someone to put in long hours, give up holidays, and pay them only $8,000 a year."

Whenever a program demonstrates that it can successfully deal with a problem, it usually faces enormous pressure to expand its service. It is important to avoid the "more is better" school of thought. "You have to resist the temptation to overexpand; otherwise the program deteriorates." The intensive, on-call nature of the program requires that caseloads remain low so that staff do not spread themselves too thin and in the process lower the quality of the service, decrease interaction with the other therapists, and increase the burnout rate.

# 8
# COUNSELING/ EDUCATIONAL: Domestic Abuse Project

**T**he Domestic Abuse Project deals with the problem of spouse abuse in and around Minneapolis, Minnesota. It is a private community agency that operates through the partial support of a state-sponsored grant to provide services to families in which spousal violence occurs. Specifically, the program serves men who batter their wives, and it also assists the victims and children of the assaulter. The program offers four major components:

• A therapy program for abusers, their wives, and children
• A self-help support network for abusers and their wives
• A community intervention program
• A 24-hour crisis phone service

The program was designed to be both long-term and intensive. The full program takes from nine to twelve months to complete. Attendance is required several times a week during one portion of the program to reinforce the learning and to remind the clients that the program is an important part of their lives. All services are free, except the structured therapy program, which is offered on a sliding fee basis.

## DEVELOPING THE PROJECT

The Domestic Abuse Project grew out of the frustration felt by the program director, Mary Pat Brygger, during her work as a family therapist. She, and others who worked with battered women, noticed that traditional family counseling approaches often put more emphasis on the victim's role than the abuser's behavior. The attitudes of many therapists toward the victims convinced her of the need to start a whole new organization that would focus only on family violence. At the time, she was very involved in working with battered women and had begun working together with a local psychologist, Phil Oxman, to provide treatment for the men also. In 1976 she had taken a part-time leave of absence from the family service agency where she worked to develop a shelter for battered women.

Drawing from their experiences, she and her colleagues identified the components of a comprehensive domestic violence program. Clearly, something had to be done to work with the men so the cognitive-educational approach used by Phil Oxman was one component that would be included. However, many people who provided therapy seemed to overlook the community and cultural reinforcement that was very powerful in perpetuating abuse. Therefore, another key component of a model program needed to be a community intervention segment that offered both case and class advocacy for the victims. "I think that if other resources in the community are doing an effective job of class advocacy, working with the court system and training professionals, then community intervention doesn't have to be included as part of a program for men. But without that mindset, without understanding the historical and cultural system, without understanding the traditional blaming the victim, without remembering it in our day-to-day work, then the advocacy component needs to be housed with the program." The self-help component came from observing Henry Giaretto's sexual abuse program in California as well as from battered women's groups. "Many women's shelters threw out the idea of formal therapy because so often it included the attitude, 'I know what is best for you.' But in my heart, I knew that putting a group of batterers in a room and saying, 'Okay, now help yourselves,' without any professional guidance, would not get anywhere." Therefore the self-help group would include both peer and professional group facilitators. Also, in order to be available at all hours to calm the crises inherent in domestic violence situations, the program needed a 24-hour hotline.

By then the state legislature had adopted the idea of including a model program for abusive men and made it a budgetary item in the state-funded battered women's program. Together with Lynn Powers, the current coordinator of the women's and children's program, who was then serving on the State Task Force on Battered Women, Mary Pat and Phil decided to apply for the funds to implement that model program. They presented their proposal, which incorporated the Domestic Abuse Project, in June 1979 to the State Advisory Task Force of the Department of Corrections, which is responsible for determining how the funds are distributed to battered women's programs throughout the state. Their proposal was accepted with funding granted at $85,000 a year for two years. "That was enough for us to begin the counseling and self-help portions of the program, but they stipulated that all four components had to be operative in order for us to receive the money." That sent them scurrying for additional funds, which they obtained from private foundations. They began hiring when the state funds were received in October 1979 and opened their doors to clients in January 1980. Figure 8.1 depicts the organizational structure of the program.

## PROGRAM DESIGN

The Domestic Abuse Project was designed to develop and implement treatment modalities that are most effective in ending abuse, to train professionals in the use of the treatment methods developed, and to network an effective community systems response which strongly discourages battering and enforces sanctions against it. The philosophy that guides the program is based on a belief system that differs sharply from the more traditional conceptions of wife battering. For example, they believe that violence is not caused by poor marital relationships, job frustration, unemployment, alcohol, or other drugs, but that battering is the result of rigid sex-role culturalization, that it is a learned behavior passed on within families, and that men who batter seldom stop battering without outside help.

All services are housed in eight rooms of a large renovated two-story stone building which is shared by other professional services and organizations. During the day the rooms serve as offices for the staff and at night they are used to hold group meetings. General services are offered from 8:30 A.M. to 5 P.M. Monday through Friday, with self-help and therapy group meetings scheduled Monday through Thursday evenings. Hotline and crisis intervention services are available when the agency is closed. The staff is composed of males and females who have Bachelor, Master, or Doctoral degrees.

Program staff have been experimenting with the content and interface of the four components that make up the program. They plan to evaluate their experiences and make some modifications in the pro-

---

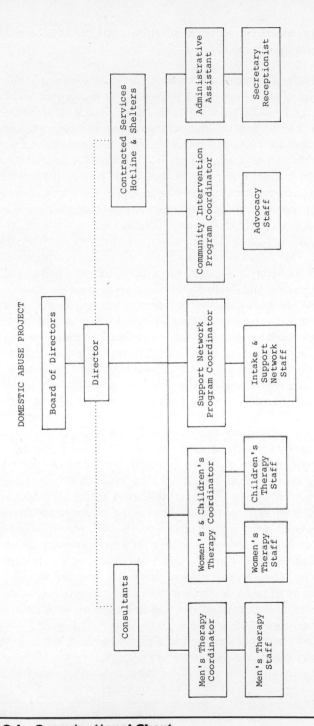

DOMESTIC ABUSE PROJECT

Board of Directors

Director

Consultants

Contracted Services
Hotline & Shelters

Men's Therapy
Coordinator

Women's & Children's
Therapy Coordinator

Support Network
Program Coordinator

Community Intervention
Program Coordinator

Administrative
Assistant

Men's Therapy
Staff

Women's
Therapy
Staff

Children's
Therapy
Staff

Intake &
Support
Network
Staff

Advocacy
Staff

Secretary
Receptionist

**Figure 8.1   Organizational Chart**

gram. The following sections describe each of the components as they originally operated.

**Self-Help Support Network**   The goals of the self-help support network are to provide a peer support group that breaks down isolation and builds trust, to serve as an initial orientation to the program, and to provide the confrontation and ongoing supportive environment needed to integrate the new learnings from the therapy groups. There are separate self-help groups for husbands and for wives which meet once a week from 6:30 to 9 P.M. The size of the groups varies from ten to twelve people. Currently, ten self-help groups operate on one of two nights a week that they are scheduled. The groups are open-ended and include people who are in various stages of the program; clients participate throughout their stay in the program. This component is staffed by a female coordinator (M.S.W.) who also facilitates groups, by three male and two female facilitators (mostly M.A.'s), and by two interns from graduate school.

Because most dropouts occur during the first month that clients are in the program, an orientation group was added to keep the open-ended self-help groups as cohesive as possible. Depending on the number of new clients admitted to the program each week, the orientation group may contain between ten and seventeen people, with an average of twelve. The orientation groups are ongoing, but participants transfer to their permanent self-help groups after four weeks.

**Therapy**   Therapy is available for all family members, individually or together, so that they may all deal with the effects of the violence. Three therapy segments take place during a sixteen-week period: individuation (eight weeks, two times a week), couples group (four weeks, two times a week), and family group (four weeks, once a week). During the sixteen-session individuation phase each family member works in his or her own peer therapy group. There are two men's, two women's, and three age-specific children's therapy groups. The therapy groups are closed and the number is limited. Each adult group is limited to twelve participants (but averages nine or ten members) and the children's group is limited to eight. The groups meet twice a week from 6:30 to 9 P.M. and are held in conjunction with participation in the once-a-week self-help group. A new therapy group begins every six weeks.

Those clients who are involved with a spouse or partner enter a four-week couples group following the individuation phase. Five couples are admitted to each group, but through attrition that number usually stabilizes at three or four. The couples group meets twice a week for a total of eight sessions. In addition, the couples continue to participate in their self-help groups once a week.

The final four weeks of the therapy segment are for those people with children in the program. They meet in a multiple family group once a week and continue in their self-help support group once a week.

The therapy program is directed by two coordinators (one M.A. and one Ph.D.); one is for the men's therapy program and one for the women's and children's therapy program, and they also provide treatment. In addition, there is one full-time therapist in the men's program, one full-time therapist in the women's program, and two half-time therapists in the children's group. Each therapy program also includes an intern who is affiliated with one of the local universities.

**Community Intervention**  Intervention into the community legal and social service systems is provided by a full-time coordinator plus four half-time workers. The coordinator is a full-time employee of the Domestic Abuse Project, but the program pays funds to four shelters in the area, enabling each shelter to supply the Domestic Abuse Project with a person who will work half-time in the community intervention component of the program. Their aim is to facilitate a community response that sets external limits on violent behavior. They encourage court prosecutions and mandated referrals, and they train police and courts on the issue of battering. They also provide advocacy for individuals within the program and assist the extended family network that is available to the men and women in setting limits on the violent behavior and in offering their support. They advocate on behalf of the individuals in the program and coordinate with the shelters for advocacy of nonshelter women and children who are referred to the program. They are also charged with providing community education and training to other professionals.

**24-Hour Crisis Phone Line**  The project contracts with a volunteer organization known as Men in Violent Relationships Hotline to handle after-hours and between-session problems. They take crisis calls and provide suitable intervention. They are also available to give information and make referrals to other community re-

---

sources. Their line is open to both batterer and battered, members of their families, and human service agencies in the metropolitan area.

Self-help and therapy staff are expected to work two evenings a week. During the day they conduct intakes and talk with individual clients, in the early evening they see families and couples, in the evening they conduct their groups, and from 9 to 10 P.M. following each client group meeting they participate in a process group for staff. Several people are employed half-time or quarter-time, specifically to facilitate the evening groups. Individual program units meet for an hour and a half every week and the full staff meets for an hour and a half every two weeks. Thursday afternoons are set aside for staff meetings, which include in-service training sessions. Most people who are employed by the program hold advanced degrees, and two hold Bachelor's degrees; however the degree is less important than the experience and knowledge that they bring to the job.

## STAFF TRAINING

Initially the staff received two weeks of training about violence, the use of a cognitive/behavioral/affective model, child abuse and working with protective services, chemical abuse, and available community resources. As other needs became known, a series of in-service sessions was planned. Although the program hires consultants, many in-service training sessions do not require that people be brought in from the outside. They draw on their own staff and focus on ways to keep their system running smoothly. For example, they discuss processing court-ordered and non-court-ordered referrals, how the goals of community intervention impact on the other program components, or special problems such as substance abuse. The self-help staff give training to part-time people concerning intake procedures and also acclimate them to the style of leadership expected when they are working with the self-help groups so that the groups can receive similar experiences.

New staff receive an informal orientation and training period. They work closely with one of the coordinators to ensure continuity of approach. They co-facilitate group sessions with an experienced staff person for the first two months before they branch out on their own.

Staff are encouraged to attend local conferences and professional workshops, especially those that focus on physical and sexual assault.

"The unfortunate thing is that in the last six months, rather than going to conferences to learn, the staff are going to conferences to present information." There is no specified amount of time alloted to conference attendance; it depends on the needs of the program and the individual.

## LINKING CLIENTS AND PROGRAM

Referrals to the Domestic Abuse Project may come from the courts, from battered women's shelters, from community agencies, and from self-referrals. Approximately 25 to 30 percent of the clientele are mandated to enter the program by the court. However, the program director believes that no one really enters the program willingly. "Whether a man is mandated to be here by the court or mandated by his wife, he is not coming because he is dying to participate. Most men do not see their violence as a problem. It takes several weeks in the program along with the support of other men before they see it that way." The staff insists that the man call and request service for himself. They have found that the firmer they are at the beginning, the lower is the dropout rate. "As men call us we do a lot of what some people might consider "discouraging." We let them know how long the program is, how intense it is, that we want the whole family to participate, and we tell them that there are other sources we will refer them to. We found that more and more people are coming back saying, 'This is the place we want,' which is the opposite of what we expected." Because so many people request service, it usually takes two weeks from the time of their telephone inquiry before they see an intake person. Consequently, the initial telephone calls are used to offer immediate assistance. According to the self-help coordinator, "The men call and sometimes act as though all they want is an appointment, but they really need to talk right away, so we spend a lot of time on the phone talking about what is going on with them and their violence. Usually the man has just lost his wife or girlfriend, or is afraid of losing her. That's their main concern. So we talk about a control plan with them, what alternatives they have to becoming violent." The worker helps the men realize they are not as out of control as they fear. They focus on cues, that is, noticing changes in themselves emotionally and physically as their anger increases. "Some people are really in touch with their bodies. They might say, 'My jaw gets tight' or 'I start sweating' or 'I clench my fist.' We tell them to be aware consciously that their hand should be open so that they are thinking about their hand instead of doing something with it." The workers suggest that when the men feel that their emotions are escalating, they take a time-out period. They should leave the room or the house and cool off. Their mates need to be informed about this time-out procedure before it occurs so that they do not feel they are being abandoned.

The staff schedules two intake sessions, each lasting an hour and a half. Before beginning the intake, the men complete attitude and personality questionnaires. In the first session they discuss the current situation, the type of violence engaged in, and how to avoid violent interactions. "When he walks out of the first of those two intake sessions the man has on paper a contract that he has signed which includes some new ideas he might have about the cues that lead to his violence and the alternate ways he has of dealing with it before he reaches the point of no return." (See Figure 8.2.) The women are invited to talk with another intake worker and by the end of the first session are also able to identify those cues and make protection plans for themselves and their children, that is, determine what actions to take for protection prior to and during violent incidents. (See Figure 8.3.) During the second intake session they discuss the family background, the way they were treated as children, their use of drugs and alcohol, and any special physical abuse, especially child abuse or incest. The intake workers also tell both the men and the women about the program's separation policy and position on firearms. (See Figure 8.4.) During the first eight weeks of participation in the program, the couple is advised to live in different places. This separation gives the couple the encouragement and the safe space needed to focus on their own individual issues rather than on the relationship. It reinforces the emphasis that the violence is not the result of relationship problems and moves the men more quickly toward accepting responsibility for their behavior and for learning violence control.

When the men and women enter the self-help program, each is assigned to a peer orientation group for the first month. The men or women can participate regardless of whether their partners do. "We want to identify clearly that it is not the woman's problem, that she is not responsible for the violence; so we encourage, but never coerce, the women to participate." Orientation groups acclimate the men to the program. People who have been in the program for several months talk with the people in orientation to help them understand what to expect when they begin subsequent portions of the program.

CONTROL PLAN

AGREEMENT TO BE NON-VIOLENT


CUES THAT INDICATE VIOLENCE:

    Physical:


    Fantasy/Images:


    Emotional:


    Red Flag Words/Situations:


PLAN FOR CONTROLLING VIOLENCE:

    Y.E.S. Hotline - 339-7033




I agree to use this control plan to be non-violent while
participating in the Domestic Abuse Project.

Participant's Signature _____

Intake Counselor _____

Date _____


This agreement includes being non-violent with children and
others, as well as your partner.  Information and assistance
about non-violent discipline is available.

Advocates are available to help you with problems in the
following areas:  legal, police, welfare, emergency housing,
child protection and other referrals.  Call Denise, Jo, or
Cheryl at 784-0763.

**Figure 8.2**                                              157

PROTECTION PLAN

The objective of our program is to prevent future violence.
We know from research and experience that violence repeats
itself and gets worse.  Now is the time to plan what to
do if there is further violence.  Protection Plan is a
means by which you can protect yourself and your children,
by using personal and community resources and by becoming
aware of signs that usually precede a person's violent
actions.

1.  What are some behaviors or circumstances leading up to
    an explosive situation in your home?  (Time of day,
    chemical use, money, children, issues, location, own
    reactions, stress level of partner, etc.)




2.  How have you protected yourself and/or your children
    from being hurt in the past?




3.  What has been effective in the past?


4.  What people or organization do you know that you can
    turn to for help?


5.  Are you familiar with legal protection available to you?


6.  Are you familiar with the medical services available
    to you?



If I am in a situation where I am afraid violence will
occur or is occurring towards me or my children, I know
that the following options are available to me:




Name _____  Date _____

**Figure 8.3**

DOMESTIC ABUSE PROJECT

POSITION ON FIREARMS


In the interest of the safety of the clients we serve at
the Domestic Abuse Project, we strongly recommend that
any and all firearms be removed from your home by the time
you enter Phase I groups, and that they remain outside the
home until completion of the program, at which time this
agreement may be re-negotiated.  We are not in any way
suggesting that these firearms will be used as weapons
against your partner or yourself; yet, we do not have
sufficient information on clients entering our program to
make this determination on a case-by-case basis.  In the
event that the firearms in your home are not your property,
the intake counselor will be willing to discuss possible
alternatives with you.


SIGNED: _____    _____
                    Client                            Date


          _____    _____
                Intake Counselor                      Date


POSITION OF SEPARATION


The Domestic Abuse Project strongly recommends that couples
beginning our program live apart for at least the first
eight (8) weeks of their involvement here.


We have found that couples who follow this policy are much
more successful in the program and at ending violence.  It
helps the individuals sort out their feelings and keeps
the tension down while dealing with hard problems.  When
living together, the everyday stresses make it more difficult to do these things.


We understand that this separation causes some couples
hardships and we would like to offer our assistance in
helping you accomplish this important part of our program.

---

**Figure 8.4**                                            **159**

At the end of orientation the men enter a self-help group. At the same time they also begin the twice weekly therapy component of the program. This involves a physical transition as well as an emotional one. "It is important to separate the men so that destructive coalitions in the group don't form. Usually when someone is ready to leave orientation, we consider which self-help group would be best. We explain to the participants at the beginning of orientation that the participants will not necessarily stay together when they enter self-help and therapy groups. Generally, it means a change of group members, and for some, a change of meeting night." The women make the transition more easily than the men. For them, going into another group does not represent too much of a problem because they feel a sense of togetherness with the other women in the program. The men don't see it that way, however. "They have a real fear of abandonment both from their wives and from us, so they really want to stay connected with the original counselor."

The men's and women's self-help groups are structured the same: one member of the group is named the chairperson. He or she is elected by the group and serves for six to eight weeks. The chairperson's function is to welcome the members, encourage the members to talk, and facilitate the discussions in the group. A professional consultant, who is a member of the staff, sits in also as a backup person to provide support and guidance such as cutting through denials and helping members work on heavy emotional issues.

The goals of the men's therapy program are to end the violent behavior and the threat of violence, to change attitudes that lead to violence, and to deal with other issues which are indirectly related to the violence. The eight-week individuation therapy component is a structured, sequential program that covers sixteen sessions. The therapists use a session-by-session outline that stresses cognitive-behavioral principles. According to the men's therapy coordinator, "The techniques we use are not unique, but the combination and the way we structure them probably are. They reflect our view of aggression which is based on a social learning theory model. We believe that aggression is a learned response to conflict. It is learned principally through the family of origin and is maintained by cultural norms. There are powerful short-term rewards for the behavior, including a release of anxiety and tension, and gaining control or 'winning.' This is not an instinctual or inherited trait; it is not something that results from frustration-aggression drive theory. We believe we have to teach them new ways of responding to conflict. That is why we adopted a teaching model as opposed to an insight model."

The first three or four weeks focus on behavior. After spending the first session on introductions and outlining of the therapy program, the wives are invited to join their husbands for a time during the second session, when the therapist explains about the cycle of violence and cues of anger arousal. Later in that session the men and women return to their separate groups and the men choose a "buddy" whom they can call during the week. They also use that session to engage in imagery work related to anger. "We ask them to imagine their anger, get a picture of its form, shape, and color. Then we ask them to draw it and then we talk about it. It is a way of externalizing the anger. The men have to talk about their drawing in the first person. For example, 'I am Joe Smith's anger. I am very big and powerful.' Then the therapist asks questions like, 'What do you do for Joe? If you protect him, how do you do so? What would happen if Joe didn't have you any more or if you were a lot smaller?' It is a powerful exercise."

The second session generally spills over into the third session, which teaches progressive relaxation. Participants are asked to keep a daily log of their tension levels. The men are given relaxation tapes to play at home every day for the first six weeks of therapy and then every other day. Then the partners come together again to discuss cues and how they are responded to.

The fourth session revolves around an analysis of a situation chart. (See Figure 8.5.) The men are asked to talk about the worst incident of violence in order to help them deal with some of the shame they have felt. Part of the chart is a section about benefits, what they gain from the use of violence, and disadvantages, what they lose as a result of resorting to violence.

The fifth session teaches about self-talk. "Probably the principal cognitive aspect of the behavioral stage is the central focus on self-talk. We borrow a lot of techniques from Ellis. We focus on that because of the men's obsession about anger and events. They can't seem to let go of the anger; it continues to build and build. I had a call this morning from a man in the program who had an argument with his girlfriend last night. He did all the right things to prevent the argument from leading to violence, including sleeping apart. But this morning he was still angry and with hardly any words between them at all he became verbally abusive toward her, kicked her out of the house, and dumped all her things out of the bureau drawers. I'm certain that what he was doing all night long was obsessing about things. The mistakes a lot of people make is to label it impulsive behavior when, in fact, it may be something related to the obses-

ANALYSIS OF SITUATIONS

| DESCRIBE THE SITUATION WHERE YOU USED PHYSICAL FORCE AND WHO WAS INVOLVED | WERE THERE ANY EVENTS WHICH LED UP TO THIS SITUATION? | DID YOU KNOW YOU WERE GOING TO USE PHYSICAL FORCE? | WHAT KIND OF PHYSICAL FORCE DID YOU USE? | WERE YOU USING ALCOHOL OR OTHER DRUGS BEFORE OR DURING THE SITUATION? | ADVANTAGES OF USING PHYSICAL FORCE IN THIS SITUATION | DISADVANTAGES OF USING PHYSICAL FORCE IN THIS SITUATION |
|---|---|---|---|---|---|---|
| | | | | | | |

**Figure 8.5**

sion." So they teach the men to recognize the thoughts and words they say to themselves that reinforce their beliefs about what happened. "We ask people in the group to volunteer some incidents and then have them think about what they said to themselves and the emotional consequences that followed. One man related that he and his wife were going to a wedding. In his mind the man believed that it was going to be a hard night, that it was going to be a problem, and that his wife wouldn't understand. The emotional consequences were that he was nervous, anxious, and upset. At the wedding he became drunk, passed out, got into a gigantic hassle with his wife, and finally assaulted her. By this time she was frightened and angry. She called the police and he said, "See, I knew she wouldn't understand."

Session six represents the end of the behavioral section of therapy. The men are asked to revise the control plan they had developed during intake to reflect their new and expanded knowledge. During that session the men also learn to combine relaxation techniques with visual imagery that can be used in stressful situations.

The next two sessions represent the insight portion of the structured therapy. Participants focus on their family of origin and the men recall in detail what they learned about emotions and love, about anger and how to express it, the consequences of their behavior, and the role they played in the family. They call to attention those behaviors that still linger from childhood learning and discuss their appropriateness in adult situations. Following this session, their homework assignment is to give up anger for a week. "I call them anger junkies. The idea is to give them a different tool, take away the anger, and see what happens."

There is an exchange of therapists during part of the ninth session. The men's therapist talks to the women's group and the women's therapist talks to the males' group. The exchange is one way to deal with the dynamics that both partners are changing.

Next the men enter the skill acquisition phase, which is the third and final aspect of individuation and begins with assertiveness training. "Most programs that take an educational approach," commented the men's therapy coordinator, "usually start with the skill training and the assertiveness. I think that is too soon. I think you have to give them some controls first or at least have them understand their behavior and what is happening inside and give them some clear-cut, behavioral, structured controls." The men learn and practice assertive behavior both within the group and with their spouses.

The twelfth session deals with sex-role socialization. The thir-

---

teenth session is concerned with sexuality. It starts with a discussion of the messages they received about sexual behavior as they were growing up and ends by talking specifically about their sexually abusive behavior toward their wives. The fourteenth session deals with the issue of control. "It is possible to terminate the physical violence fairly quickly in therapy. Emotional, psychological, or verbal abuse persists for a longer time, but even when that decreases you still find a lot of controlling and manipulative behavior that continues for a long time." The men participate in an exercise called "commander-robot." One of the men plays commander and one of them plays robot. For five minutes the robot does everything the commander says to do. Then they change places. The exercise is used to stimulate discussion about control and power in their relationships. The final two sessions are concerned with an evaluation of their experiences and with leave-taking.

During the eight-week period each person is seen individually at least twice for an hour each time. The first individual interview is spent on their reactions to the program, family of origin material, and disruptive or counterproductive group behavior. The second individual session is principally an exit interview. They are retested with the tests they took when they were accepted in the program.

The women engage in a similar process in their therapy group. Their concerns are focused on protecting themselves from violence, recognizing and expressing feelings, using support systems, increasing their self-worth, increasing their independence and decision-making ability, and exploring parenting issues. Their activities include reading books that explain the battering phenomenon, learning about the cycle of violence, developing protection plans and means for withdrawal, practicing assertiveness skills, analyzing anger and its expression, and connecting with the various feelings they experience.

Not everyone who completes the therapy group goes on to couples therapy. Some don't go on because they do not have partners in the program and others because, in the opinion of their therapists, they are not ready to go on (usually because they have not taken responsibility for their violent behavior). Four or five couples meet in a group twice a week for the four-week period. The goals of the couples program include the teaching of effective communication skills; the processing of current feelings, especially those related to anger, hurt, or fear; the discussion of relationship issues and dynamics; the discussion of sexual issues; the sharing of the effects of violence; the learning of ways to relate interdependently rather than overdependently.

The first session is introductory and seeks to build group cohesion. The next two sessions focus on the effects that violence has had on the couple. In the second session each person is paired off with a member of the opposite sex, but not his or her own partner. The task is for the women to talk to the men about how the violence has affected their life. The men's job is to listen without interrupting. When the women have finished, it is the men's turn to tell how the violence has affected their life and the women are instructed to listen without interrupting. Then as a group they process what has happened. The same exercise is repeated during the third session, this time with their own marital partners. The next session is concerned with communication and how each of them impairs or enhances communication with the spouse.

The fifth session focuses on the positive and negative attachments to the relationship. "We ask them to identify what is good that keeps them in the relationship and what keeps them in the relationship that is bad. Not what is bad about the relationship, but what keeps the person in it that is not healthy for him or her. Generally for the men that is emotional dependency and for the women it is security." The next session addresses the issue of sexuality in the relationship. The therapists use a structured question format and ask the men and women to discuss it separately for half the session before coming together and talking to each other in partners. In the seventh session they discuss and practice the assertive behavior with each other that they have been learning in their peer groups. The final session is basically evaluation and follow-up of where each couple is in the relationship.

The multiple family groups are designed to deal with parenting issues and to heal family wounds caused by the violence. The parents learn violence-free conflict resolution techniques, the children discuss their reactions to the violence that had occurred, and they all learn techniques for showing caring among family members and becoming more cohesive as a family unit.

Throughout their therapy sessions the men and women attend their own self-help group once a week. That is where the integration of the therapy experiences occur. Therapy sessions often trigger thoughts, feelings, and questions which can be aired and discussed in the self-help group. Actually, because the therapy group is more educational therapy than psychotherapy, the self-help group provides the forum for process therapy. The group deals with some heavy psychological issues. Once they have completed couples group and/ or family group, clients continue in self-help for several more months. Termination from the program occurs when the therapists, group members, and individual believe the goals of the program have been met. Graduation is both a formal event involving the giving of diplomas and a festive occasion in which food is served and the family members attend.

## CASE EXAMPLE

Joan and John are both 33 years old. John is a successful skilled laborer and Joan is a housewife. The couple were married five years ago. This is Joan's first, and John's second, marriage. John had been physically abusive with his first wife and the marriage ended in divorce. However, the abuse was minimized during the divorce proceedings and John was awarded custody of the children. The children, a boy aged 12 and a girl aged 10, currently share the home with Joan, John, and their 2-year-old son.

John was raised in a farm family in which he experienced and witnessed violence. The mother was beaten periodically by the father, who also used belts and other instruments regularly to punish the children. During adolescence, John was known to be violent toward his mother when his father was not around. Joan was raised in a family where there was very little violence. Her father never assaulted her mother; however, he did hit her brothers and sisters more often than he hit Joan. She was spanked every once in a while, but never severely. There may have been some inappropriate sexual activity between the father and Joan's older sister, but it has never been discussed openly.

The marital violence began on their honeymoon. It was triggered by the dissatisfaction about the cost of the honeymoon and the couple's sexual relationship. John choked Joan to the point of her passing out and also banged her head against a wall. The violence erupted every few months during the marriage. In addition to hitting, there was a great deal of shoving, pushing, and grabbing. John frequently followed the physical abuse with forced sexual relations. Joan usually did not fight back. However, one time she felt so angry and fed up following one of John's attacks that she threw an ashtray at him. It missed and put a hole in the wall. In addition to beating his wife, John was a strict disciplinarian and administered severe spankings to both of his sons.

Prior to calling the Domestic Abuse Project the couple had tried marital counseling once for nine months and a second time for a year. With the first counselor violence was not raised as an issue. With the second counselor it was but was treated as though Joan caused it. The counselor would listen to a description of the violence and then ask Joan what she had done to provoke it or what she got out of keeping the violence system going. Counselors described John as smooth and very likable; it always looked as though Joan were the crazier one. John spoke of being able to convince both counselors that he really didn't have a problem, that everything was under control, and that it was Joan who had the problem. The counselor finally decided that the couple would derive greater benefit from a group program and referred them to the Domestic Abuse Project.

When they entered the Domestic Abuse Project, both John and Joan were minimizing and denying the severity of the violence. At first John claimed he never abused anyone other than his present wife; only much later did he acknowledge the physical abuse to his mother and his first wife. Initially, neither acknowledged that forced sex occurred and neither mentioned that police intervention had been needed. Denials were made by both parties. John denied ever threatening the use of other punishments, such as withholding money or taking the children away, although his wife claimed he often did that. Joan in turn denied how badly the marital relationship had deteriorated by claiming that John never threatened to leave the marriage, whereas John stated that he frequently threatened to leave. The attitude questionnaires administered by the program personnel revealed that both John and Joan held rigid, traditional sex role stereotypes.

John experienced several meaningful revelations during his stay in the program. One occurred when he entered the self-help group, saw the fourteen other members, and realized that he was not the only one who acted violently toward his wife. Even though he was still denying the violence verbally, he claimed "it turned his head around" and his violence decreased. Later, during the therapy program, some of the exercises the men were asked to do made him aware that many of the things he told himself internally did not match reality. He also began to recognize that acting on those distorted thoughts had brought about much of the verbal and physical abuse he showered on his wife. A third important piece of insight occurred when the group members confronted him about his smoothness and the superficiality of his feelings. He had skated through the first few months of the program by being supportive of other group members, occasionally confronting group members, and saying that he took responsibility for the violence. However, he had not been very self-disclosing and the men confronted him about it. He couldn't relate to what they were saying until once, during a group meeting, the men were given a list of words that described feelings. It shocked him to learn there were so many feelings because the only feelings he had ever experienced were "happiness" and "anger." The men's confrontation was the first he had ever encountered. Until then he had managed to convince people, including his wife, that everything was all right and that he was changing. Another major revelation occurred during couples group, when he was required to sit and listen as his wife described the effects of the violence on her. Her disclosure had a profound effect on him as he began to tie together the violence he had experienced as a child and the abuse he had inflicted on his children and his wife.

Joan began the program several weeks after John started. Her prior counseling experiences made her reluctant to enter another counseling setting in which she might once more be blamed for causing the violence. However, she noticed that since starting the program, John was less abusive toward the children and she decided that this program might be different from her other experiences. For the first month she was very quiet and did very little sharing. Finally, she told the group of the shame she had felt because her husband had convinced her that she was inadequate as a wife and mother and that she was responsible for the violence. During the therapy sessions she identified the degree of sexual abuse she had suffered, which was far more extensive than was realized at the beginning. Later, she started getting in touch with her anger about the control. She had already dealt with her feelings about the violence, and now she was realizing how much control her husband kept over her behavior. She related that her husband continued to intimidate her by raising his arm as he came toward her or by yelling and putting his face in her face. Earlier he had used violence to force her to do things that he wanted. Now, his intimidation was meant to prevent her from being more active socially. He wanted to keep her home with him. Like many battered women, Joan was afraid to show her anger because she equated angry feelings with violence. It was almost as though thinking about violence was as bad as committing violence and she was afraid of what she might do if she allowed her angry feelings to surface. The support group was especially important at this phase because it helped clarify what was happening to her and in her relationship with John. Through the assertiveness training, she gained the skills she needed to confront him without being aggressive.

The Domestic Abuse Project holds formal graduation ceremonies for the men who complete the program. Prior to graduation, the men are required to make an assessment of their goals and accomplishments in the program. As part of his assessment John noted that he was now able to get along better with people at work as well as those at home, that he felt more comfortable with people, and that he had developed friendships both in and out of the program. He also realized there were certain people he could not associate with because they would reinforce his earlier attitudes and "macho" image. At the graduation ceremony, Joan and the children watched as John received his diploma. John continued his involvement with the program by leading a self-help group.

## TREATMENT ISSUES

Initially, the client attrition rate was a major problem for the therapists. "When I first started working with this population," said the men's therapy coordinator, "we had an attrition rate of 50 percent. Now we get very little dropout; we have 90 percent retention in therapy groups." Two factors seemed to account for the difference: better screening, and the four weeks of orientation before entering the structured therapy portion of the program. The change in screening procedure has been toward longer telephone counseling prior to intake to help the men get through the crisis period and gain some control over their actions. This delay helps cool the situation and establishes a bond with the program. They attempt to screen out people who are chemically dependent (drugs or alcohol) or those in whom there is clear evidence of psychosis or a chronic history of severe mental illness. For the others, the counselors make clear the time commitments and emotional demands of the program to discourage those people who are ambivalent about seeking help. The second factor, the four weeks in orientation, was implemented to accommodate the large number of people who sought entry into the program and to maintain group cohesiveness in the ongoing self-help groups. "If people drop out of the program, chances are it will be within the first four weeks. A lot of men come once or twice, feel better because they get rid of a lot of pent-up emotions, and think they are cured. Or else they feel threatened because of the intimacy of the group experience and then take off. So those who remain beyond orientation feel an increased commitment to the program."

Counseling personnel involve as many family members in the program as is possible (whenever it is *safe* to do so), but experience has taught them that focusing on the relationship too early only reinforces the violent pattern in the family. It keeps the issue secret and covert and keeps the blame and the responsibility on the victims. "We used to do marriage counseling at the beginning of the program, but we discovered that it only escalated the violence because we would be encouraging the women to describe the violence and discuss issues that the men were not prepared to admit. Then the threats and the escalation would occur after they left our office. Now we take it on a step-by-step basis. We separate the family members at first, putting them in a safe environment in which to express their feelings, because if they discuss these things together initially they are not safe. Timing is critical. Even though looking at the relationship issues is important, we are doing that only after the violence is under control so that the threat of violence isn't used to perpetuate the old system."

Minimization is a common feature among abusers, especially in relation to the frequency and severity of the abuse. The Domestic Abuse Project counselors found that minimization was most pronounced on the subject of sexual abuse. The men rarely acknowledged the sexual abuse that frequently accompanied the physical abuse they inflicted on their partners. "The women will tell us about marital rape where he sticks sharp things up her vagina or ties her to the bed and brings in a dog to have sex with her, but the men won't say anything about it until they have been in the program for many months." When asked to describe the sexual abuse, some of the men are likely to describe a romantic scene that has nothing to do with abuse. When they finally reach a point where they can acknowledge the marital rape, most men describe a power struggle. One man said, "First we started playing and then I started playing rougher. She pulled away and it started to be a power thing. I went after and penetrated her with all my force and shouted, "I'm going to get you, bitch. I'll get you, bitch." It took that man seven months in the program before he could talk about the incident as well as the shame and guilt he felt about it. Once a few people are willing to talk about sexual abuse, it triggers a discussion by several group members.

However, without prodding, it is a subject that may never spontaneously come up for group discussion.

Another important issue is the men's victimization in their early childhood. Approximately 70 percent of the male clients have experienced or witnessed abuse in their family of origin. However, they do not offer much information about their victimization until they have been in the program for several weeks because they don't identify or interpret it as abuse. The men describe abusive situations during the intake period, but at that point consider them appropriate discipline. For example, one man described being beaten regularly with a razor strap that had metal prongs at the end. He said the only bad thing about it was the metal parts at the end that hurt him and cut his skin, and he interpreted the beatings as appropriate punishment because he had been naughty. "Here again, timing is very important. We used to start discussing the issue of their victimization at the beginning of the program, thinking that it would serve as good empathy training for the men. Unfortunately, all it did was confuse them and they would start talking about being a victim of their partner. Now we wait until after the control phase, when they have learned some basics about controlling the violence and have some tools for preventing violence, and after they have begun to examine some of the ways they were socialized. Then we discuss family of origin material." The men often have an emotional investment in avoiding the fact of early abuse. "They have a lot of anger toward the father that they are trying to deny and a lot of shame about being like their father." Acknowledgment might sever or jeopardize their relationship with their parents, especially their fathers. At some point in the program, however, the men stop interpreting the beatings they received as discipline and begin to realize that they were abused, that it was not an appropriate use of force. Uncovering the abuse puts them in touch with the hurt they felt and how they dealt with it. "He needs to get in touch with that victimization of his own, with the pain and the feelings of powerlessness he felt then, in order to understand and empathize with the feelings of victimization that his partner is having now as she receives abuse from him. That's a critical turning point for the man. It's an important issue in the couples group. The relationship just will not work until the woman is certain that she is safe, that the violence is under control so that she can talk about the effects the violence has had on her, and until she knows that he will listen and not become defensive or deny. Only then can she really start trusting him again."

Since working here," said a self-help counselor, "I have learned to look past a person's behavior and get in touch with the person who is exhibiting it without being repulsed—to realize that they aren't just walking around being terrible, abusive, mean people." In this job, counselors need the ability to look for the good parts of the client and to work through their own feelings about the violent behaviors their clients have performed. "To do this job you have to listen to awful stories and really be able to hear them, not stop them or shorten them by saying, 'Uh'hm, I understand.' And not only to listen, but to probe and ask for more information. So you'd better be able to deal with your own reactions and not let them get in the way."

However, it is also important to maintain a balance so that the counselor does not become emotionally overwhelmed by the clients' experiences and feelings. "One thing I learned early," explained the self-help coordinator, "is that you have to take care of yourself professionally; otherwise it is like being a mechanic who doesn't wash the grease off before he leaves the garage. He would be taking the grease home to his family and getting it all over everybody." To provide for the emotional care of group facilitators, they all meet for an hour to an hour and a half following each evening group meeting for a debriefing. Because most counselors felt unable to request help for themselves directly, it was structured as part of the debriefing session. "We start by saying, 'Okay who needs time today?' Usually everybody says, 'I do.' It is a very safe place for us as professionals to show our feelings. Sometimes a person will cry because he or she is feeling responsible for the safety of a client and knows the client may be in danger. If we didn't meet together, each person would carry all those feelings home and feel totally responsible. So, instead of making the client the main focus of those meetings, we make the main focus the counselors' emotional protection."

## ADMINISTRATIVE ISSUES

**Funding**  With an annual budget of $350,000, the project has fund raising constantly at the top of the list. "I am supposed to be the idea person," said the director, "but more and more of my time goes to finding the money that will keep the agency doors open. I don't even have time to see clients any more." When planning for funding it is also important for the director to stay connected with what is going on in the battered women's movement. For example, working with the State Coalition for Battered Women to get a whole package of programs for battered women and men who batter, plus an increase in the existing program, and to have that pass the legislature and the governor, would increase the total amount of money available to the Domestic Abuse Project. There is a Family Violence Task Force operated by the county and it is necessary to coordinate activities with them in asking the county for funding. The fact that the program has so many components and offers service to the entire family is an appealing feature to many funding sources.

**Board of Directors**   Selecting a board of directors takes time and careful recruiting. The board members should meet two qualifications: having an understanding about domestic violence and having a skill that would enhance the implementation of the program, e.g., financial management, fund raising, legal issues. For example, "We have two financial experts on our board, but each serves a different function. One is a CPA who helps us to monitor the books and to set up our annual audit. The other person is an investment manager and she helped us invest some of our grant funds until it had to be used in the program. As a result, we made a few hundred dollars that we could add to our budget. Both people help us with fiscal management, but in different ways." The board represents a broad spectrum of the community. The program began with a board of seven but has expanded as the committee work load increased. Committees meet monthly and the board as a whole meets for at least two hours each month. The board members need to be well informed in order for the board to do its work well. "You have to do as much communication, education, and information sharing with the board as you do with other parts of the community. Their decision about making policy has to be well informed; otherwise you are in serious trouble."

**Coordination**   Because the Domestic Abuse Project contains so many components, an enormous amount of administrative time is spent making certain that all parts of the program are communicating with each other. The transfer of case information is vital. "Because our program is so integrated, we need to have the information from the women's group because the men's therapist needs that and from the men's therapist because the women's therapist needs that. The man may be saying, 'Well, we had a little tiff' but the woman says, 'I spent the weekend in the hospital.'" The need for effective coordination is made even more necessary by virtue of the large number of part-time staff employed in the program. The majority of program personnel work from one-quarter to three-quarter time. "It would have been much easier on us to have fewer bodies here. When you have three staff people, you only have nine lines of communication. The more people you have, the more the number of lines multiplies and it is tiring for the staff. But it is also more stimulating." It puts a lot of pressure on the people who hold coordinator positions to make certain they have all the information they need and remain connected with everyone. "There is an atmosphere here that we are working together; we're dependent on each other to get the work done. I think that tends to tie in the part-time people and governs the service they give. It might not happen in an agency where services were not so dependent on each other. The big problem is energy. It is more draining to do it this way."

## ELEMENTS FOR SUCCESS

To develop a program that works effectively with abusing men requires at least three key ingredients: community support, a particular perspective concerning abuse, and a support system for family members. The first step is assessment of community support. "There has to be an awareness of the issue of battered women. There has to be safety for the women whether through shelters or safe home networks. There has to be some beginning contact with the courts and law enforcement system to help respond and set external limits on the men. There has to be a commitment from somewhere in the community to keep all those elements going. Once you have that, then you can start talking about what you are going to do therapeutically."

The therapeutic model should be one that clinically incorporates the cultural, historical perspective of spouse abuse instead of viewing the problem from the traditional medical model perspective. Maintaining that mindset involves ongoing connectedness with the shelters, the Family Violence Task Force, and the regional coalitions. "We have to be politically active in the sense of making it known that it is not just the responsibility of shelters and women's programs to talk about the problems of battered women, but also of men's programs. We have to convey the message that although we are here to help the men, the way to help them is to make sure that they are taking responsibility for the violence, that limits are set on their violence, and that the issue of abuse of women is kept in focus." That makes the running of this type of program a more politically administrative job than is the operation of more traditional social service agencies. "To run an organization for men who batter, you have to be involved actively with the local coalitions for battered women, to lend support to legislation that establishes financing and statutes that set limits on behavior. You may not be able to lobby for it actively, but your interest should be visible in terms of letters of support."

The final ingredient is a support system for all members of the family that is housed within the same facility that provides service for the men. "You cannot leave out other members of the family. All family members are affected by the violence." They need the opportunity to talk about their experiences and feelings, to feel that they are not alone, and to interact with the abuser so that changes can occur in the family.

# 9
# INPATIENT SETTING:
# Sex Offender Program

The Sex Offender Program is housed at Western State Hospital in Fort Steilacoom, Washington.[1] It uses a guided self-help approach in the treatment of convicted sex offenders, of whom approximately 45 percent have offended against children in the home as well as in the general community. The program is long term; the average completion time is four years. Unlike the other programs described in this book, this one includes a lengthy inpatient stay as well as outpatient service. The major components are:
• A 90-day evaluation period
• An inpatient phase which lasts a minimum of eighteen months
• A work release phase which lasts a minimum of three months
• An outpatient phase which lasts a minimum of eighteen months
It is a highly structured program that uses peer groups as the therapeutic vehicle through which changes occur. As part of its service to the community, the program provides community education to lay and professional groups.

## DEVELOPING THE PROGRAM

Since 1951 the state of Washington has had a sexual offender law which permits the court to commit sexual offenders to the state hospital for a 90-day observation period. When indicated, treatment can follow this period until the offenders are considered safe to be at large in the community. During the 1950's most of the sex offenders went to jail; those who were sent to the hospital were considered psychologically unbalanced and were committed for treatment. The hospitals viewed them as dangerous criminals and kept them in locked wards, isolated from the rest of the patients. Until 1958, the "treatment" received by sexual offenders consisted mainly of security for those who were considered dangerous and, among the very few who were not considered dangerous, an industrial assignment in the kitchen, laundry, or elsewhere in the hospital complex. The hopelessness of their situation led to many attempted and successful escapes by the sexual offenders. In 1958 Dr. Julio di Furia, the newly hired clinical director of male services, asked one of his psychologists, Hayden Meyes, to provide therapy for the sexual offenders. Even with the addition of psychotherapy once a week, some of the offenders continued to escape from the facility, creating an uproar in the community.

Realizing that traditional treatment methods held limited value for rehabilitating sexual offenders, di Furia and Meyes convinced the hospital superintendent to house all the sex offenders on the same ward and to treat them with group methods rather than individually. Using the group as the medium for change, the men could assume more responsibility for their actions and, ultimately, gain more freedom. "We were able to tell these patients that even though they could probably escape from the facility, once they were apprehended they would automatically be sent to prison with no chance of being returned to the program, but if they stayed, maybe they could learn something about themselves and their behavior. At least that way they might gain something from being here." They initiated group sessions with the sex offenders. The men were told: "You are not mentally ill like the other patients in this hospital. You have learned to behave in ways that are not acceptable to society. Through the group process you can learn more acceptable behavior. We are not here to take care of you (cure you) so you better start taking care of yourself (be responsible for changing). We can teach you how to change your behavior, but you are the ones who have to do it." From then on the men were allowed to run their own group sessions, which were held not just once a week but every day, and not always during the day when staff were present but in the evenings when nothing else was going on. All the sessions were tape-recorded so the staff could hear what had happened even when they were not there. "At that time we had about 29 patients on that ward.

---

We divided them into three groups and within each group assigned one man who seemed more responsible as the senior member to run the group. That established the idea of the self-help group." Both family visiting privileges and group therapy for the wives of the sex offenders were instituted early in the program. "Our feeling was that if the patient was kept isolated it would disrupt his family and cause his tie with the community to die. It is more difficult for a person to return to a community with which he has had little contact." The result was that there were fewer escapes, the men were given ground parole, they had more freedom, and they had their own ward.

However, the program met with obstacles from outside sources. At first it did not receive much support from the legal system. Judges did not always follow hospital personnel recommendations when the sexual offenders returned to court following their 90-day observation. "If our report indicated that a particular sex offender was too much of a con man, too ingrained in his activities to benefit from our program and we requested that he be sent to prison, the judges often returned the man to us for treatment. And vice versa." It took two or three years before the prosecuting attorneys and judges began to follow the program doctors' recommendations. Until they did, the program pretty much had to accept who was sent. A modification to that rule came in 1964, when the program developers were able to change the law pertaining to the length of treatment. "Although the judge still has the ultimate right to send the sex offender for treatment, we added a clause that said the superintendent would declare when the patient had received the maximum benefit from the hospitalization. Then the patient would be returned to court for further disposition. So, even if the judge sent us a person for treatment whom we found was inappropriate for the program, after a few months we could send that person back to the court as having received the maximum benefit from the hospitalization."

Opposition to the program was encountered within the hospital, also. At that time the hospital was overcrowded and understaffed. Many people believed the small group of sex offenders was receiving too much attention, taking up too much staff time. Also, because the sexual offenders were given industrial assignments in the kitchen and laundry, they were taking those jobs away from other patients. The opposition decreased when the men in the offender program began performing needed services in the hospital. For example, they spent four or five hours a week assisting in the geriatric unit. They became volunteer firemen in the hospital; they gave blood for other patients.

As they showed their concern for others, they became more accept-able to the hospital community.

Personnel shifts by the program initiators took place in the 1960's, when di Furia was appointed hospital superintendent and Meyes ac-cepted a university appointment. Without their constant supervision the sex offender program began to deteriorate. A "con" system devel-oped. The senior members who ran the groups became a privileged group themselves. They were the only ones who could talk to the staff, they received the best jobs, they had the best places to sleep, they appointed junior members to act as their assistants. The patients began to get into trouble. To regain control of the program, Dr. George MacDonald, the senior clinical director, was assigned responsibility for the sex offender program in 1965. He completely revised the group system. The basic assumption that sex offenders had a learned disorder remained the same, but the rest changed. He disbanded the con system by giving everyone equal status in the group. There were no more senior members; group leadership changed every three months. He outlined the four program components and the steps within each stage. He developed therapy supervisor positions among staff members so that each patient group reported to a professionally degreed staff person. The self-help group treatment model as it now exists evolved under his direction. MacDonald remained in charge of the program until 1976, when he stepped down. H. R. Nichols was director until he resigned in September 1977, and then the current director, Maureen Saylor, assumed responsibility. Figure 9.1 shows the current organizational chart.

In December 1966, because the program was working so well, Western State Hospital was given statewide responsibility for evaluat-ing and treating sex offenders. Consequently, the patient population, which had ranged between 20 and 40, quickly rose and reached an all-time high of 212 in 1977. To ease the overload, two groups of 24 patients along with two therapy supervisors were transferred to East-ern State Hospital near Spokane. Now Eastern State operates a small sex offender program containing 40 to 50 patients and the popula-tion at Western State is approximately 180 sex offenders.

## PROGRAM DESIGN

The Sex Offender Program is designed to help convicted sex offend-ers learn more appropriate and responsible sexual and relationship behaviors in an environment that replicates and confronts as much as

---

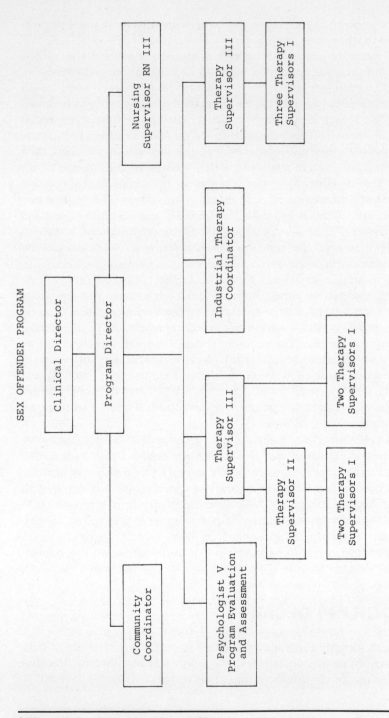

SEX OFFENDER PROGRAM

**Figure 9.1    Organizational Chart**

possible the realities of living in the community. The core of the treatment model is a peer group therapy called guided self-help, which relies on offenders treating other offenders under the direction of a therapy supervisor (B.A., M.A., or Ph.D. with a behavioral science background). The use of a peer group model is based on the belief that learning happens best when the learners themselves are expected to carry the major responsibility. Under this system the role of staff is to organize, guide, and assist the self-help groups as they progress through the four major stages of the program from evaluation to discharge.

Three locked wards in the hospital house approximately180 sexual offenders. All therapy takes place on those wards, which also include the offices of the program director, the therapy supervisors, and the nursing personnel. Each ward contains sleeping quarters, a large day room, kitchen, dining area, bathroom, resident lounge, and rooms for conjugal visits.

**Evaluation**   Sex offenders who are referred to the program spend their first 90 days under observation by the staff and the group members to determine whether they would make suitable candidates for the program. During that time the men are admitted to one of the guided self-help groups to participate in group therapy. Approximately twelve men are admitted for evaluation each month, and they are evaluated by the members of both the peer group and the professional staff. Two case reviews of the offenders on observation status take place at evaluation and treatment conferences held by the staff. One conference occurs near the beginning of the 90-day period to determine whether the offender meets the program's criteria as a security risk; the other conference takes place toward the end and evaluates the offender's appropriateness for continuation in the program. The men are confined to the ward during the observation period but are allowed visitors.

**Inpatient Phase**   Approximately two-thirds of the men who are evaluated return to the program. The minimum stay on inpatient status is eighteen months, with an average inpatient stay of 20 to 24 months. The men rejoin the peer group in which they were originally placed. Currently there are ten peer groups; each contains fifteen to 20 men. The groups are open-ended. Approximately one new person is admitted to each group every month. Controlling the number of new people admitted to a group each month minimizes the amount of disruption to group process.

Each person on inpatient status is given a work assignment during the day which occupies his time from 7:30 A.M. until 2:00 P.M. The men are not paid for the work they do, but neither do they pay for the treatment they receive.

The men participate in approximately 25 to 30 hours of group therapy each week. Groups meet from 2:30 P.M. to 4:30 P.M. on Monday through Friday and from 7:00 P.M. until 10:00 P.M. (and often longer) Monday, Wednesday, Thursday, Friday, and Sunday. Tuesday evening is couples group for those men who have wives or women friends and, on Wednesday or Thursday evenings, people on outpatient status return to participate in the groups.

The following is a typical daily routine.

| Time | Activity |
|------|----------|
| 6:00 A.M. | Wake up, dress, make bed |
| 7:00 A.M. | Breakfast |
| 7:30 A.M. | Work assignment |
| 11:30 A.M. | Lunch |
| 12:30 P.M. | Work assignment |
| 2:30 P.M. | Group meeting |
| 4:30 P.M. | Dinner |
| 5:30 P.M. | Unstructured activities |
| 7:00 P.M. | Group meeting |
| 12:00 A.M. | Lights out |

One therapy supervisor, a member of the professional staff, is attached to each group. He or she usually attends three of the five afternoon meetings and an occasional evening meeting. However, the group runs exclusive of the therapist. Each meeting is tape recorded and a member of the group takes extensive notes. The therapy supervisors use the notes and tapes to review what transpired and then give their groups feedback. On Tuesday mornings the two leaders or representatives from each group meet with the therapy supervisors to discuss problems, procedures, and techniques.

Each group has developed written policies and guidelines for its members over the years. The longer the group has been in existence, the more massive the number of policy decisions related to structure and process it has developed. All of the policy development occurs under the guidance of the therapy supervisor. Therapist and group members operate as a team or partnership. The better functioning the group, the less the staff member interferes. But at, at the same time, members know that the therapist is the final authority and that everything is subject to his or her approval.

Treatment goals are accomplished by progressing through a clearly defined ten-step procedure which each group develops in collaboration with the therapy supervisor. Achieving each of the steps results in gaining certain privileges. Everything is earned, nothing is given without effort on the offenders part, including work details and visiting privileges. Every 90 days two group members, who have attained step 4 or higher, are voted into leadership. The two are responsible for setting up the group format and running the meetings.

Each ward houses a room for conjugal visits. This room gives a couple privacy in which to talk or to have sexual relations. Only married couples are allowed to use the room. "We're not prudes," said the program director, "but this concerns the reaction of the whole community. Several years ago program personnel thought they would try the conjugal visiting room for the very inadequate person who has limited sexual contact, in the hope that the experience would be helpful. However, that stipulation wasn't made clear and as a result some of our swinging, wheeling-dealing rapists, who had no trouble making contact with women, were bringing in some new woman every weekend. As soon as the director got wind of it, he put a stop to the whole thing." In addition to the rooms for conjugal visits, each ward also contains a room, called the resident lounge, in which the men can masturbate in privacy.

The men may not carry more than $20 on their person at any one time. "They have accounts, but we set a limit on what they can carry with them. If they want to buy something for themselves or have money for their families, that is not a problem, but we don't want someone who manipulates others running around with a lot of money."

**Work Release Phase**  Once a person has completed all the steps of progress to the satisfaction of the group and the staff, he is eligible for work release. This step necessitates another court appearance. If the court concurs, the man is placed on probation and allowed to work or attend school in the community during the day and return to the hospital at night. Work (school) release lasts a minimum of three months. Each group develops steps of progress that apply to the work release phase. The men in work release are expected to participate in the evening group meetings on the ward. If they display behavioral difficulties in the community, then they may be pulled back into the inpatient program.

**Outpatient Phase**   When a person has demonstrated that he is able to adjust to his work and to the community, he is placed on outpatient status. This is the final phase of the program and lasts a minimum of eighteen months. As with the other phases, the men must complete certain steps of progress before they can be released from this phase. They are required to attend an outpatient meeting at the hospital each week (the number of meetings they attend per month decreases the longer they are on outpatient status) and if they are in couples group then they are expected to attend those meetings also. In addition, at least twice a week they have to be involved with people from their own group who are on work release or outpatient status. They are expected to work and live in the immediate vicinity. When the men are discharged from the Sex Offender Program, many continue to remain on probation for an additional year.

# STAFF TRAINING

Newly hired staff are initially assigned to another therapist, who helps them learn the policies, procedures, and routines and to whom they can take their questions. They are supervised by a senior therapist in the program. Additionally, they are given a copy of the therapy supervisor handbook, which describes procedures and policy. "We don't have that formal a training packet. We try to hire people who have adequate backgrounds so that all we have to do is acclimate them to the procedures and policies." The most preferred experiential background is one that includes both work with sex offenders and work with groups plus academic training in the behavioral sciences.

All staff receive ongoing in-service training which deals with current needs of the staff and the group. That might involve issues of planning, psychodynamics of the sex offender, or group observation. Most of the information is generated by the workers within the units themselves, but they also have two consultants who provide information.

The therapy supervisors are on a nonscheduled work week. The average day is from 8:30 to 4:30 or 5:00 P.M., but they are on call 24 hours a day. They also work in the evening once a week for couples group and once a month for outpatient group.

New workers earn one vacation day a month. They are permitted to take compensation time for their evening work. However, time release and compensation for conferences vary according to the state budget, and remuneration for attendance at conferences is not guaranteed.

## LINKING CLIENTS AND PROGRAM

Although this section will discuss each phase of the program, it will focus most heavily on the evaluation and inpatient phases of the treatment process. All referrals to the Sex Offender Program come through the courts; self-referrals are not possible. "At one point in the early developmental stages of the program," explained the program director, "there was an attempt to admit some voluntary people. But it turned out to be just absurd because the program is very intense and highly structured, so that if people could leave that's exactly what they did. Unless there is some kind of legal hold over the people we see, then they're going to opt to leave. It was principally on the basis of our experience that we stopped taking volunteers." Under Washington state law a person who has been convicted of committing a felonious sex offense, such as rape or indecent liberties, may be remanded to Western State Hospital for 90 days to ascertain whether he is a sexual psychopath, that is, whether he has a neurosis or a psychopathic personality which predisposes him to commit sexual offenses to the degree that would be a menace to the health or safety of others.

In addition to undergoing a psychiatric assessment and some psychological testing, the offender completes a very thorough social history with the therapy supervisor during the early part of the observation period. This social history, which is a combination of the person's account of his past and how he perceived his development plus other available reports and assessments, enables the therapist to form initial impressions of the newly admitted person and also to gain insight into the reasons for the exhibited behaviors as well as to determine future treatment needs. Figure 9.2 presents an outline of the social history.

As soon as the individual enters the hospital for the three-month observation period, he is immediately assigned to one of the ten guided self-help groups. No attempt is made to match the person to the group. Each person is placed in whichever group is at the top of rotation. "There has been some discussion from time to time that we do it differently," commented the program director, "but our experience has been that the combination of the more aggressive and the

SOCIAL HISTORY OUTLINE

Identifying Data:

Statement disclaiming confidentiality

Childhood Background (up to 12 years of age):

Place, date, and order of birth. Father and mother's age,
occupation, personality traits, special problems, and
relationship to patient. Others who have played special
role in rearing patient and their relationship. Siblings -
relationship. Family environmental situation and special
family problems, isolation, constant moves, etc. Special
illnesses.

Life Adjustments:

School achievement - intellectual attainments, adaptation
to teachers and playmates, social and sports participation,
dating patterns, truancy or delinquency

(Following to be placed in chronological order)

Work experience - special training, specific problems on
the job (being fired), relationship to employees and workers

Criminal record and admitted offenses; use of drugs and
alcohol; military background - rank, duties, AWOL, etc.;
violence

Religious affiliation, special problems, major changes in
lifestyle, medical problems, mental health involvement,
handling of personal problems, relationship to peers

Sexual and Marital History

Age at first introduction to sex, first sexual instruction
Age at first masturbation
Chronological record of sexual relations
Dating patterns
Age at marriage, length of courtship, relationship with
  spouse and children
Sexual adjustment - frequency of sex, sexual dysfunction,
  rigidity in sex
Reasons for divorce or separation, ability to form rela-
  tionships after separation
Problems - infidelity, jealousy, religion, etc.
Description of sexual deviancy, precipitations, factors,
  and development, type of victim, pattern (patient's
  version and police reports)

Significant People:

Important relationships (long term)

Resources:

Financial interests, property, skills or special abilities,
support of family or friends, goals

**Figure 9.2**

more passive personalities leads each to learn behaviors from the other. I think the more passive people learn that they can speak out, express themselves better, and in like kind the more aggressive offenders learn a less violent, less hurtful way of operating with other people."

During his stay, the offender is expected to admit why he was sent for observation and begin to discuss other deviant sexual behaviors he has committed. "We get all the material, such as the victim's statement and presentence report, from the prosecutor's office," explained a therapy supervisor. "If the men are not completely honest with us, then they are confronted with that material, so they are expected to take responsibility for what they've done and begin to elaborate beyond that. Additionally, we expect that they are going to involve themselves in the treatment process, begin to talk a bit, and participate in the ward work. Obviously, we don't expect them to be totally self-disclosing about everything they have ever done, but we do expect that they will tell us a fair amount of what they have done sexually. That really goes back to our premise that we can't treat someone who won't take the responsibility for his own behavior." The offender completes a 20-page biographical data sheet by the fourth day and writes a lengthy (approximately 80-page) autobiography by the fourteenth day of the evaluation period. Both documents are read and approved by the group. The data sheet asks for information about such things as the person's criminal and juvenile offense record, educational, employment, and armed services experiences, psychiatric history, home experiences, marital experiences, sexual experiences, and a self-evaluation of his personality. The autobiographical material is expected to go into great detail about the offender's background. The standard autobiography outline specifies:

- Write about your home life and environment, the people who were in the home as you grew progressively older.
- Give a brief description of living conditions, money situations, type of neighborhood.
- Describe the type of work your father (and mother) did.
- Start writing about the earliest memories of your life, progress to the age of 16, putting in everything including the feelings you can remember at the time of any and all incidents.
- Write about the most important incidents of your life after the age of 16. Be sure to include all sexual experiences, and crimes, acts of violence, vandalism or theft, etc. Be sure to write about the feelings during these incidents.

During the observation period the person is confined to the ward and is allowed no ground privileges. He is also assigned a "buddy" who helps to acclimate him to the program and ward policies and with whom he must be at all times. Observation members, under the direction of more senior group members, clean and maintain the program wards.

Toward the end of the 90-day observation the group evaluates whether the individual meets the criteria for remaining in the program, that is, he (1) is a sexual psychopath, (2) is not safe to be at large in the community, and (3) is amenable to treatment. The group members make formal written votes in which they describe for the therapy supervisor and the other members of the staff how they arrived at their decision. With that vote in mind, plus the other information that is available, the therapy supervisor makes a presentation to the staff with recommendations regarding the individual. Then the total staff makes its recommendation, which is processed on to the court. (See Figure 9.3.)

Cases in which the staff finds that the person is not amenable to treatment in the Sex Offender Program but should not be at large in the community present a difficult situation for the staff. "We try to work very hard with people during the 90-day observation period and to motivate them toward getting involved in the process. That is one of the reasons the self-help process works so well, because you've got about twenty people (in the group) working to convince the person that this is the way to go. But, if we find him not amenable for any number of reasons, such as he won't cooperate or he doesn't want anything to do with this place and would rather go to prison, then he is returned to the court. The judge makes the final decision and may impose the deferred prison sentence or place the person on probation."

If the court returns the man to the program, then he is reassigned to his original group, where he formally begins the program. The days are carefully structured to include both industrial and group therapy activities. Initially, work assignments are confined to the locked wards of the hospital. As the men progress in the program, work assignments are made to the other areas of the hospital, such as the kitchen.

The men also continue to work on the ten steps of progress. (See Figures 9.4a and 9.4b for examples of steps of progress that have been developed by two different peer groups in conjunction with the staff.) The steps involve teaching the individual some of the basics about himself, why he did what he did, his basic pattern of operation, how he got to the far end of the spectrum, e.g., taking the

---

**Profiles of Programs for Abusers**

Dear Judge Jackson,

   Mr. Daniel J was admitted to the Sex Offender Program at Western State Hospital on November 3, 1979, for a 90-day period of observation and evaluation to determine the existence of sexual psychopathy. Mr. J had pled guilty to the crime of indecent liberties on September 15, 1979. Deputy Prosecuting Attorney, Robert Williams, used this crime plus the evaluation done by Washington Valley Counseling and Psychiatric Services as the reasonable cause basis to file the petition for determination of sexual psychopathy per R.C.W. 71.06.020. In accordance with the statute we are reporting our findings and conclusions to the court regarding Mr. J.

   The committing offenses involved Mr. J molesting three minor females, ages 11, 9, and 8, during a one- to two-year period. Mr. J fondled the genital areas of the girls, committed oral sodomy, attempted sexual intercourse with one of the girls, masturbated in front of the girls, had the girls read pornography to him, and forced his son to simulate sexual activities with one of the girls. These victims were his nieces by marriage and the activities took place while he was baby-sitting with them.

   Upon admission to Western State Hospital, Mr. J began our standard evaluation process, which includes both assessment and treatment. Mr. J was evaluated by professional staff members concerning the psychiatric, psychological, social, and medical elements relative to his sexual offending. He remained on a locked ward where he was

With the exception of the program name, the names of all people and places mentioned in this letter were changed to maintain confidentiality.

**Figure 9.3   Assessment Letter**

continually observed as he participated in treatment with a functioning treatment group of committed sexual psychopaths. Their schedule includes approximately 25 hours of group psychotherapy each week, and following a patient's observation period his treatment group also gives their opinion to the staff relative to the question of sexual psychopathy. In addition to the data gathered from these standard procedures, we have obtained the routine prosecutory materials, including victim statements plus the evaluation done by Washington Valley Counseling Center, and a summary of Mr. J's Seattle State Hospital treatment. Our conclusions and recommendations result from combining the data from these various sources.

The primary evaluation questions addressed were: (1) does Mr. J meet the statutory definition of the sexual psychopath; (2) what type of risk does he currently present in terms of sexually reoffending; and (3) what treatment setting, if any, is best suited to help Mr. J.

The definition of the sexual psychopath, according to R.C.W. 71.06, states that this person "is affected in a form of psychoneurosis or in a form of psychopathic personality which form predisposes such person to the commission of sexual offenses in the degree constituting a menace to the health and safety of others." The Sex Offender Program feels that our responsibility for identifying the sexual psychopath is to discover those elements in a person's behavioral history and personality makeup which, in fact, predispose that person to sexual crimes. This prediction of future behavior is imprecise, but in our opinion the best single indicator of future dangerous

---

**Figure 9.3   Assessment Letter,** *continued*

sexual behavior is a clear history of past dangerous sexual behavior.

Mr. J has revealed a pattern of sexual deviancy beginning at approximately age 8. These acts include incest with a sibling, molesting both boys and girls while babysitting from age 9 until the present, bestiality as a child, plus being a sexual victim himself approximately twelve times when in the Seattle State Hospital. In the last several years, as the court knows, Mr. J has molested his nieces and he has also molested both his children. The only absolutely verifiable activities are those with the nieces. However, Mr. J's disclosures of these activities have come only through our standard processes of interviews and intensive group therapy sessions, and we have a high level of confidence in the ability of these procedures to bring forward the truth.

Mr. J's personality profile is that of a fearful, often depressed, and maladjusted person. His academic level is so low that he has been mistaken for retarded in spite of the fact that his tested IQ was in the normal range. Functioning in an unstable manner for most of his developing years, he became psychotic and dangerous when he was 19 and spent nearly nine months at Seattle State Hospital. Since that time he has been involved in various treatment programs on a nearly continuous basis. As an adult, he has been sexually confused and sexually retarded, and he suffers from chronic low self-esteem. Mr. J, as had been disclosed, began getting his sexual needs met from children at a very early age. As an adult he seems to relate better to children then he does to adults, and his position of

---

**Figure 9.3   Assessment Letter, *continued***

power over children has given him license to sexually exploit them. This has developed into a very powerful, compulsive pattern.

In summary, then, to go along with Mr. J's history of
dangerous sexual behavior, a study of his personality re-
veals serious disturbances and a very fragmented picture.
Thus, we believe he qualifies both behaviorally and psychologically to the R.C.W. 71.06 definition of the sexual
psychopath.

SAFETY TO BE AT LARGE:

The danger Mr. J presents to children, both other
children and his own, seems very great at the present time.
In addition to his multiple personality deficits, the support system in the community does not seem adequate for
the protection of children while Mr. J is present. As
reported by Mr. Davidson of Washington Valley Counseling
Service, Mr. J's wife did not feel his behaviors caused
any real damage and was not able to see the signs of child
abuse occurring before her; neither was the mother of the
children involved who is Mr. J's sister-in-law. Hopefully,
both of these individuals have been helped in their understanding of these matters; yet, in our experience, we have
found that chronic sex offenders can easily deceive and
manipulate even very conscientious spouses and others in
order to return to their offending. Although Mr. J feels
he can be treated in the community, we do not feel that he
could maintain himself, and we feel that he would wait for
others to allow him access to children and soon reoffend.

**Figure 9.3   Assessment Letter,** *continued*

AMENABILITY TO TREATMENT:

Mr. J has been observed for over two months in order
for us to evaluate the three main areas of amenability to
treatment in the Sex Offender Program, which are:  (1)
ability to learn and respond to our treatment approach,
(2) willingness to participate in treatment and willingness
to begin to modify his behavior, and (3) amount of progress
or change that has taken place over the period of evaluation.

As assessed by our staff psychologist, Mr. J has sufficient intellectual capacity to learn and respond to
treatment in the Sex Offender Program.  His low academic
ability will quite likely make his progress through treatment slow; however, it will not prohibit him from effectively learning what he needs to do to become a healthy
individual.  In addition, we have a schooling program
available so that Mr. J could upgrade his academic skills.

Mr. J has followed all of our rules and guidelines
and shows every willingness to continue to be a cooperative and hard-working member.  He has had to put out extra
effort in certain areas because of his inability to read
and write, and he has shown that he is willing to take
these extra steps.

The total amount of change that has occurred in Mr. J
has been encouraging.  The large amount of self-disclosure
is a very positive sign for future success.  His willingness to begin to examine his behaviors and his personality
has proven to be fruitful so far.  The two weak areas, thus
far, have been his limited observable expression of guilt
over his offending and his inability at this point to

**Figure 9.3  Assessment Letter, *continued***                           193

openly express his feelings on a consistent basis. We do not feel these problems are permanent nor do they seem insurmountable.

On February 3, 1980, the Sex Offender Program treatment staff reviewed Mr. J's case and determined the following specific conclusions and recommendations:

1. Mr. J does conform to the statutory definition of the sexual psychopath.
2. He has been assigned the diagnosis of: sexual deviation, pedophilia.
3. He is not safe to be at large.
4. He is amenable to treatment at Western State Hospital and we feel he should be recommitted for treatment in our specialized program for the sexual offender.

We hope our conclusions and recommendations have been helpful to the court in this matter. Should you have any questions concerning our report, please feel free to contact us. Mr. J's evaluation is now complete and he is available for transport at your convenience.

Sincerely,

Director
Sexual Offender Program

Clinical Director

**Figure 9.3   Assessment Letter,** *continued*

1st Step - WORK PAROLE

A. Honesty, effort, and concern.
B. Completion of autobiography, understanding of group words and on and off ward policies.
C. One in group therapy on outlet and image of a man.


2nd Step - 1 HOUR G.P. (Ground Privileges)

A. Be able to tell the difference between hurtful and selfish behaviors and responsible behaviors.
B. Be able to tie outlet into hurtful and selfish behaviors.
C. Trust group members and/or accept them or know why I don't.
D. Commitment to self, group, and society.
E. Know G.P. and association limits and boundaries.


3rd Step - 2 HOURS G.P.

A. 30-day log on recognition of behaviors and problems with feelings.
B. What is the cause, effect, and result of my behavior.
C. Definite knowledge of basic problem.


4th Step - 3 HOURS G.P. (ESCORT)

A. Definite knowledge of how G.P. ties into self-concept.
B. Knowledge of behavior pattern.
C. Demonstrate application of controls over deviant be-haviors, pattern and basic problem.
D. Definite knowledge of escort responsibilities.
E. Know and relate basic life pattern of each member in group (must have read each inpatient's autobiography).


5th Step - 5 HOURS G.P.

A. Honesty, effort, and concern.
B. Definite knowledge of modifying deviant behavior pat-tern, compensation in negative result.
C. Demonstrate application of stop signs.
D. Show progress in developing a realistic self-concept.
E. Explain how previous lifestyle relates to outlet pattern.


6th Step - 5 HOURS G.P.

A. Definite knowledge of inadequacies and how they tie into self-concept.
B. Definite knowledge of conflict structure and how it relates to feelings.
C. Definite knowledge of assertive behaviors (must read "When I Say No I Feel Guilty").
D. Further application of modifying deviant behaviors through assertion.

**Figure 9.4a   East Group Steps of Progress**                    195

## 7th Step - 6 HOURS G.P.

A. Show progress in developing a realistic self-concept.
B. Demonstrate ability to solve personal conflicts.
C. Demonstrate pattern of responsible resolving of conflicts.
D. Show modification of behaviors in previous lifestyle in relation to outlet pattern.

## 8th Step - 6 HOURS G.P.

A. Honesty, effort, and concern.
B. Definite knowledge of insecurities and how they tie into self-concept.
C. Definite knowledge of peer group structuring.
D. Definite knowledge of how person's stop signs tie into deviant behavior pattern (show good examples).
E. Show further development of assertive techniques.
F. Lay out autobiography in group.

## 9th Step - G.P. CLEAR (SENIOR STAFF)

A. Demonstrate realistic approach to peer group and tie into self-concept.
B. Demonstrate practical application of responsible reaction pattern to insecurities.
C. Demonstrate adjustment to a responsible sexual outlet.
D. Preliminary release plan based on positive and appropriate goals.
E. Has written a treatment autobiography and laid out in group.

## 10th Step - DISCHARGE TO WORK RELEASE

A. Review of discharge plan inpatient (with special emphasis on unexpected problem areas and how a person plans to cope with them).
B. Demonstrate how your present self-concept and nonhurtful pattern of behavior will work in various social settings.
C. Demonstrate positive self-presentation (show good example).
D. Present realistic short- and long-range goals for work release.
E. Questioning left open.

---

**Figure 9.4a   East Group Steps of Progress,** *continued*

STEP ONE

A. Must have completed biographical data sheet and written and oral autobiography.
B. Show a willingness to communicate both in and out of group.
C. Understanding of words, terms, ward, and group policies.
D. What is ECHO?

WORK PAROLE

A. Must lay out security and off ward policies.
B. Return from court for full-time treatment.
C. Hand vote by group and approval by therapist.

STEP TWO

A. Show an understanding of the hurtfulness of my outlet and tie in the lack of ECHO.
B. What are the four controls and how do they work?
C. Know the association limits and boundaries and the ground privilege boundaries and buildings I may enter for pleasure.
D. What are my goals group and program are helping me to obtain?
E. Must have read policies and know why they are important.

STEP THREE

A. Know my three main and related behaviors and know the seven main therapy questions.
B. Through examples how have I applied ECHO in getting my treatment?
C. What does it mean to be assertive and how does being assertive relate to the four controls?
D. Must have started reading autobiography (inpatient, work release, outpatient).

STEP FOUR

A. Must know escort responsibilities.
   1. Knowledge of program policies.    4. Group charge.
   2. Security of group.                5. Charge of quarters.
   3. Head count.                       6. Pop refrigerator.
   7. Responsible for all off ward activities and other responsibilities required by group.
   8. Must know emergency procedures.
B. Explain what I have learned about my outlet tieing my three main behaviors.
C. What is meant by the term basic problem?
D. Show where I have used the four controls in dealing with both positive and negative feelings in and out of group.
E. Explain how devious thinking leads to deviant behaviors.

STEP FIVE

A. Show ability to apply the four controls to interrupt my deviant behavior pattern.
B. Cite examples of how I have both recognized and communicated about my basic problem and show how it ties into my deviant behavior pattern.
C. What extra privileges and responsibilities come with this step?
D. Must have working knowledge of discharge contracts.
E. Must have completed reading all autobiographies (inpatient, work release, and outpatient).

**Figure 9.4b   Echo Group Steps of Progress**                    **197**

STEP SIX

A.  Explain what is meant by the term culture bearer and
    why this function is important to my therapy group.
B.  What stereotypes about men have I identified that I
    have applied to myself that have contributed to my
    deviant behaviors and how have I dealt with them?
C.  Explain specifically how I have dealt with my basic
    problem (through examples).

STEP SEVEN

A.  How is my present self-concept different from the one
    I had when I went to outlet and how did my previous
    self-concept contribute to my outlet and how is my
    now healthy self-concept going to help keep me out of
    my outlet.  (Written form.)
B.  Demonstrate a positive attitude toward social·inter-
    actions and how this attitude has appeared in my
    behavior.
C.  Demonstrate how I have passed down ECHO GROUP culture.
D.  What is a friend and how to make and maintain a friend?

STEP EIGHT

A.  What changes have occurred in my ability to relate
    to others and what changes have occurred in my
    feelings as a result?
B.  Who am I closest to and on what basis?
C.  Show adjustment to responsible outlets through examples.
    (Sexual and nonsexual.)
D.  Demonstrate how I have interrupted my outlet behaviors
    using the four controls and assertive behaviors.

STEP NINE

A.  Must have relaid out oral autobiography.
B.  Examples of how I have recognized questionable situa-
    tions and the stop signs I will use to stay out of
    them.
C.  Detailed outline identifying changes in my lifestyle
    essential to maintaining my nondeviant behaviors in
    the future, controls for hurtful behaviors, and apply
    controls in specific community interactions.
D.  What are the values changes I have made in treatment,
    both those I had to and wanted to make?
E.  Must have discharge contract based on positive and
    appropriate goals.

STEP TEN (LETTER TO COURT)

A.  Explain plans to maintain a healthy self-concept once
    I'm on work release and outpatient.
B.  What changes have I made while on inpatient (detailed
    review of treatment) and how have these changes pre-
    pared me for work release.
C.  Before requesting this step, review discharge contract
    (inpatient, total outpatient, and marriage group, if
    applicable).  Also present summary of Minnesota Multi-
    phasic Personality Inventory feedback and how it fits
    in my behavior.
D.  Must have sample authorized leave in preparation for
    return to court.

---

**Figure 9.4b   Echo Group Steps of Progress, *continued***

rejection at one point and ending up by molesting a child at another. "He learns some typical cues in his behavior at which he can intervene sooner and sooner to stop himself from marching down the road to his outlet." The emphasis in the first half of the progress steps is learning about himself and what goes on in his mind. "It is important to understand what goes on in the person's head because, as a group, sex offenders have spent a great deal of time with a fantasy life. They masturbate to deviant fantasies and reinforce their whole process that way. So we interrupt and attempt to teach them how to eliminate deviant masturbation fantasies and how to substitute appropriate sexual fantasies." During the second half of the progress steps the offender focuses on his self-concept and learns how to develop better social skills, become more assertive, and learn how to communicate better with others. "By the time they are midway through the steps, we are taking a look at what in their past lifestyle precipitated or assisted in creating the problem for them, and then we begin to help them restructure how they will live in the future to prevent it. We do a lot of interfering and restructuring of people's lives, their jobs, or whatever they may need to change to prevent them from going back to their former sexual outlets. And, we let them know that early on. Obviously, if someone is a child molester, then he is not going to be a janitor in the local grade school. So we do interfere. If someone has molested kids, we let him know that part of his discharge contract is going to be that he cannot date women who have children. We try to create a high level of anxiety in people relative to their outlets and outlet objects. Even here on the wards when families visit on the weekends, the child molester is not allowed open socialization with children. They need to withdraw and not become overinvolved with kids so that we teach them right here on the ward that withdrawal is the first line of defense in dealing with children. They need to develop constructive relationships with adults rather than resorting to children."

The group decides when the person has satisfied the requirements for each step of progress. The individual makes a formal request in group, which is voted on and then presented to the therapist for final approval. Each completed step brings with it some desirable reward in the form of a certain amount of ground release time. At the initial steps, ground privileges cannot be taken alone. The men leave the ward in groups of four. At least one of that group is a person who has reached the fourth step and is allowed to perform escort service. The escort takes responsibility for the other three. All ground privileges take place on the hospital grounds. During the last 30 days of their inpatient stay, after final staff review, they are allowed to walk around the hospital grounds unescorted.

"In addition to the overall treatment objectives and steps of progress, each individual identifies specific behaviors that he himself needs to change. These behaviors are worked with and tied into the group's steps of progress. The treatment group and staff assist the individual in identifying those things within his life that support and reinforce his deviant acting out. It is imperative that these elements be identified early because they may require significant changes that affect the way the individual will operate in the future. For example, if he is an alcoholic or problem drinker, he must plan never to drink again. If his particular occupation or employment has created problems, he must be prepared to seek other employment. If he has molested children, either in his home or elsewhere, he must be prepared for some very specific controls relative to his interaction with children for the rest of his life." The steps of progress address the two main issues that must be resolved during the program: learning to control oneself and restructuring the individual. The men can learn to stop the sexual offending, but if there is nothing to substitute in its place, then there has not been the restructuring that will prevent their return to the former patterns.

Sexual needs are dealt with via conjugal visits and masturbation. Conjugal visitations are available once or twice a week to couples who have participated in the couples group for at least two or three months. All men are permitted to use the resident lounge for masturbation.

Because so many sex offenders are psychological isolates, several aspects of treatment are designed to break into the "loner" style of the offender. "He has little or no time to himself and is constantly involved in sharing with his peers. He is forced to live, work, sleep, attend therapy, and be involved socially with the fifteen to eighteen members of his group as well as other groups that may be housed on the ward. Confrontation is used to deal with behavior on a day-to-day basis so the individual is unable to retreat either from his own behavior or the behavior of others. If he refuses to deal with inappropriate behavior that he sees in another group member, he will undoubtedly be confronted for condoning the behavior."

Confrontation is the technique most used by the members of the peer group. It is a way of calling attention to a person's behavior and making him take responsibility for his actions. Unlike the brutal confrontations used by some counseling programs, the peer group members use a form of supportive confrontation. For example, "When I said 'Hello' to you this morning you didn't return my greeting. What was going on with you then? Were you angry at me?" Sometimes it is a stronger confrontation such as, "Why were you late to the meeting?" or "Stop yelling at Joe!" Confrontations are made in good faith and out of concern for the other person. Group members avoid sarcasm and, when they see something in the person's behavior they like, they are quick to compliment that person. However, they make no attempt to soft-pedal or water down the statements they make to each other. Each person is required to carry a notebook to log the confrontations he receives, and these are read at the group meetings daily.

The therapy supervisor plays a special role in relation to the group. "The therapist really does not do therapy in the classical sense. The responsibility of the therapist in this program is to teach, to guide the group so that they do the counseling with each other; to help them develop the needed structure, process, and treatment plans; and to approve or disapprove of what they are doing. Essentially, the therapist's client is the group, and if the group remains healthy then the members can give one another treatment."

The therapist determines the boundaries within which group decisions can be made. "We attempt to be relatively subtle, but at the same time they know clearly that the therapist is the final authority, that anything that happens is subject to the therapist's say. At times we interfere directly with what the group is doing, if their plans are not appropriate, and redirect their planning. There is a real team or partnership process that goes on between the therapist and the group. The better functioning the group, the less the staff member has to interfere."

The therapy supervisor promotes a therapeutic culture which sets appropriate limits while encouraging behavioral and feeling changes. "The relationship between the sex offender and the therapist is like that between the adolescent and the parent in that he will frequently test limits to be sure they are there. However, indirectly the group pays much attention to the way the therapist behaves, and groups frequently take on the characteristics and behavior of the therapist. It is important that the group learn from the therapist how a healthy, normal, responsible human being behaves. Be the therapists men or women, it is important that they are secure enough within themselves that they do not reinforce the strong stereotypes that the offenders bring to treatment with them. Often it is clear that the sex offender is a gross exaggeration of what he believes to be manliness. Much of his unproductive behavior has been an attempt to live up to what he believes to be masculinity. Presenting the group with a model of an integrated person, accepting of oneself, is one of the more important functions of the therapy supervisor."

When the group meets, the members discuss issues of personal and group concern. They discuss behaviors and experiences of the various members, new confrontations, identified problem areas, program format and policies, and topics of special interest. Group members are expected to give their full attention to the issues discussed at the meetings. They are not allowed to eat or smoke during the sessions. They are also expected to make periodic layouts (talk to the group) around their thoughts or plans or sexual feelings. One member, for instance, may be asked to lay out his fantasies, goals, or anxieties, which are then discussed by the whole group with suggestions given for changing or maintaining certain behaviors. Special attention is given to helping group members deal with thoughts and feelings about their sexual outlets (the targets of their sexual release). Each man is expected to talk fully about his sexual outlet. He is taught to take action toward changing his behaviors around his sexual outlet. For example, he may be told to stop masturbating when fantasizing about the outlet, to disclose to the group when he has not successfully done so, and to talk about the process leading up to masturbation.

Many times the group members discuss aspects of the program to determine whether changes are needed. For example, one group discussed the amount of time available for recreation to decide whether there was a need for extra recreation time during periods of stress or whether it should remain at four hours each week. No matter what issue comes up for discussion, it is treated seriously and is resolved by a group vote. Some groups have developed their own "Bill of Rights" concerning member participation. One such document states:

1. In every respect, each member has the same rights.
2. There will be no segregation or discrimination.
3. All members have the same right to be themselves within the limits of the program values.
4. Each member has the same right to speak openly without fear of reprisal.
5. Each member has the right to be free of intimidation or coercion.
6. Each member has the right to confront questionable situations or conduct at any time or place without the fear of reprisal.

---

7. Each group member has the right to protest any action or decision to the total group or staff.

Sometimes a group member will ask for a meeting to be called around a special area of concern. As an example, one meeting focused on suicide. Some incident on the outside had triggered the subject for one group member and he asked for a special meeting so that the whole group could talk about their own experiences and feelings regarding that topic.

As the men complete the inpatient phase, they direct their thinking to the development of goals in the work release and outpatient portions of the program. Each of those phases requires the successful negotiation of additional steps of progress, the attainment of which continues to be determined by the group and the therapy supervisor. The steps of progress in this phase might include demonstrating effort toward obtaining employment, applying controls to their behavior in social situations, interacting responsibly with other members of the program who are in the work release and outpatient phases, and establishing financial stability. Figure 9.5 illustrates the steps of progress developed by one of the groups. Prior to leaving inpatient status, the offender drafts a contract with the group and the therapy supervisor which he must fulfill during the work release and outpatient phases of the program. The contract specifies behaviors, whom they can see, what they must continue to do in their group (see Figure 9.6). "Some groups begin to think that the end of inpatient is the end of the program, but we believe a person is only half done when he leaves the intensive treatment setting."

Because the program does not offer the men vocational rehabilitation, they must locate their own jobs just as any other person might by going to the employment office, perusing the want ads, or using whatever connections they might have. They must find work within the county where the hospital is located. The majority find work within three weeks of the time they are discharged to work release.

Transfer to work release status requires another court appearance, in which the judge places the offender on probation. During their time on work release (and the subsequent outpatient phase) offenders are jointly supervised by the therapy supervisor and probation officers who work exclusively with the Sex Offender Program.

When a person has demonstrated a satisfactory adjustment both in his work and in the community, he is placed on outpatient status. As with the other phases, the men must complete certain steps of progress before they can be released from the program. These steps include maintaining commitments, demonstrating responsible choice

EAST GROUP STEP OF PROGRESS FOR WORK RELEASE AND OUTPATIENT

STEP 1: To be accomplished during the first thirty (30) days.
    A. Show application of controls in various settings.
    B. Demonstrate initiative in developing a socially acceptable behavior pattern.
    C. Definite time of involvement with outpatient.
    D. Accurate log turned in for work and business A.B.'s.

STEP 2: To be accomplished during the second month.
    A. Show progress in developing responsible social adaptation.
    B. Show control or application of control for outlet pattern.
    C. Questioning left open.

STEP 3: To be accomplished during the third month.
Part 1: Requested through work release.
    A. Show financial stability, be able to show evidence of same.
    B. Show positivie proof of established residence.
    C. Outpatient commitments.
    D. Show development of responsible lifestyle.

Part 2: Requested through total outpatient.
    A. Outpatient commitments.
    B. Questioning left open.

STEP 4: Minimum of six (6) months outpatient, out one (1) meeting.
    A. Demonstrate how present self-concept keeps self out of outlet.
    B. Further progress in maintaining a responsible behavior pattern around self.
    C. Outpatient commitments.
    D. Questioning left open.

STEP 5: Minimum of (9) months outpatient, out two (2) meetings.
    A. Show further progress in strengthening a realistic self-concept.
    B. Show development of a secondary support system.
    C. Outpatient commitments.
    D. Questioning left open.

STEP 6: Minimum of twelve (12) months outpatient, out three (3) meetings.
    A. Definite application of a responsible lifestyle.
    B. Show further progress in development of a secondary support system.
    C. Present a realistic plan in preparation for discharge.
    D. Outpatient commitments.
    E. Questioning left open.

STEP 7: Discharge from outpatient.
    A. Show how present self-concept reinforces behavior pattern.
    B. Show modification through comparison of discharge categories in relation to past and current lifestyles.
    C. Present short- and long-range goals to continue responsible lifestyle to stay out of outlet.
    D. Questioning left open.

**Figure 9.5**

TREATMENT CENTER FOR THE SEXUAL OFFENDER

DISCHARGE CONTRACT

NAME _____ GROUP  East  DATE COMPLETED  9/6/79
                                                             -

INSTRUCTIONS:  To be filled out in triplicate and submitted to
inpatient groups, oupatient group, marriage group, and therapy
supervisor prior to discharge request and appearance before senior
staff.

WORK RELEASE   min. 3  MONTHS

EMPLOYMENT    USUAL TRADE   Drafting, Carpentry, Laborer

Describe your plans:  Will look for work in drafting or carpentry in

the Tacoma area.

RESIDENCE AFTER WORK RELEASE

Address _____ Phone _____

Name and relationship of person(s) you will be living with: _____

_____

EDUCATION OR TRAINING PLANS  Will look into continuing education at a

community college or vocational school in a technical field.

SOCIAL AND RECREATIONAL PLANS  Back packing, scuba diving, camping,

falconry, archery and other outdoor activities.

CONTINUED THERAPY PLANS

Outpatient   min. 18 months

Marital  Will attend marriage group if I establish a committed rela-

tionship

Other  Will be involved with W/R & O/P at least twice a week, one to

be initiated.

SPECIAL CONDITIONS  Will not hitchhike or pick up hitchhikers.  Will

not drive around without a destination or long distances alone at

**Figure 9.6**

night.  Will not drink or go places where alcohol is the specialty, i.e., taverns, lounges, etc.  Will not use drugs other than those prescribed for me by a doctor.  Will not associate with minor females unless otherwise approved by group.  Will not date women with minor female children.

PROGRAM DECISION

|  | APPROVED | DATE | SIGNATURES | COMMENTS |
|---|---|---|---|---|
| Inpatient |  |  |  |  |
| Outpatient |  |  |  |  |
| Marriage Group |  |  |  |  |
| Staff |  |  |  |  |

**Figure 9.6,** *continued*

of sexual outlet, becoming integrated within the community, and developing a secondary support system.

In addition to attending weekly group meetings at the hospital, the men must be involved twice a week with people from their own group who are on work release or outpatient status. These meetings are social: for example they may go out to dinner or invite a person to their home and just talk about what has been going on during the week. The social contact is vital. "They absolutely have to maintain involvement with their peers," said the program director. "Two visits during the week are minimum. If the outpatient group contains five or six people, we would expect that each person would be seeing four or five people during the week. The group becomes a family for the individual, and outpatient is the extension of that. The connectedness has to continue in the community. In fact, those men who begin to drop away from it invariably are the people who have trouble."

The men are required to introduce their friends from the program to people whom they meet and are required to tell the women whom they date about their involvement in the program. Part of their discharge contract stipulates that if a man becomes involved in a committed relationship with a woman, then they must both attend the weekly couples meetings. He is also expected to introduce the woman to his fellow outpatients. "Getting into that whole hiding, devious business is probably the worse thing that can happen with a sex offender, so we just build in conditions all over the place and it becomes a matter of course that if they become good friends with someone that person will know who they are and what they are about."

The men are not able to leave the immediate geographic vicinity. "Over time we have found it particularly crucial that the individual not be allowed to move out of the sphere of influence too early. The first six or eight months of outpatient are absolutely essential in assisting his readjustment to the community. Very often old lifestyle patterns recur. Unless he is under the scrutiny of both his therapy group and his peers in the community, he can fall too quickly. If he withdraws from his system of support and controls too soon, he will more than likely reoffend." Only after they have demonstrated that they are capable of behaving in accordance with the program goals are the men discharged.

# CASE EXAMPLE

**Intake**   Mr. John S is a 40-year-old white male charged with First Degree Statutory Rape of his 8-year-old stepdaughter.

Mr. S was raised in a Midwestern city as one of six children. His parents divorced when he was 12. He learned that his father had been involved in an incestuous relationship with one of the daughters. Mr. S felt that his mother favored his sisters and protected them more. He describes himself as a loner both at home and at school. As a juvenile he experienced some legal difficulties when he broke into a hardware store, and he was placed on probation. During his preadolescent and teenage years he was involved in fights off and on and ran away from home. When the parents divorced, the children were placed in foster homes. He was returned to the mother's home when he was 14 but became very upset to find her living with someone else. As a result he broke into another store in hope of being picked up and sent back to a foster home he had liked. Instead, he was sent to a school for boys for eighteen months. At age 16 he returned home again. His mother had remarried. He did not like his stepfather and was in constant conflict with him. He quit school and joined the Army, where he spent 22 years until he was retired with an honorable discharge. However, he did not attain a high rank because he was busted many times as a result of difficulty in getting along with superior officers.

Mr. S married at age 19. The marriage lasted for twelve years and produced three children who currently reside with the mother. A year after his divorce he married again, and this union lasted for seven years. His present wife, whom he married two years ago, is not sure she wants to stay with him. She has talked about divorce but has done nothing definite at this point.

Mr. S's first sexual experience occurred with his sister when he was 6 and she was 10. She asked him to have sex with her. They had sexual contact periodically until he was 8. He later learned that her interest in sex was the direct result of the incestuous relationship with his father. He also had sex with a younger sister when he was 10 and she was age 6. Later, while in a foster home, he had a homosexual experience with a younger boy who lived there. When he was in his early 30's his first outlet occurred, a young girl of 8 or 9 who lived nearby. He states that she approached him for sex because she had had sex with a number of older boys in the neighborhood. The encounter consisted of mutual fondling and mutual oral sex. Although he did not continue the relationship with this girl, he was involved in peeping and wandering around the neighborhood looking for young girls he could watch. He began a relationship with his stepdaughter when she was 7 while he was living with his present wife. He managed to manipulate her into oral sex and had encounters with her several times for three months. Then one of the child's friends told her mother, who in turn told Mr. S's wife. Mr. S went for psychiatric treatment and was released as "okay" three months later. A short while later the incidents with the stepdaughter resumed and continued until the child told her mother and Mr. S was then turned in to the authorities.

**Observation and Evaluation Phase**  Since his admission John has gone through a number of changes in relationship to the program. Early on he seemed to realize that he needed help and began to express that he needed to be here. He has struggled a great deal with his relationship with his wife, but she has agreed to stay with him as long as he receives treatment. At his evaluation his treatment group voted that he should continue in the program. He will more than likely have some difficulty in the program because the therapy supervisor is a woman. He is very resentful of women as a group and feels that women have had far too much control over his life. In addition, he resents other people's pointing things out to him and attempts to put them off by projections and snide remarks. In the past he has been given to striking out at people when he resents what they do.

## Inpatient Phase

*6-75:* John returned to court and was recommended for full-time treatment. In addition to daily group therapy, he and his wife have begun attending marriage group. One session was especially intensive for him. His wife began talking about her feelings of hurt because of his outlet. He became angry and attempted to lead her from the room. He felt he had managed to bury the outlet by not talking about her and he did not want it brought back up. In the ensuing marriage groups he seems to be comfortable and less upset by feelings that may be expressed in the group. He has started work assignments off the ward, seems to enjoy them, and does them well. He is becoming more open and less defensive in group. He still does not talk enough about his outlet and suppresses feelings. These are areas he will need to work on in the future.

*1-76:* Since the last report John has continued to participate in at least 25 hours of group therapy each week plus attend marriage group. He has stepped forward as being quite interested in making sure the group stays on the straight and narrow. He attained the second step of progress. He requested a visit with his outlet victim (his stepdaughter) with his wife present. The visit went well and John handled the situation appropriately. However, it was very anxiety-provoking for him and he spent some time in the group afterwards talking about the feelings he had when he saw her. His stepdaughter visits on one day of the weekend, always with supervision by the mother, and John is establishing a better relationship with her. Two months ago John went up for his third step of progress but was unable to complete the layout. This caused him a good deal of disappointment. Later that month he made a layout regarding the arousal he felt by another group member's daughter. Apparently he had begun to recognize desires for the young girl three weeks before but did not lay them out to anyone until it began to cause him considerable discomfort. Part of his pattern has been to believe that if you don't talk about things they will go away. He again attempted his third step of progress but stopped himself halfway through his layout because he was speeding, was not able to answer questions put to him by the group, and did not feel comfortable continuing with the step. During the past month he has, with some regularity, made a weekly layout on recognitions and desires including a layout about sexual contacts with his oldest son in 1969 as well as outlet with a dog. John and his wife continue to attend the marriage group and work on their problems. In general, John has shown progress in that his sarcasm has decreased, as has his tendency to project hostility and intimidate. However, a few days ago he did have a blowup in group. He was being confronted about a situation and was called a liar by another group member. John verbally intimidated the person by saying, "If you call me a liar again, I'll flatten you." He was confronted by another group member, immediately straightened himself up, and was no longer intimidating. He was grounded on the ward as a result of that behavior. Later, in group meeting, he apologized for the outburst and explained his situation and where he was coming from. The group accepted his apology.

6-76: John continues to participate in group therapy and marriage group. He has continued to lay out his recognitions and desires, especially about any minors that come on the ward. He has gotten in touch with how his outlet has been hurtful to his stepdaughter and describes himself, at times, as feeling dead inside. His relationship with his wife seems to be improving. Their communication is more open with one another and they seem to enjoy each other sexually. They have been given the assignment of writing down how a man and a woman are supposed to behave and how that relates to the way in which they interact with one another. John received his third step of progress and six weeks later the group approved his fourth step of progress. A few weeks later he was voted into leadership by the group. He accepted the responsibility, although he protested that he did not want it. The position of leadership has triggered his former "Army sergeant" image, in terms of needing to be in control of things, and he is having to work this through. He has not made any layouts about the leadership situation and was confronted about it. He was also confronted for not arranging to get job reports. During the last month he has had significant problems in leadership. On several occasions he asked to be relieved of the position. Despite his own feelings about leadership, the group members think he is doing a good job. A major problem did arise a few weekends ago concerning the adequate supervision of his stepdaughter. On visiting day the girl wandered down the hall to play catch with another group member. She was unattended and out of sight of either parent. When the confrontation was brought into group the next day, John became quite angry and came close to walking out of group. However, he did gain control of himself and has been dealing with the issue. We spent time dealing with the issue at the couples group meetings, identifying how it had occurred and why John and Mrs. S were not managing their responsibilities as they should have.

*1-77:* Problems in leadership continued. John and his co-leader were not communicating well. John gave inaccurate information at policy meeting, was uninformed on a few issues, and tried to lie his way out of the situation. He was confronted heavily and as a result of this and other problems in the group, the group was grounded for three weeks. He and his wife had a major confrontation at couples group because he had neglected to inform her about the grounding. When she arrived early, so the two could visit together before the meeting, she was asked to leave the ward because John was not allowed visitors prior to the meeting while he was grounded. She felt this was a repeat of his old behavior of not caring about her and once again brought up the issue of terminating the marriage. John was reevaluated by the group and, after a split vote, was retained at step 4. He was not placed back on leadership because it was felt he needed to work on other issues. However, he was informed that he would be expected to go back into leadership at another time and handle it better than he had this time. The group developed a treatment plan for John that involved modified fifth step requirements, particularly around demonstrating definite knowledge of modifying deviant behavior patterns and the application of stop signs. They also expected he would complete two layouts per week. Mr. S has been working well with the treatment plan. In couples group he discussed with Mrs. S how fearful he is about the stepdaughter and how he will handle the situation when he returns to the home in the future. He requested that his stepdaughter no longer visit him until he has time to resolve his fears.

*6-77:* John's industrial therapy assignment has involved being a member of the Escort Team and he has experienced some feelings about it which he has shared with the group. Two months ago he went up, and was approved, for his fifth step of progress. Last month he was placed in leadership again. At this time he seems to be handling the responsibility much better. While leadership is not something he relishes, his feedback to policy meeting has been accurate and he has been working with the other leader to keep their communication open so the group functions better. At times he almost seems to be enjoying himself. He has a position of responsibility in the group and others look to him for information.

*1-78:* He came out of leadership during this period and felt very positive about the experience. There had been a several-month lag since he went up for his last step of progress, but when he finally went up for his sixth step the group turned him down. He was angry about the turn-down but was able to get on with planning to go up for the step again. Two months later his attempt was successful and he is now at the sixth step. His relationship with his wife continues on the upswing. At times he voices feelings of insecurity about re-entry into the home; however, visits with his stepdaughter have resumed without major incident. John's industrial therapy assignment was upgraded to Group Charge. He is responsible for monitoring group activity during the day and for supervising the men who are on observation status. He has been struggling with the Group Charge position both in terms of organizing the work and dealing with some of the observation members who are somewhat rebellious. On a few occasions he found himself becoming verbally intimidating with them and had to back off and walk away from them. He has brought the problem into group for help and seems to be trying to work it through. However, John set very high expectations for himself and was disappointed in his performance as Group Charge. The position has forced him to come to grips with frustrating situations and work through rather than suppressing his feelings and then letting them seethe.

6-78: A situation between John and his stepdaughter occurred. He was confronted for having her stand next to him with his arm around her. John maintained he was not thinking about the consequences of what he was doing and wanted to give her some additional attention. Later, he admitted that while he had not been using the behavior to groom her, it had not been appropriate and that as a family they were going to have to meet and discuss proper father–daughter be-havior. Mrs. S was quite concerned with her own lack of awareness around this issue and is working in concert with her husband to make the situation more appropriate for the girl. Mr. S's functioning in group has lessened and he has not participated as actively as he has in the past. There had been some problem between him and his wife because of the delays in running his next step of progress. How-ever, when he did go up for the seventh step it was approved and the following month was a positive period for John. He was very enthusi-astic about the prospect of his wife's locating a home nearby. Mrs. S has expressed a lot of frustration about the commuting distance in-volved to visit her husband. She recently became quite angry be-cause she arrived for a visiting day and John had group commitments that prevented them from spending all the time with each other.

*1-79:* John spent a month laying out his autobiography in anticipation of moving toward his eighth step of progress. He ran his step successfully and he continued to show high motivation. He is looking toward work release and outpatient status in the near future and has already placed his name on the board to have his ninth step of progress run. Apparently there are no special problems in his relationship with his wife, but he does seem to depend on the couples group to lay out the status of their relationship. Mrs. S is beginning to raise issues about the adaptive changes that will be necessary when John returns to the home. They both understand and accept that John cannot be home alone with his stepdaughter, who is his outlet victim. Even though he handles his group responsibilities, John's involvement with younger members has been down and his overall participation in group has also decreased. John expressed much frustration because of the amount of business the group had to take care of which prevented them from allowing him to run his ninth step. His feelings were intensified because of pressure he was receiving from his wife to complete the necessary steps so that he can be placed on outpatient status. Twice he went before the group to run his ninth step of progress and both times they turned him down because he failed to adequately address the section on his contract regarding alcohol use. He was angry and sullen when his step was not approved, but he controlled his feelings and again pursued the information he needed to run the step a third time. This time he was successful.

*6-79:* During this period John was presented to treatment staff for Ground Parole Clear. The request was held in abeyance until a graduated reentry plan was developed for return into the home. Approval for GP Clear was further delayed because his group was grounded and all steps were frozen until the grounding was completed. John handled the frustration well and was able to assist the group in accomplishing its goals. When his request was reconsidered, it was approved and John is now at the tenth step of progress. John has been dealing with the issues of integration into the home and the potential problems of relating to his stepdaughter in an appropriate way. The child has many problems and individual psychotherapy does not appear to have been too helpful. Recently, the child has been experiencing gastrointestinal problems and John is convinced that his pending work release may be contributing. Mrs. S has leased a house and is quite anxious for John to obtain work release in spite of the problems it will generate on the home scene, especially with her daughter.

*1-80:* The staff recommended John for work release, and at his court appearance the judge granted the request. He obtained work with a construction company within two weeks of his release. A month later he was laid off but managed to find a job as general laborer almost immediately. Both Mr. and Mrs. S were excited about the opportunities they would have to spend time together alone in their home during John's authorized leaves from the hospital. They continued to be actively involved in couples group. Four months after being placed on work release John obtained his second step of work release, which made him eligible for weekends at home. However, he lost the privilege of spending the first weekend at home because he violated the reentry plan that had been established earlier by spending too many evenings at home when his stepdaughter was there. Mr. S continued to have some difficulties working with his deviant sexual desires. Often, on his way to work he passed the same two minor girls who were standing near a corner waiting for a bus. He received a heavy confrontation from the group around his reluctance to change his route to work. He reacted very defensively at first but eventually agreed to change the route. Toward the end of this period Mr. S attempted to run his third step of work release, which would have been the last step prior to outpatient status. The step was called off because John could not remember the requirements of the step. Also his authorized leaves for one weekend were turned down because he violated a group agreement that he not sign a contract for over $50 without the group's permission. Against his wife's wishes and without the group's consent, John had obligated himself to $500 of indebtedness for furniture. For a few days, consideration was given to pulling him off work release, but he settled down and has begun to deal with the bad decisions he has made. It was decided that John would have to demonstrate a minimum of 30 days of responsible decision making before he could be considered for his next step of progress.

*6-80:* Mr. S was at a loss about how to control his stepdaughter's aggressive behavior. The girl surfaces a lot of the family's problems and has been scapegoated by Mr. and Mrs. S. The S's informed their community psychotherapist about the problem so the couple could more intensively work on this issue. Mr. S has been managing his personal affairs more responsibly. His behavior stabilized over a two-month period and his request for outpatient status was approved.

Shortly afterwards, the stepdaughter went to stay with her natural father temporarily while the S's worked on the problems that caused the need to scapegoat the child. Currently, Mr. and Mrs. S seem to be handling their conflicts very responsibly. Mr. S has been closely observed by the other outpatients in his group and maintains contact with the inpatients. As long as the stability he is now experiencing in his lifestyle continues, he should have little difficulty progressing through the remaining steps of outpatient status.

## TREATMENT ISSUES

Most people in the helping professions expect to deal with issues of client manipulation and limit testing at some points during the therapeutic process. Within the sex offender program, those issues are constant. According to one of the therapists, "Our people are fairly manipulative in their transactions with the rest of the world. They are always testing limits and trying to bend the rules in some way." Many times it is over something very minor such as how many cups of coffee they can have at a given time or smoking in a restricted area. Sometimes they use manipulation to mask underlying feelings of insecurity and inadequacy. "You'll see it even in the way the group votes. They are clearly testing the therapists. They need to feel that those limits are there and they can bounce off of them. Part of the whole treatment process for them is learning to work with the fact that you can't always have what you want and can't always be immediately gratified." Some of the manipulation is related to the inpatient status and forced participation in the program. "I think it is fair to say that no one wants to be here, given the choice," said a therapy supervisor, "so I think that part of the manipulation is geared toward getting out of here as rapidly as possible. They may become very ingratiating. They have their own agendas. Some prefer to be here instead of prison and will put in a year or two in our program, even though they are not fully invested in it, with the hope that the courts will consider their stay here as equivalent to a completed jail sentence." People who work in this setting for any length of time develop a healthy skepticism toward client motivations. The group process sometimes helps to counteract the manipulations. Because everything happens in the presence of others, there is less opportunity for one group member to say, "Well, my therapist said I don't have to do that any more."

An adjunct to the limit setting is the placement of every newly entering person into the group that happens to be at the top of rotation. Once people are placed in a peer group, they are not permitted to change to another group even if personality clashes develop among some of the group members. The director acknowledges that some problems might arise because of the arbitrary placement but foresees even greater problems if the offenders were given options. "We would have our people playing musical groups. They would find a reason to change every time they didn't like the color of somebody's eyes. But life is full of potential personality conflicts with their bosses or their wives, so part of the process here is adjusting and learning to deal with whomever happens to be in their immediate group."

Skill training in sexual areas is one aspect of the program that the staff feels should be dealt with more than they are able to in the current program. Presently, the men are taught how to substitute for deviant sexual fantasies more socially acceptable ones. They are encouraged to use the more acceptable fantasies when they masturbate. Some of the men do not exhibit any sexual dysfunctioning. Others, perhaps in the context of their marriages, may have been ejaculating prematurely or had difficulty maintaining an erection or experienced a temporary dysfunction with their wives during the time the men were involved with their daughters. The most difficult offenders to work with are those who have had no sexual experiences with adults or are dysfunctional with any adult female. It is hard to help a person structure his sexual fantasies when he has had no sexual experience with an adult and may not even have had sexual desires for a peer partner. Those who have had inadequate or unpleasant experiences with women at least have the beginning of a fantasy which can be more fully developed. Each therapist provides sex education for his or her group as needed. For the single offender, sexual dysfunction can be approached only through masturbation and developing appropriate fantasies. Married men can be assisted more directly because they are allowed conjugal visitations. Volunteers from the community assist through role playing and psychodrama to help the men learn more appropriate social skills.

Both qualified males and females are hired as therapy supervisors. Having a female therapist can alter the functioning of the group initially. "My experience is that the men frequently have to come to grips immediately and directly with some aspects of male–female relationships they have difficulty with. The rapist, for example, has difficulty with women in authority, and, as a therapist, you are automatically in that role. I think the men have some pretty solid stereotypes of how women should behave, so it is important that the female therapist does not reinforce those stereotypes. Someone who is very fluffy and flirtatious would be counterproductive to our aims, but the woman who is an assertive person and who has come to grips with herself and what she wants in life is an extremely valuable person in our program because it forces the men to deal with a lot of their own insecurities. When I first began to work here, the group wasn't as concerned about talking about their offenses in front of me as they were about whether they had to clean up their language. That was the subject of a rather lengthy discussion.

Some therapists find that one of the most difficult aspects of the job is resolving the conflict of being in a position of providing treatment and establishing a therapeutic relationship and at the same time being constantly reminded of the behavior that brought people to the facility in the first place. Said one therapist: "I deal with human tragedy, not necessarily from what the men bring us themselves, although their lives are often tragic, but from the kind of things they do to get here. I had one fellow who was admitted to my unit who did an absolutely horrible thing. After I read the victim's statement, I could not interview him immediately because I had such ill feelings about him. There is no way you can be exposed to that kind of information and not personalize it to the loved ones in your own life. I have sometimes, in my mind, put the faces of people I know on some of the victims I have read about. In this job you can't distance yourself from it because you have to deal with it day in and day out."

Groups tend to take on the qualities of their leaders. At some level, the groups' actions are the therapists' actions. Sometimes the sense of responsibility is overwhelming. "You have to decide who is the patient. Is it the person who is here, or is it the community, or is it the victim? I spend a tremendous amount of time agonizing over whether or not these guys, as they terminate the program and move toward reentry into the community, are safe or whether they are going to hurt someone else. If they reoffend and hurt someone else, then I feel a part of that. After all, we have the power to hold them here. I know of patients who, after release, have hurt someone. The staff people who had supervised those cases go through a lot of guilt over what occurred. I don't think there is any way one can escape that, especially if you believe in things like modeling and social learning."

# ADMINISTRATIVE ISSUES

**Funding**   Programs always need additional funds to add greater depth and quality to the services provided, and the Sex Offender Program is no exception. However, because it is part of Western State Hospital's budget, ongoing funding for the $300,000 a year program is not a major issue. The problem comes in convincing the funders that the program needs additional monies to conduct research and to add equipment. The program director would like to add a behavioral research laboratory because it is difficult to provide individual behavior work in a group setting. "We'd also like to develop some modular work with sex education, social skills training, and assertiveness training. Even though we are doing some of that in each group now, it is not on a consistent basis." As part of the state system, the hospital is subject to the current legislative and budgetary climate, which is not much different in the state of Washington than it is anywhere else in the country. "There just is no money for anything and the governor is talking about a budget cut. In normal times it is difficult to get additional monies and it will probably be even more difficult in the future."

**Hiring and Firing**   The program is subject to other rules that govern state-operated agencies. For instance, the director cannot hire just any qualified person who applies for a job with the Sex Offender Program. First choice must be given to job applicants whose names have been placed on the state register by the Department of Personnel. To qualify for the register a person must have at least six months employment with the state and possess the minimum qualifications of the particular job description. Only if there are not at least three names listed on the register can the job be opened to the public. "Sometimes specifications for a position are not as tight as they should be. For example, the job classification used for a therapy supervisor is the same as that used for the mentally ill offenders program, so we may not find applicants who have had experience with sex offenders. Unless one of those three people waive their right to an interview or employment in this program, we have to take one of three people offered, even if none possesses the specific qualifications we want." The state system makes firing as difficult as hiring. At the end of four months the director has the option of telling new employees whether or not they can continue, but after an employee successfully completes his or her six-month probationary period in the program it is difficult to force a person out. "I think that is much easier to do in the private sector. You just tell somebody, 'You are just not working out' and they resign or are fired. In the state you really have to show cause and come up with gross incompetence in order to force a person out. There is almost no such thing as firing someone."

**Security**  Because the offenders present a danger to people in the community, tight security is a big issue. The security system was altered in 1974 when a man escaped from the grounds and murdered two young women in Seattle. It was at that point that all people who were on observation status were confined to the ward for the full 90-day period and that they instituted the "buddy" system. The medical or nursing staff hold the keys and let people in or out of the ward. From May 1977 to September 1980 the program was without an escape. Whenever escapes occur, the groups and the staff do what amounts to an autopsy after the fact. They go back over the person's behavior and frequently find three or four minor signs that had been overlooked. They then spend several group sessions deciding what changes or additional measures should be taken to prevent subsequent escapes.

**Public Relations**  With this type of program, the director believes that it is absolutely essential to have one person designated to perform public relations functions with the community. The PR person talks with groups of people, explains the program, and visits the court and judges. Initiating a full-time position for public relations has made a big difference in creating a more positive image for the program. The program was featured in a newspaper article, a television program, and radio shows. "It not only keeps the program visible, but visible in a positive way. We are sitting on a powder keg. If someone escapes or reoffends, understandably it creates an uproar in the community and we come under attack." With a public relations person, program personnel can provide community education rather than respond only to crises, as they must when one of the men escapes or reoffends.

# ELEMENTS FOR SUCCESS

The successful running of this type of program begins with a core of dedicated staff. "I don't think the professional discipline is as important as the individual persuasion of the people involved," commented the program director. "We look for people who are basically learning-theory oriented, who are willing to investigate approaches and learn what works in which types of situations." Given the state of the art, it is still difficult to find experienced people. Those with prior work experience specifically related to sex offenders are best, but others with behavioral backgrounds and some work with criminal offenders do well also. It is essential that the program director have prior experience working with sex offenders.

Another crucial element is being highly selective when choosing the initial patient population. "At the beginning you really do need a pilot group with a high probability of success because they form the nucleus of your program. You can set yourself up for failure if you don't know how to select the appropriate clients." To accomplish this requires the freedom to decide whom to accept and whom to reject, a luxury not permitted in many systems when the courts have so many people and so few resources.

"I would also recommend that the program not be in a prison setting," advised the program director. "Treatment in a prison setting is almost antithetical to the goals of the program." It is difficult to teach people to be honest, open, and concerned about others and to confront behavior within the values of the prison culture. "If you confront somebody else or interfere in his business, you may end up with a knife in your back." The program needs to exist in a setting that is free from the counterproductive elements of a general population that would undermine the therapeutic process.

# 10

# FAMILY CAMP: Family Life Educational Program

The Family Life Educational Program provides a family camp experience to ameliorate physical and sexual child abuse among families in Pasadena, California, and the San Gabriel Valley.[1] Selected families are invited to participate in four camping weekends that take place over the course of a three-month period. The program is sponsored by Foothill Family Service but operates as a multidisciplinary effort with several community agencies. The program includes:
- Twelve hours of group therapy
- Twelve hours of family life education
- Six hours of informational workshops
- Four hours of dance and drama
- Structured recreation

There is a fee for those who can afford to pay. In addition, the program provides community education by offering a course on child abuse at a local community college. The course is open to the general public.

## DEVELOPING THE FAMILY CAMP

The idea for the Family Life Educational Program was a collective one. Its roots began when the program coordinator, Audrey Oppenheimer, became a sponsor for a Parents Anonymous group. "An hour and a half a week just wasn't enough time to deal with the cascade of crises that faced these parents. I didn't see sufficient follow-up by community agencies and felt the need for more coordination in service delivery." She called several of the community agencies, including community mental health and the police department, and proposed a community network that would better meet the social and emotional needs of these families and close some of the gaps between the agencies. The idea was well received; however, no formal arrangements developed at that time.

The specific idea for a camp occurred as an outgrowth of the feeling that the abusive parents needed to be removed from their stressful environment. A colleague who had recently bought a camper casually remarked, "It would be nice if they could all go to the mountains." Why not! She began thinking of the broad parameters of a program that took place away from the agency. "It should be a happy program, a family program where children are welcome. Let's take them all away where they won't have distractions and they can concentrate on the crucial problems that bring them into the program. Let's give them a sense of family that they can enjoy." The idea called for the merging of five community agencies which would combine forces for the benefit of the abusing family. They would not duplicate each other's services or infringe on each other's territory but would consolidate their services to maximize each other's strengths and efficiencies. In that way they would be able to give unified service to the abusing family—something they did not have yet. The idea received support from the agency director, Michael Miller, and the board of directors, as well as the four other community agencies that would be participating: Pasadena Police Department, Los Angeles County Department of Public Social Service Protective Services unit in Pasadena, Parents Anonymous, the Pasadena Mental Health Association.

The original program called for a camp experience with educational and recreational components that would meet for four weekends over a period of several months. It was perceived as one way to help parents recover their children who were in placement, to provide modeling for the parents, and to give families a respite from the burdens of parenting. The plan was shown to the co-founder of Parents Anonymous, who said: "This is beautiful, but you don't think you are going to get to the heart of the problem without counseling, do you? I would never be here today if I hadn't had some confrontative and deeper experiences." At that point the therapeutic component of group counseling was added and in May 1977 a local foundation funded the program for one year at the $10,000 level.

Integrating the five core agencies became a main order of business. The agencies gave their workers compensatory time to attend the weekend camps. Each agency served clients who could use the type of program that was being proposed. In order to establish equitability, representatives from each agency attended monthly meetings to develop criteria for the selection of families who could be accepted into the program. If any family was selected whose children were in foster home placements, the Department of Public Social Services agreed to release the children during the camp weekends and allowed that time to be used as visitation with the parents. The group spent four months gearing up for the camp program after the funds were authorized. Figure 10.1 shows the organizational arrangement of the program.

Just talking about the camp generated considerable interest among people who wanted to help in some way. A member of the board involved a neighbor who ultimately helped the agency find additional private foundation funds. The president of the board made a personal donation and produced a typist from somewhere. What started with five agencies grew to include the cooperative efforts of ten or twelve community organizations. Some groups assisted with child care, one group supplied the toys, and another donated the arts and crafts materials. Many professionals and paraprofessionals volunteered their time and services during the camp weekends.

The first camp weekend was held August 24, 25, and 26, 1977, and included six couples plus four single parents, all with their children. The last weekend of the first series was held in October 1977. The program was repeated for two additional years. After that, the depletion of funds necessitated offering a modified version of the program.

# PROGRAM DESIGN

The project goals were set at two levels. At the service delivery level it aimed to demonstrate the value of an integrated approach in providing service to families in which children were neglected or abused. At the therapeutic level the objective of the Family Life Education Program included the immediate goals of teaching parents new and constructive parenting skills, fulfilling the total social and emotional needs of the parents, and eliminating the child abuse

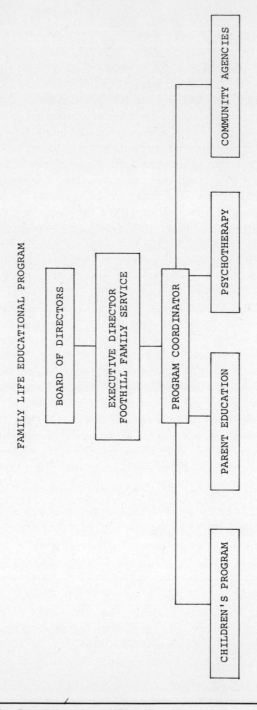

FAMILY LIFE EDUCATIONAL PROGRAM

BOARD OF DIRECTORS

EXECUTIVE DIRECTOR
FOOTHILL FAMILY SERVICE

PROGRAM COORDINATOR

COMMUNITY AGENCIES

PSYCHOTHERAPY

PARENT EDUCATION

CHILDREN'S PROGRAM

**Figure 10.1   Organizational Chart**

practices of 90 percent of the parents who attended the camp. The long-range therapeutic goals were to provide a framework in which individuals could learn self-worth and experience their own growth as well as the growth of others. To achieve those goals, personnel from various disciplines provided professionally supervised group experiences for the parents, modeled normal male–female and parent–child relationships, provided day care for the children, and offered parents supportive relief or "time off" from their children.

The camp site is a county facility located in the San Gabriel Valley close to Los Angeles. The facility was chosen because it was funded by a grant that enabled the county to provide lodging and meals for the weekend for only $10 per person. The camp site was a former probation facility for juveniles and housed the males and the females separately. Because it was not set up for shared heterosexual residence, the families had to be split, with the men and boys living in one set of dorms and the mothers, daughters, and children under the age of 5 living in another set of dorms and cottages across the compound. Counselors and their children also lived in the dorms. The size of the facility determined the number of people selected for the camp experience. The camp could accommodate 12 to 15 families and 12 counselors (between 50 and 60 people).

The camp experience consists of a series of four weekends each of which begins at 6 P.M. Friday and ends at 1:30 Sunday afternoon. Both recreational and therapeutic activities are available to all family members. The same families participate throughout the four weekends. During their stay the parents are expected to participate in the basic activities that form the core of the program. Although the program content may vary according to the availability of personnel and funds, the program contains the components described in the following sections.

**Group Therapy**  Saturday mornings from 9 A.M. to noon the parents meet in a structured group therapy experience that is conducted by two therapists, one a male (Ph.D.) and the other a female (M.S.W.). Their function is to help parents rapidly connect with their emotions, especially their anger and self-contempt. Each group therapy session focuses on a specific concept: self-esteem, self-gratification, mutual sharing, and empowerment. The therapists are paid personnel who arrive early Saturday morning and leave Saturday afternoon. They do not see the group participants outside of the camp setting.

**Dance and Psychodrama**   Saturday afternoons from 2 to 3 P.M. sensorimotor specialists (B.A. plus professional training) teach dance and psychodrama to adults and children. Their function is to help the less vocally articulate and the more disturbed clients plumb their emotional systems still further. They teach them specific dance movements and combine self-worth attitudes with the movement to music. They use psychodrama to recreate family scenes. They believe it is possible to teach even the youngest children family life education through psychodrama and work with them in small groups. The sensorimotor specialists are also paid personnel.

**Informational Workshops**   Informational classes are conducted on Saturday afternoons from 3 to 4:30 P.M. by resource people from the community. The content varies according to the interests of the group and the availability of speakers from the community. They have had workshops on budgeting, human sexuality, and beauty care. The workshops are meant to be instructive and practical. The people who conduct the workshops do so on a volunteer basis.

**Parent Education Class**   On Sunday mornings from 9 to 10:45 A.M. the parents gather for a parent education class that is conducted by the program coordinator (M.S.W.) and a male therapist (M.S.W.) who is also on the staff of the Foothill Family Service agency. The instructors use a modified behavioral approach plus some concepts described by Haim Ginott. They also stress the development of active listening and communication skill building among the participants. The class is intended to teach parents how to change their children's behavior through a reinforcement system that does not rely on physical punishment. The instructors use films, books, and homework assignments to get their points across. During the last 30 or 40 minutes of each session the older children are invited to the parents' group, where they interact with the adults to increase parent–child understanding.

**Structured Recreation**   Built into the program are periods of supervised recreational activities for children and for parents and children. For the children, these activities include stories, songs, nature walks, and outdoor games. A variety of parent–child recreational activities are offered during periods when families have free time. These include outdoor games such as baseball and volleyball, hikes, and campfire songs. Participation in the parent–child activities is voluntary.

In addition to the therapeutic and educational elements, recreational performers are brought in sometimes, and at other times camp members participate in folk dancing or outdoor singing. The parents are expected to attend the morning sessions. However, participation in the afternoon sessions is voluntary. Parents may use the afternoons and evenings as free periods to pursue their own interests.

Child care specialists provide day care for the children while the parents are involved in other activities. The children are placed in one of four clusters: infants and toddlers, 3 to 6 year olds, 7 to 11 year olds, and 12 to 16 year olds. Each cluster is staffed by a unit leader (M.A.) who is part of the paid personnel. Two or more volunteers are assigned to each cluster to assist the unit leader and provide individual attention when it is necessary. To give the child care staff some free time, parents are expected to supervise their own children during mealtimes, bedtimes, and staff meetings. Figure 10.2 provides an example of the deployment of child care personnel and a typical schedule of daily activities.

Staff meetings are scheduled on Saturdays from 4 to 5 P.M. The staff meetings serve to integrate the observations that various personnel have made about specific families and family members. Staff members compare notes about how the parents are relating to their children and to each other, how the children relate to siblings and peers, and the type and depth of parent and child participation in the camp activities. The observations help to pinpoint family dysfunction and family strengths. "One year," recalled a counselor, "we had a mother who totally left her children on their own. She wouldn't eat with them, she wouldn't do family activities with them, she put the older one in charge of the younger ones and she was off doing her own thing. And you could see the children just falling apart as the weekend progressed." Staff can then deal with the behavior directly when they see it exhibited in the future. Staff meetings also serve a supportive function. By Saturday afternoon staff are tired and need a breather. The meetings help them cope with the stress of constantly dealing with family members' disturbed behavior. During staff meetings parents are responsible for looking after their own children.

Follow-up of the families who are admitted to the program is done via the network of core agencies at their monthly meetings. Also, after the camp experience the referring person is asked to write an evaluation summary of the case plan that had been proposed at the

People in Attendance

Six couples (12) + (4) single parents = 16 adults

Children will be assigned to four clusters as follows:

| | Ages 2-6 | Ages 2-6 | Ages 7-11 | Ages 12-16 |
|---|---|---|---|---|
| Approximately | 6 | 6 | 6 | 6 |

| Basic Care of Children | | | | |
|---|---|---|---|---|
| 1. | Child care person | Child care person | Case-worker, L.C.S.W. | Case-worker, L.C.S.W. |
| 2. | Student | Student | Student | Student |
| 3. | Volunteer relief | Volunteer relief | Volunteer relief | Volunteer relief |

Breakdown of Responsibilities

Friday Night - Arrival

6:00 p.m.    Dinner is served. Parents will supervise children.

8-10 p.m.    Orientation by professionals and students: One hour for ice breaker activities where four clusters are taken as a group to see camp-grounds and introduced to one another.

One hour for breaking into separate clusters and quiet activities such as story or quiet games.

10 p.m.    Children will be put to bed by parents and supervised by parents with volunteer relief offered from 10 p.m. to midnight.

Saturday Morning - Resource Specialist and Child Care Attendants Arrive

8 - 9 a.m.    Breakfast, with parents supervising their children.

9 - 9:30    Dramatics for 12 children, ages 2-6.

In the camp in which this example was used, there was no need for infant and toddler cluster. Two-year-olds were placed in the 3–6 age clusters, two of which were required for adequate care.

**Figure 10.2   Example of Staff Deployment**

| | |
|---|---|
| 9:30 - 10 | Dramatics for older children. |
| 10 - Noon | Child care person and students work in separate areas with their groups - two to three activities will be offered per hour, such as story, songs, nature walks, or outdoor games.<br>Volunteers to offer relief at 10 and 11 a.m. |
| 12 - 1 p.m. | Lunch in dining hall with parents supervising. |
| 1 - 2 | Nap and quiet time for all children. Supervision by child care person, students, and/or professionals. |
| 2 - 3 | Optional participation in "Mommy and Me" dramatics class or remain in cluster with students and child care persons - volunteers can assist with dramatics workshop. |
| 3 - 4 | Human relations staff workshop - optional attendance for children or choice of remaining in their own cluster. Volunteers can assist in workshop. |
| 4 - 5 | Free time for families and/or group games will be offered by teenage group for boys and fathers; professionals may initiate the activities with students assisting. |
| 6 - 7 | Dinner - indoors or outdoors with parents supervising. |
| 7 - 9 | Family entertainment time. |
| 9 - 10 | Child care persons and parents will assist with settling children in bed. After 10 p.m. parents will take responsibility for children but will be assisted by volunteers. |

Sunday

| | |
|---|---|
| 7 - 8 a.m. | Optional sunrise fellowship, possibly conducted by teenagers. |
| 8 - 9 | Breakfast. Parents will supervise their children. |
| 9 - Noon | Children will meet in their clusters. Child care persons, students, and/or professionals will assume responsibility for activities. One volunteer will offer relief to one group for an hour during this time. |
| Noon | Lunch and departure. |

**Figure 10.2  Example of Staff Deployment,** *continued*      **229**

time of referral. When finances permit, an informal evaluation takes place when the parents are invited to a Christmas party reunion held at the family service agency. Formal program evaluation began in 1979, when a Ph.D. candidate was hired to evaluate the program. He administered a self-concept scale and a personality scale to the parents at the beginning and the end of the camp experience. He also asked the parents to complete a goal attainment scale. They selected five goals they wanted to accomplish and within three months following the camp experience the parents were rechecked to determine how close they were to achieving those goals. Most people reached their goals at the predicted levels or better.

## STAFF TRAINING

All the volunteers and program personnel receive formal preparation at meetings held on three different occasions prior to the first camp experience. The meetings deal with the practical problems that can be anticipated at the camp. They discuss the children and what types of behavior to expect. They receive some background information about the families. They discuss the supplies that will be needed. They also review the problems that had been encountered the year before. "These meetings also gave the counselors and volunteers an opportunity to look across the table at each other and begin to fashion a team."

Many of the volunteers have also taken the course on child abuse that the program coordinator teaches. The content of that course includes an understanding of child development and the motivations that lead to child abuse.

## LINKING CLIENTS AND PROGRAM

In order to be eligible for the program, the clients must already be involved with a social service program in the community. Personnel from the participating agencies initiate most referrals to the program. Self-referrals are accepted from members of Parents Anonymous. Program participation is voluntary; there are no mandatory referrals. All referrals are accompanied by a Parent Child Observation report from the referring agency. This report includes a social history of the family, an assessment of the potential for child abuse, the type of child abuse that has occurred, and an evaluation of the community service needs of the family and also the inner strengths the clients need to develop. (See Figure 10.3.) A committee composed of representatives from the participating agencies meet monthly to review the referrals. They attempt to select people who represent all levels of the abuse spectrum, from self-referred to court referred, as well as all socioeconomic levels. "We mixed populations and included middle-class matron types as well as people who were on welfare. They mixed well. Everyone looks the same when they all wear blue jeans. Despite economic or educational differences, they begin to see that they were responding to stress in similar ways and that their children were being caught in the crossfire." Generally from 40 to 60 percent of the families chosen are single-parent families. Very often the parents are interviewed by the program coordinator prior to a decision about their acceptance.

Two weeks before the first camp weekend the parents are invited to a Parents Night at the Family Service agency. "Since many of the families do not know each other, we try to do some ice breaking. We introduce them to some of the staff and prepare them for the camp facility and the sleeping arrangements. It is important for them to know it isn't a vacation, that there will be a lot of hard work as well as pleasure." Each family receives written guidelines that help them prepare for the camp experience. (See Figure 10.4.)

Friday evenings are very busy, especially during the first weekend, with people unpacking, meeting each other, and then having dinner. To make the initial transition easier, each family is assigned a volunteer who shows them to their quarters and helps them feel comfortable. Friday nights are informal, with gatherings of group singing and marshmallow roasts or people in small groups taking walks, playing cards and games, or just drinking hot chocolate and talking together. "It is a very nurturing experience that leaves most people feeling good."

The formal part of the program begins after breakfast on Saturday morning. (See Figure 10.5 for a sample outline of the camp activities.) The parents leave their children in the play area with the counselors and then they attend their group therapy session. The therapists use a structured approach which incorporates both supportive and confrontative elements to develop a sense of self-affirmation, rage reduction, and mutual sharing. They use a transactional approach to teach about parent—child or spousal interactions. The therapists rapidly encourage the parents to discuss the history of their own betrayal and victimization, and to release some of the anger which arrests their own emotional growth and keeps them

PARENT-CHILD OBSERVATION REPORT
FOR EACH FAMILY REFERRED TO FAMILY LIFE EDUCATION CAMP

## Social History

1. Members of household, including sex, age, and relationship.
2. Adequacy of income.
3. Parental relationships, child-rearing ideas, and family
   dynamics.
4. Involvement or isolation of parents and availability
   of help or relief of stress.
5. Parents' own childhood experiences (especially methods
   of discipline used on parents by their parents).
6. Recent family stresses.

## Potential for Child Abuse

A. Parents

   1. Has previously demonstrated inability to cope with
      child.
   2. Inadequate or missing parent bond.
   3. Wall of isolation.
   4. Unsupporting spousal relationship.
   5. Low self-image.
   6. Role reversal with child.
   7. Parents' lack of awareness of child development.

B. The Child

   1. Special; e.g., "wanted" for parental needs.
   2. Seen differently; e.g., scapegoat.
   3. Is different; e.g., slow developer.

## Situation

Are problems so overwhelming that the parent is unable to
recognize the child's needs adequately?

## Type of Child Abuse

Single assault, repeated assaults, psychological violence,
neglect, sexual offense.

## Caseworker Recommendation

1. What special services does the client need in the community such as advocacy, psychotherapy, medical, etc.?

2. What inner resources does the client need to develop
   to mobilize, to function better, and to more adequately
   meet the needs of the child?

**Figure 10.3  Parent-Child Observation Report**

FOOTHILL FAMILY SERVICE - FAMILY LIFE EDUCATION CAMP

We have reserved the Oak Grove Conference Center through the courtesy of the Los Angeles Commission on Human Relations for our five weekend camping trips:  August 24-26; September 14-16; September 28-30; October 12-14; October 26-28, 1979.  The Camp is also called the Julius Klein Conference Center.


## GUIDELINES

### AUTOMOBILES

Cars brought to the center will be directed to the nearest parking area where you may leave your cars while registering.  Cars will remain parked as the center gate is usually closed during all of the sessions.


### SLEEPING ACCOMMODATIONS

Dormitory style with indoor plumbing and heating.  Individual beds and mattresses are provided; the camper will be expected to furnish sleeping bag or blankets.  Blankets can be borrowed from Foothill Family Service, if necessary. Beds should be made and cleanup finished either before or immediately after breakfast.  A cleanup crew can be formed to clean restrooms or empty trash each day.


### DINING

Food is prepared by a qualified cook and served cafeteria style in a large dining hall.  All serving of food, washing of cooking utensils, and cleaning up will be the responsibility of campers, volunteers, and professional staff.

KP'S (4-6 plus 1 supervisor) should report to the kitchen, 15 minutes before each meal.  The same KP'S clean up after each meal.  It is the supervisor's responsibility to see that garbage is placed in a container separate from paper and cans, and that all tables are cleaned, the floor swept, and utensils dried (paper plates are used for dishes).  At the conclusion of the last meal the floor should be mopped. Please do not take food out of the Dining Hall.


### SMOKING

Permitted in designated areas.


### OFFICE

Main office is off limits to everyone except Human Relations Staff and the nurse.

**Figure 10.4**                                                    **233**

TELEPHONE

Please use the telephone for emergencies only.

TO BE SURE OF A COMFORTABLE AND ENJOYABLE EXPERIENCE AT
THE CONFERENCE CENTER, BE SURE TO BRING THE FOLLOWING:

Sleeping bag or 2 blankets and sheets. Pillows optional.
(No pillows are provided by the conference center.)

1 or 2 towels

Warm pajamas and robe

Warm jacket or sweater

Swimming suit (river wading, no swimming pool) and shower
slippers, old shoes for river wading

Comfortable shoes or sneakers (2 pairs, if possible)

Several changes of socks, underclothes, etc.

Toilet articles including soap, toothbrush, toothpaste,
combs, brushes, shaving equipment, hair care supplies,
etc.

Writing tablet and pencil for note taking

Casual clothes for a comfortable conference

FOR BOYS:  jeans, bermuda shorts, and shirts

FOR GIRLS:  slacks, jeans, bermuda shorts, blouses, skirts

OPTIONAL:  Musical instrument, hand mirror, sunburn pre-
           ventive, sunshade and/or dark glasses, flash-
           light with batteries, camera and film

IMPORTANT:  If you have a health or medical problem which
            requires special attention, please notify the
            Conference Director as soon as you arrive in
            the Conference Center.

No money needed

YOU MUST limit baggage to one suitcase.

PLEASE mark all of your belongings for easy identification
to prevent loss.

Please call Audrey Oppenheimer, 795-6907 if you do not have
enough blankets or sheets for your family for the weekends.

You might wish to bring your child's rubber balls, baseball gloves, or frisbees to use.

---

**Figure 10.4,** *continued*

All clients of the State Department of Public Social Service are invited to Camp Oak Grove at no cost. We are requesting that the other families contribute as much as they can to cover the expense of food and lodging for their family. The cost per person, over age 4, is $10.00 for the weekend.

RESPONSIBILITY FOR DAMAGES

No gambling or possession of alcoholic beverages is permitted within the campgrounds. Infraction of this rule may result in termination of the group's program. This applies to drugs also. Smoking marijuana will result in the expulsion of participants.

WEATHER AND CLOTHING

The weather will vary and you should be prepared for cool mornings and evenings as well as sunshine.

WORKSHOPS

Sessions meet from 9:00 to 12:00 on Saturday and Sunday mornings. Afternoon workshops are scheduled from 2:00 to 4:00 p.m. Free time for family visiting will be held from 4:00 to 6:00 p.m. Meals are served at 8:00 a.m., 12:00 p.m., and 6:00 p.m.

SOCIAL FUNCTIONS

You are invited to a welcoming party on Friday, August 24. There will be ice-breaking activities, a tour of the camp, and a wonderful opportunity for all to get acquainted. On Saturday, August 25, from 7:30 p.m. to 9:30 p.m. we have arranged for special musical entertainment for parents and children. The recreation lounge will be open thereafter until midnight for parents to visit.

We look forward to seeing you at Camp Oak Grove.

Sincerely,

Audrey Oppenheimer
Camp Coordinator

SAMPLE OUTLINE OF CAMP ACTIVITIES

FAMILY LIFE EDUCATIONAL PROGRAM

Friday

6:00 p.m. or after:    Arrival time.  Check in main recrea-
                       tional room for registration and as-
                       signments.  Dinner will be served.

8:00 to 10:00 p.m.:    Social hour and orientation.


Saturday

8:00 to 9:00 a.m.:     Breakfast.  Families are to supervise
                       their own children during meals.

9:00 to Noon:          Parents: Group therapy.
                       Young children: Recreation outdoors at
                       the right end of the main recreational
                       hall.
                       Teenagers: Plan their own activities.

12:00 to 1:00 p.m.:    Lunch

2:00 to 3:00 p.m.:     *Parents*: Optional choice - Dance and
                       drama (adults only OR dance and drama
                       for "Mommy and Me" OR "Dad and Kids"
                       play volleyball, baseball, or foot
                       races.
                       Teenagers:  Class in dramatic expres-
                       sion or jazz dancing OR hike through
                       the trails and possible overnight
                       spent in mountains.
                       Small Children:  Nap followed by
                       free play.

3:00 to 4:30 p.m.      Optional class:  Budgeting and Home
                       Economics Workshop OR Sexuality Work-
                       shop.

6:00 p.m.:             Dinner - Indoor or outdoor barbeque.

9:00 p.m.              Outdoor singing, folk dancing.


Sunday

7:00 to 8:00 a.m.:     Breakfast.  Optional religious service
                       will follow.

9:00 to 10:45 a.m.:    Family Life Education: Understanding
                       Childhood Growth.

12:00 to 1:30 p.m.:    Lunch and departure.

---

**Figure 10.5  Sample Outline of Camp Activities**

bound to the original parent. The sessions are focused around specific themes. The first is on self-esteem and attempts to broaden each individual's awareness of self. The second session is concerned with self-gratification. The participants learn ways to gratify their psychological needs themselves and reduce their emotional dependence on their children. The third session is devoted to the idea of mutual sharing. The participants learn how to use support systems to counteract personal loneliness and to diminish the feeling of being overwhelmed. The final session focuses on the concept of empowerment. Group members are told that they have the ability to take responsibility to guide and direct their own lives. They consider the means by which they may assume personal responsibility in meaningful and constructive ways.

The dancing and psychodrama activities may include only the adults or only the children or interactions between children and adults. In conjunction with the dancing, participants are asked to say something nice about themselves. The exercise sometimes triggers very powerful emotions. "I remember one woman who broke out in tears because it was so difficult for her to see herself positively. Later, toward the end of the exercise, she was able to commit verbally some comment about herself that she liked and she felt so guilty that she completely broke down. That woman went on to get a job and was able to trace some of her self-worth to that experience." The psychodrama episodes might recreate everyday situations. "One incident was very moving," recalled the coordinator. "A group of four children play-acted what it was like when mother came home from work. The daughter of one of the abusive mothers played the role of the mother and saw her as a bossy, bossy lady. She gave a perfect rendition of her mother pounding the table and saying, 'Where's dinner!' The real mother was watching from the next room in disbelief. That weekend the mother embraced her daughter for the first time in ten years."

The parent education class begins with the identification of negative behavior. Parents are taught to differentiate between behaviors and emotional feelings. Group members are given a copy of Gerald Patterson's book *Living with Children* and the accompanying workbook to use throughout the parent education meetings. They select one behavior exhibited by their child that they wish to change. They become aware of their reactions to the child's offensive behavior and may be given a homework assignment to keep track of how often the negative behavior occurs and under what circumstances. During the

---

second weekend they talk about the behaviors they had observed since the last camp weekend. Many parents begin to realize that their negative reactions have a lot to do with compounding the problem. They focus on new ways to deal with the identified behavior in the future by developing a reward reinforcement system. The parents also learn the technique of "timeout" as a disciplinary tactic to use when children become very resistant or throw tantrums. The third weekend the parents discuss how well they were able to implement the skills they had learned the time before. During the third session the parents identify another behavior they want their children to change. They learn to transfer tangible rewards, such as money or candy when the child performs well, to social rewards like hugs or praise. The fourth weekend is a review of how the parents now function with their children.

Toward the last half hour of each parent education class the older children come in to the group to talk with the parents. The instructors use a fishbowl arrangement in which the children sit in the middle and answer questions put to them by the instructors. They might be asked, "What is different about your family when they are here at camp?" or "What would you like to see happen at home once you leave camp?" Each child takes a turn and answers the question put to him or her. The answers encourage a parental response and a continuing dialogue between the parents and their children.

There is an identifiable process of parental behavior change that takes place during the course of the four weekends. The first weekend everyone enters feeling frightened but quickly allows the nurturing of the weekend to affect him or her. "The experience itself is so enriching that they begin letting their defenses down and become more open. It is like some sort of group honeymoon." The second weekend is characterized by critical and testing behavior. "By the second weekend we would begin to hear criticisms of the camp, like the food is too spicy or the accommodations are uncomfortable. One person had brought marijuana to the camp and another said the family had made other plans on Sunday and asked to leave camp early. Although some of the complaints were legitimate, many just masked underlying fears associated with close living and the need to trust other people." The program personnel instituted a parents' meeting on Friday nights of the second, third, and fourth weekends to air some of the grievances. By the third weekend parents seem to exhibit a breakthrough in confronting and understanding some of their destructive behavior. Very often by this point things reached a peak and, as a result, people began to act more loving toward their spouses and more respectful toward their children. The final weekend is "a real high," a feeling of exuberance and camaraderie. "The group has become a large family and even though they are leaving they will carry those feelings into their homes." There is a feeling of hopefulness that the learning and growth that began in the camp will continue to flourish in the future.

The children, also, exhibit predictable behavior during the four weekends. The first weekend they are very upset. Some scream even if their mothers move only a few feet away. The children are calmer during the second weekend. They do not cling so tightly to siblings and they allow the substitute caretakers to pick them up. By the third weekend the children are embracing the other children. "Everyone at camp needed a second family and that always happens. When I saw them embracing children of different ages and ethnic backgrounds I knew that something good was happening." By the end of the camp experience they are able to reach out and to share.

## CASE EXAMPLE

Twenty-five year old Mickey was referred to Foothill Family Service for intensive counseling by the Child Protective Services of Pasadena's Department of Public Social Services. She was seen jointly with her nonlegal mate, Dan, aged 32, for three sessions in the office. Mickey was also seen individually for a total of twelve sessions. The couple were the parents of 15-month-old Annette, who was currently a ward of the court because she had received multiple bruises and lacerations from numerous "accidents" since she was two months old. The couple had been living together for five years. Dan had married previously, had four children in Wyoming, but was not divorced from the children's mother. He did not pay child support either to Mickey or to his wife. He barely supported himself through his work as a mechanic and stock car racer. Mickey was bright, active, and a conscientious clerk for a travel agency.

In individual and joint sessions I learned of the frequent quarrels that plagued the relationship, often with physical beatings to Mickey by Dan. Dan complained of Mickey's poor mothering, her tendency to pick on him for his shortcomings, and her unfounded jealousy of other women. During one particular episode Annette was dropped during the heat of a battle. The mother was in the process of making a sandwich and was at the refrigerator getting a mayonnaise jar, holding the baby in her arms. Dan was shouting at her and approached menacingly as if to assault her. The mayonnaise jar fell to the floor and the child fell from the mother's arms. Annette suffered cuts on her spine from broken glass and required 20 stitches. Because this was only one in a series of injuries the child had sustained during the past year, the court placed Annette with Mickey's older sister until such time as the parents separated or stabilized their relationship, improved their self-esteem, and acquired additional child development knowledge. Mickey and Dan were allowed visiting privileges.

By the time both came for joint counseling, their relationship was souring, but neither one knew how to let go of the other. In the few individual interviews we held with Dan, he was guarded, suspicious, and defensive. On an intellectual level Dan was aware that he was endangering his job by the excessive use of alcohol, but he admitted he did not know how to control his drinking. Mickey was alternately depressed and frightened but made efforts to share emotionally charged or painful material with the worker in individual sessions. During one joint session, in the hope that a discussion of a financial conflict would lead to some resolution of their differences, Mickey talked of their money problems. Dan was enraged that she would give such an accurate version to the counselor and, after leaving the agency, subjected Mickey to a physical beating. Shortly after this episode Dan lost his job and moved to another city. He attempted to kidnap Annette one weekend when the baby was visiting with Mickey, but Mickey pressed charges and had the police place him under arrest.

During the first two camp weekends we worked on Mickey's problems in the areas of low self-esteem and symbiotic relationships. Mickey was raised in a middle-class home, one of three daughters in a military family. When her father was abroad, her mother was described as critical, depressed, and bitter. After ten years her parents were divorced. Mickey entered the family camp experience with a lifelong Cinderella complex, that is, that she was an ugly duckling compared with her two older sisters, who were "more beautiful, more clever, and certainly more loved" by their mother. The themes she expressed at group counseling sessions revolved around her loss of a truly caring maternal figure. While never the victim of an abusive physical act by her parents, she sustained severe emotional neglect. She traced her present overdependence on Dan to her feelings of potential loss in the past. She knew that he was a rakish fellow and a user of women, but he gave her existence a sense of aliveness and excitement. As she began to shed her depression and anger over her earlier rejection by the parents, she asserted her independence on a spontaneous and natural basis. She did not need a man to make her feel alive. She made significant autonomous decisions concerning Annette's care, her office, and her home life. Ultimately, these two individuals uncoupled and went their separate ways, geographically and emotionally.

Mickey attended all group experiences offered to her in Parents Anonymous and came to three of four camp weekends. Men and women at camp liked her, reached out to her, and she began to see the enormous therapeutic value of networking as a tool to help her grow. Child management was quickly achieved through her reading and participation in the Family Camp parent education program.

Although Annette was still in the custody of her aunt, she was allowed to be with Mickey during the camp weekends. When she was first brought to camp Annette screamed so sharply and incessantly that it was hard not to be aware of the child's intense separation anxiety. Interestingly, the child did not shed genuine tears, but she would wrinkle her face and wail at the slightest opportunity. Aware that Annette was still unused to living with her, Mickey developed a plan to help Annette's adjustment to the maternal home. She took Annette to the community mall, to the supermarket, and gradually increased the time she placed Annette in her stroller outside their screen door. As she did this, she offered Annette considerable loving attentive behaviors as well. By the third time Mickey appeared at camp, the child was relaxed and could be picked up easily by caretakers.

A review of Mickey's growth indicated that she achieved the inner stability that she was seeking, and that the Child Protective Services required of her. She was more centered within herself, her consciousness was raised, and self-actualization had been achieved. From the mousey, frightened child-woman we saw at intake, she had grown into an adult. She was assertive and had mastered her anxiety over the loss of approval by others that she had felt during her early weeks at camp. From a quiet participant, in the corner of a group, she became a vocal, effective group contributor. She transferred these qualities into her job situation and secured a rapid promotion. After the final camp Mickey developed a series of shallow alliances with various men, but within a few months she discontinued these and focused on personal growth by upgrading her job skills, by acquiring new women friends who also were single parents, and by securing her first apartment on her own. Her child was returned to her custody. She appeared to blossom into a graceful swan and no longer talked about herself as an ugly duckling.

## TREATMENT ISSUES

During the first night at camp the stress of the whole family is reflected in the behavior of the children. The younger children are anxious; they cry, they scream, they fight, or they cling to the parents. With the infants and toddlers, separation from the parents can be traumatic because both the place and the counselor are new. "At the first camp," recalled the program coordinator, "I was distraught by the fact that for the kids it was just agony. Here it was a new place and then Momma goes too. We have tried to ease that by having our volunteers attach themselves to each of the families so they can get to know the children. That way the child doesn't become frightened when the parent leaves for group therapy."

Although child care is the primary responsibility of the counselors, they are also available to the parents, especially after therapy when many adults feel upset. "I used to kid the therapists," said the program coordinator. "I would say you open them, you close them, and then you leave, but the drainage and the bandaging and the convalescence the rest of us have to do all weekend." Many times unit leaders and counselors are called on to pick up the pieces following an emotional encounter. For example, one couple characteristically dealt with each other manipulatively in passive-aggressive ways. The husband tried to make contact with his wife, but she had her hidden angers because he had failed to live up to her expectations in the past. One weekend, in an attempt to avoid emotional contact with her husband, the woman spent hours cleaning the dormitory area. She swept the foyer, hung up a sheet in her room to gain privacy, and decorated the room with flowers. The husband grumbled under his breath, "You try, you try, and look how she acts." The group therapists confronted the woman about her tendency to run away from intimate encounters. "I remember that she was red-eyed during the coffee break," recalled one of the counselors. "I hadn't ever seen her that way. I talked with her a little bit and she said that she had never had an experience like this before. She told me that, for her, participation in Parents Anonymous was like chipping away at a block of ice, but this particular weekend was as if the ice were cracking and melting away. Later I saw her holding hands with her husband."

Counselors often find that parents do not want to become involved with their children. Some of their withdrawal is caused by the therapy experience which opens up an emotional area they want to work through. During the process of working through, they relate less to the children. Staff need to retain their sense of professionalism and refrain from becoming angry. "You have to give the parents time and not force the issue. The peer pressure from other parents may help them do it more easily." However, sometimes the reverse happens and the parents become overly solicitous about their child's welfare. "One thing that amuses me," said a unit leader, "is that these parents who have so much trouble managing their children think that no one else is good enough to take care of their child. They say, 'I only want so and so to take care of her' or 'You didn't see that he ate his vegetables,' even though at home the kid was lucky to get a piece of bread."

The modeling of attitudes and behaviors by the staff is very important. "If the parents have been into the abusive cycle for any length of time, the kids are in bad shape. We show them how to accept the child, and the mothers see that the child will be compliant with us." The other mothers share successful child-rearing experiences with each other. For example, one mother might not be able to get her child to go to bed and another mother might say, "Let me put him to bed tonight and you watch what I do."

Counselors in this type of program are prepared to make a deep commitment to each client and his or her problem-solving efforts. Such a commitment entails continual emotional support throughout the camp program. Working so intensely with people is emotionally draining for the counselors and volunteers. "By the end of the weekend," said a unit leader, "I am so tired of giving, that if a little old lady fell down in front of me I would walk around her because I just wouldn't have the energy to help one more person."

## ADMINISTRATIVE ISSUES

**Funding**  It requires an annual budget of at least $25,000 to run the family camp program. "The first year we managed on a grant of $10,000 only because we had a tremendous amount of volunteer and in-kind services." The following years the program coordinator obtained grants of $20,000 and $25,000 but found progressively less in the way of volunteer services. All the funds have come from private foundations. In 1980 the program had to be modified because there were insufficient funds available to cover the costs of the total program. "We had one entire weekend program which was excellent. We supplemented with the help of individual board members and Parents Anonymous leaders by conducting three structured dinner meetings. At these meetings, the parent education and socialization components were continued." Since then, the family camp program has been suspended for lack of funds.

**Referrals** Working with the referring agencies to clarify the nature of the program is an ongoing responsibility of the program coordinator. Both workers and clients need to be clear about the purpose of the camp. Sometimes parents agree to participate because their counselors have suggested it, not because they understand the global purpose of the camp. "One time we accepted two families who were in the twilight zone. They were in the high-risk category but were more emotionally abusive to the children than physically abusive. They did not consider themselves to be child abusers. When they saw a newspaper story about the camp and its work with child abusers, the parents became furious." Interviewing the clients helps to determine whether they have been appropriately referred.

**Staff Support** Because the intensity of the camp situation leaves people feeling drained, supporting the staff deserves special consideration. Staff meetings are a major source of support. They help staff deal with the stresses of living with people who display disturbing behaviors. "Rarely are you confronted so consistently with people whose disturbing behavior is so out in the open." The staff meetings are a place where people can share their observations, ask questions, and recharge their batteries. Staff support is also necessary if the members of the various disciplines are to function well as a team. "Psychologists may wonder why the social worker approaches a client's problem behavior differently. Or, teachers may believe that a didactic, direct approach in some situations is better, while the psychologist prefers to go more slowly." Because great respect is required for the people joining as teammates who represent other disciplines, staff are provided additional support in the form of input and education about the pathology they will be or have been witnessing. "This is acquired slowly and sufficient staff time must be allotted for cohesion to occur. Generally biweekly meetings three months before camp begins, followed by monthly meetings for six months thereafter, will accomplish that goal."

## ELEMENTS FOR SUCCESS

The first component needed to develop this type of program is community willingness to work on the problem of child abuse. According to the program coordinator, "There is a certain amount of education that agencies community wide must engage in to make this happen. When a city is enlightened, sees the connections between prevention and treatment, it springs into action via the private or public sectors. Government officials enact legislation to appropriate funds for cost-effective programs. Boards of private agencies are moved to take responsibility to raise money in their communities for necessary projects. This will not occur if trained volunteers and professionals do not engage in outreach and education projects via the media or elsewhere. When people learn that child abusers are not monsters or ugly human beings, to be kept in a class of their own like leper colonies of the past, the citizenry will be more supportive in their community. When child abuse is seen as the outgrowth of improper education or role modeling for parents, citizen groups will more easily identify with the troubled parents and make an effort to help."

Coordination among participating agencies is also vital. "There has to be some element of trust among agencies so that they can work together," said the program coordinator. "The statement, 'if we do not hang together, assuredly we will all hang separately' was never more true than when related to the need for interagency cooperation on child abuse cases. Too often, 85 percent of a community's dollar is spent on 15 percent of the community. No community can tolerate duplication and administrative waste. Achieving a measure of trust on administrative levels is necessary to begin the coordination of community programs. Line worker and casework cooperation generally exists already between public and private systems so can be mobilized for tighter integration fairly easily."

An effective screening process is a third element for a successful program experience. Program personnel need to select those clients who are best able to use the group living experience. "We try to screen out people who are too emotionally disturbed or too fragile to handle the new insights. It is necessary to reserve a project of this type only for those who will not benefit from casework in the office setting on an intensive basis. This type of project is best for people with personality problems that resist regular one-to-one counseling. Therefore, considerable thought should go into the selection of suitable participants diagnostically."

# APPENDICES

# Appendix A
# TELEPHONE PRESCREEN

_____Child Abuse - Physical

_____Child Abuse - Sexual

_____Sibling Abuse

_____Spouse Abuse - Physical

_____Spouse Abuse - Sexual

_____Sexual Abuse

_____Parent Battering

_____Elderly Abuse

_____Other

Name of service

Address

Telephone #

Person in charge

Title

Sponsoring agency

Address

Phone

Person in charge

Title

Type of agency (hospital, shelter, adult counseling, child
       guidance, community action program, family service,
       self-help, legal, etc.)

Services offered:


Service to Assaulter

   Target clientele

   When program initiated (mo/yr)

   Hours of operation

   Referral sources

   Mandatory or voluntary

   Description of services



   Fees charged


Community served (size, rural, uban, financial, ethnic)


Restriction on service (who not served)


Community response to program (supportive, detached, involved, etc.)


Client Information

   Number of clients served each month

   Maximum length of service offered (e.g., 6 visits)

   Average number of times each person is seen

Client Profile

   Age _____   Education _____

   Income   _____

   Ethnicity _____   Religion _____

Techniques that work best


Techniques to avoid


General success of program (how evaluated)


Administrative Information

   Number of personnel connected with the program

   Breakdown of personnel (type)



   Full or part-time

   Male - female

   Volunteer - paid


Organizational structure (hierarchy, cooperative, etc.)


Philosophic orientation


Source of funding


Support system for personnel to prevent burnout

# Appendix B

# SELECTED SAMPLE CHARACTERISTICS

| Type of Family Violence | Number | Percent |
|---|---|---|
| All Types | 7 | 6.03 |
| Three Types | 4 | 3.44 |
| Physical and Sexual Child Abuse | 28 | 24.13 |
| Spouse Abuse and Sexual Child Abuse | 2 | 1.72 |
| Spouse Abuse | 29 | 25.00 |
| Physical Child Abuse | 24 | 20.68 |
| Sexual Child Abuse | 22 | 18.96 |
| Total | 116 | 99.96 |

| Size of Community (Population) | Number | Percent |
|---|---|---|
| Less than 100,000 | 7 | 6.03 |
| 100,000–499,999 | 44 | 37.93 |
| 500,000–1,000,000 | 26 | 22.41 |
| More than 1,000,000 | 39 | 33.62 |

| Type of Agency | Number | Percent |
|---|---|---|
| Family Service | 28 | 24.13 |
| Community Organization | 11 | 9.48 |
| Hospital or Medical | 10 | 8.62 |
| Child Welfare | 10 | 8.62 |
| Criminal Justice | 10 | 8.62 |

| Type of Agency | Number | Percent |
|---|---|---|
| Protective Services | 8 | 6.89 |
| Mental Health | 8 | 6.89 |
| Private, Nonprofit | 7 | 6.03 |
| Private Counseling | 5 | 4.31 |
| Consortium | 5 | 4.31 |
| YMCA, YWCA | 4 | 3.44 |
| Shelter | 3 | 2.58 |
| Community Action Program | 3 | 2.58 |
| Social Ministry | 2 | 1.72 |
| Community Center | 2 | 1.72 |

| Length of Time Program in Existence | Number | Percent |
|---|---|---|
| Less than 1 Year | 12 | 10.34 |
| 1 Year | 31 | 26.72 |
| 2 Years | 19 | 16.37 |
| 3 Years | 14 | 12.06 |
| 4 Years | 11 | 9.48 |
| 5 Years | 12 | 10.34 |
| More than 5 Years | 17 | 14.65 |

| Length of Time Client Seen | Number | Percent |
|---|---|---|
| Less than 3 Months | 27 | 23.27 |
| 3–6 Months | 29 | 25.00 |
| 7 Months–1 Year | 37 | 31.89 |
| 1–2 Years | 11 | 9.48 |
| More than 2 Years | 2 | 1.72 |
| Unknown | 10 | 8.62 |

| Participation | Number | Percent |
|---|---|---|
| Voluntary | 40 | 34.48 |
| Mandatory | 11 | 9.48 |
| Both | 44 | 37.93 |
| Forced Voluntary[a] | 18 | 15.51 |
| Unknown | 3 | 2.58 |

[a] Forced voluntary = need to participate in some type of program to avoid jail or to regain custody of a child.

# NOTES

## Chapter 1

1. Raymond I. Parnas, "The Police Response to Domestic Disturbance," *Wisconsin Law Review*, (Fall 1967): 914–60.
2. Clarence M. Kelley, *Crime in the United States 1973* (Washington, DC: U.S. Government Printing Office, 1974); William Webster, *Crime in the United States 1978* (Washington, DC: U.S. Government Printing Office, 1979).
3. Donald J. Mulvihill and Melvin M. Tumin, *Crimes of Violence, vol. 11* (Washington, DC: U.S. Government Printing Office, 1969).
4. Ibid., p. xxviii.
5. Kee MacFarlane, personal communication, 1980.
6. Richard J. Gelles, "Violence Toward Children in the United States," *American Journal of Orthopsychiatry*, 48 (October 1978): 580–92.
7. Murray A. Straus, "Normative and Behavioral Aspects of Violence Between Spouses: Preliminary Data on a Nationally Representative USA Sample," mimeographed. (Durham: University of New Hampshire Press, 1977.)
8. Suzanne K. Steinmetz, "Violence Between Family Members," *Marriage and Family Review*, 1 (May/June 1978): 1–16.
9. Kee MacFarlane, "Sexual Abuse of Children," in *The Victimization of Women*, ed. Jane Roberts Chapman and Margaret Gates (Beverly Hills, CA: Sage Publications, 1978), pp. 81–109.
10. Barbara Star, et al., "Psychosocial Aspects of Wife Battering," *Social Casework: The Journal of Contemporary Social Work*, 60 (October 1979): 479–87.
11. *Los Angeles Times*, "Children Held to Injure Parents in 1 of 10 Families," 20 March 1979.

12. Marilyn R. Block and Jan D. Sinnott, eds. *The Battered Elderly Syndrome: An Exploratory Study* (College Park: University of Maryland Press, 1979).
13. "CANCO," mimeographed (Mishawaka, IN: St. Joseph County Child Abuse and Neglect Coordinating Organization, 1979).
14. National Institute of Mental Health, *Child Abuse and Neglect Programs: Practice and Theory* (Washington, DC: U.S. Government Printing Office, 1977), p. 160.

## Chapter 2

1. Rita and Blair Justice, *The Abusing Family* (New York: Human Sciences Press, 1976).

## Chapter 9

1. In addition to interviews with key program personnel, information for this chapter was derived from a paper written by the program director: Maureen Saylor, "A Guided Self-Help Approach to Treatment of the Habitual Sexual Offender," presented to the 12th Chopwood Conference, Cambridge, England, December 1979.

## Chapter 10

1. In addition to interviews with key program personnel, information for this chapter was derived from an article written by the program coordinator: Audrey Oppenheimer, "Triumph over Trauma in the Treatment of Child Abuse," *Social Casework: The Journal of Contemporary Social Work* 59 (June 1978): 352–8.

# INDEX

Techniques to avoid *(cont.)*
  touching in sexual abuse cases,
  47
Timeout technique, 129
Treatment issues, 51-55
  active vs passive, 52
  individual vs group, 53-54
  long-term vs short-term, 54-55
  mandatory vs voluntary, 51-52
  structured vs unstructured, 53
Treatment methods, see also
  Treatment techniques
  effective techniques, 39-43
  ineffective methods, 44-47

prerequisite, 38-39
Treatment techniques
  buddy system, 43
  empty chair technique, 43-44
  enhancement of self-esteem, 41
  honesty, 42
  modeling, 42
  problem solving, 41
  role playing, 42-43
  structure, 41-42
  supportive confrontation, 40
Tumin, Melvin M., 254
Western State Hospital, 176
Withers, Kent C., 95